COMPASSIONATE SATANISM

An Introduction to Modern Satanic Practice

Lilith Starr

Art by Suzanne Forbes.

Compassionate Satanism

AN INTRODUCTION TO MODERN SATANIC PRACTICE

Lilith Starr

Foreword by Lucien Greaves

LILITH STARR STUDIOS
Publishing Division
lilithxstarr@gmail.com

ORDERING INFORMATION

Quantity Sales
Special discounts are available on quantity purchases by corporations, associations, and others. For details, contact the publisher at the email address above.

Orders by U.S. Trade Bookstores and Wholesalers
Please contact the publisher at the address above.

First Edition, First Printing, 2021
Lilith Starr Studios

Page layout and design by Lena Kartzov

This book is the creative product of its artists, contributors, and author. All photos, illustrations, events, and experiences detailed in this book recount the individual experiences of the author, Lilith Starr, and contributors. This book is not a product of, approved by, endorsed by, or in any way affiliated with The Satanic Temple.

ISBN 978-0-578-91469-5

Dedication

This book is dedicated to my Satanic family all around the world — my fellow Chapter members, my Satanic friends near and far on social media, the organizers, leaders and volunteers who serve our community, and all who feel the spark of Satanic compassion flare in their own hearts. May the torch of Lucifer's wisdom light your path. Hail you, and HAIL SATAN!

Contents

Foreword i

Introduction 1

Section 1: The Rise of Satanism 21

Section 2: The Narrative of Satan 31

Section 3: Modern Satanic Ethics 59
  Tenet One: Compassion 62
  Tenet Two: Justice 67
  Tenet Three: Inviolability 73
  Tenet Four: Freedom to Offend 91
  Tenet Five: Scientific Understanding 97
  Tenet Six: Fallibility 106
  Tenet Seven: Guiding Principles 110

Section 4: The Outcast Awakens 119
  Satanic Feminism 121
  Queer Satanism 127
  Freethinkers and Atheists 133

Section 5: Tools for Practice 137
  Satanic Ritual 137
  Satanic Symbology 142

Section 6: Personalizing Your Practice 153
  Self-Compassion 154
  Self-Responsibility 157
  Break Your Chains 158
  Coming Out as a Satanist 162
  Satanic Self-Expression 166

Section 7: Taking Action 177

Section 8: Finding Satanic Community 199
    Transformation and Change 202
    Finding a Satanic Group. 204
    Starting a Community 207
    Leadership Tips 214
    Activities for Satanic Groups. 221

Section 9: In Conclusion. 237

Appendix 1: Satanic Voices 241
    Elements of Satanic Practice. 242
    Coming Out as a Satanist. 270
    Creating Satanic Art 292
    Satanic Altars 327
    Satanic Tattoos 352
    Choosing a Satanic Pseudonym 367

Appendix 2: Sample Rituals 373
    Personal Satanic Dedication. 374
    Satanic Invocation 375
    Unbaptism Ritual 377
    Satanic Destruction Ritual 380
    Initiation Ceremony 384
    Winter Solstice Self-Affirmation Ritual 387
    ĪNFLAMMŌ: A Winter Solstice Ritual. 389
    Satanic Wedding Ritual 391
    Vow Renewal Ceremony 394
    Satanic New Moon Ceremony 398
    Satanic Remembrance Ritual. 402

Appendix 3: Satanic Holidays .411

Appendix 4: Recommended Reading 415

Foreword

by Lucien Greaves

In January of 2020 I was being cross-examined, on trial, in a federal court in Phoenix, Arizona, regarding a religious discrimination suit that The Satanic Temple had filed against the City of Scottsdale where the acting City Council had refused to allow a representative of our religious organization to deliver the pre-meeting invocation, traditionally given almost exclusively by Christians. The United States Supreme Court had ruled that such public invocations or prayers are Constitutionally acceptable so long as government officials remain neutral regarding viewpoint, rendering the opportunity available to all. Of course, the Supreme Court's affirmation of pluralism went over the heads of religious nationalists who assumed they had been given an exclusive carte blanche to proselytize without the perceived indignity of alternative viewpoints enjoying equal access.

The defense for Scottsdale attempted to argue every possible excuse: that it was an administrator's error, not the City Council prejudice that was to blame for our exclusion, despite the various disparaging comments City Council members had publicly made about us; that City Councils, despite both the letter and the spirit of the law, are actually free to pick and choose who they want to grant the right of Free Expression; that The Satanic Temple actually never wanted to give an invocation, but were just trying to provoke and offend; and, of course, that The Satanic Temple does not represent a "real" religion anyways, so Religious Discrimination could not be legitimately claimed.

The last argument was particularly irksome, not least because we do, in fact, represent a "real" religion that defines us individually

i

and as a larger community, but also because individual invocations expressing, or rooted in, nonbelief and a refusal to identify with a larger religious community should be considered positions of religious opinion, protected under the umbrella of religious liberty and afforded equal access to public forums as well. Nonetheless, the defense predictably plodded on for hours, cherry-picking facts regarding our origins, pretending that authentic belief and activism are, in some inexplicable way, mutually exclusive, and painting us as a parody of "real" religion, as opposed to a religion ourselves.

Amid a torrent of facile, if not idiotic, questions that implicitly assumed that Christian practice defines true religious behavior, a lawyer happened to ask me a question that often troubles the minds of even those who are not attempting to distort facts unfavorably against us.

> *Q: What is the difference between identifying as a Satanic Temple Satanist and being an atheist?*
>
> *A: Well, I think The Satanic Temple's beliefs speak to something more generalized that is uninformed by, and I would argue untouchable by, science, in that it views this universal struggle against tyranny and autonomy, it puts these values in a balance that can't be proven, but it does speak to universal truths of the utmost importance.*

As has often been said, atheism describes what we are not. Satanism describes what we are.

Yes, "beliefs should conform to one's best scientific understanding of the world," and "one should take care never to distort scientific facts to fit one's beliefs," but the prioritization of scientific facts, how they are constructed into ethical guidelines, may forever be open to debate. Who can say that autonomy is preferable to tyranny without some predetermined values that define "preferable?" Is not Justice an abstract concept resistant to rigid scientific definitions? Why should one strive to serve the greatest good for the greatest number rather than advance their own self-interest, or that of their tribe? Indeed, some self-described "individualists" paradoxically eschew the values of equality and personal sovereignty in favor of a vision of social darwinist stratification, where the "strong," of superior will and worthier merit, are themselves free to tyrannize their presumed lessers.

Only in attempting to elevate supernaturalism over nontheistic religion would one insist that such broad and basic assumptions are too mundane, too reasonable, to be considered properly religious. Only in preferencing superstition would one insist that special privileges and exemptions are afforded only to those whose assumptions go beyond the unknowable and into the realm of a faith held contrary to knowable facts.

But are these values of The Satanic Temple not philosophical rather than religious?

Not when lives are lived in deference to them and communities ordered upon applying them. Not with ceremonies declaring adherence to them, rituals and symbols utilized to invoke them.

For anybody who has traveled out to meet the diverse, dedicated chapters that compose the ever-growing Satanic Temple community, the question of whether or not we are a real religion becomes somewhat absurd and meaningless. If our activities are merely "performative," as is sometimes suggested, then why are all of these members often engaging in them in closed groups with no "audience" other than themselves? If The Satanic Temple is merely "political," as is also suggested, why is it that so many discussions and writings emerging from our community are centered upon determining the best personal application of our ethics to everyday circumstances? In desperation, even our refusal to subject our community to authoritarian conditioning is decried as a deviation from real religion. Our rituals are too creative, collaborative, and malleable to circumstance, unlike "real" rituals, which are static, rote, and subjugating.

And what of our book? Can a religion be predicated on all of one page listing but seven tenets? Is it not required that an authentic religion will be based upon a massive prescriptive tome written in archaic dialect, full of parables, prohibitions, and demands? Again, the tactic seems to be to distinguish the ways in which we are not Christianity, and then insist that these are shortcomings that exclude us from being appropriately religious. There is a vast body of literature, from centuries old works of Romantic Satanism to modern science texts, that comprises our reading lists, but like our philosophy of ritual — and consistent with our anti-authoritarian philosophy in general — it is a list that can always grow, always be subject to revision. To insist that the final word has been delivered is to abandon inquiry and growth.

Along with that growing list of Temple canon we can happily add Lilith Starr's *Compassionate Satanism*, a thoughtful, beautiful exploration of Modern Satanism by one of our first establishing chapter heads who helped us to grow and cultivate the diverse, robust, rapidly expanding worldwide community we boast today.

When the Scottsdale decision was handed down, the judge wasted few words unambiguously affirming our religious legitimacy directly citing my testimony regarding "universal truths of the utmost importance." To the devastating inconvenience of the theocratic nationalists who wish that we would disappear and leave them to exclusive representation in public, arguments against our religious legitimacy hold no credibility. And as we continue to grow, attempts to argue against our legitimacy will be apparently more absurd, even to distant observers. As our own organizational history grows with time, and testimonials expand the record of the Satanic experience within The Satanic Temple, sociologists and religion scholars will surely marvel at how quickly Modern Satanism entrenched itself in 21st century culture after a slow, uncertain 20th century start from which it almost faded into total irrelevance until around 2013.

Now of course, Christian Nationalists who propose theocratic legislation to advance their agendas have to consider the potential for a balancing equal access claim made by Satanists who are motivated to uphold pluralism and actual religious liberty. Now, the entire landscape of the Culture War has been altered by the emergence of an unexpected, though long-denigrated and misunderstood, nontheistic religious identity. Now, those who were traditionally marginalized, outcast, and often abused by religious institutions have a religious community in which they can unapologetically and openly embrace who they are. Now, when false accusations rooted in conspiracy theories are directed at Satanists, there is an oppositional voice of reason that serves to correct the record and disabuse people of the lies.

Now, at long last, Satanism has arrived … no longer mythic boogeymen, but a movement, a cultural upheaval, a religious revolution.

To understand how we got from there to here, this book is an excellent place to start.

Lucien Greaves
3 months in pandemic isolation
Salem, MA
2020

Introduction

Say the word "Satanism," and many people envision the Hollywood image — a cult of evil, committing human sacrifice in service to the Devil in exchange for the secrets of black magic. The media loves using Satanism as a titillating device to evoke fear and horror.

But these lurid images are far from the reality of modern Satanism. In fact, the most widespread Satanic sect, nontheistic Romantic Satanism, doesn't include belief in an actual, literal Devil at all, seeing Satan instead as an inspiring literary hero described in Paradise Lost and later Romantic literature. This form of Satanism holds compassion and justice as its highest goals, and its practitioners dedicate themselves to community service and the fight for religious freedom. It is a positive force for good in many followers' lives — including my own.

This Satanic religion has literally saved my life. It gave me the strength to end a lifetime of addiction, and being part of a vibrant, compassionate Satanic community now gives me the meaning and purpose required to get through my daily struggles with chronic pain and mental illness.

This book is my way of trying to give back to the movement that changed my life. In it, I share my personal experiences with the Satanic path and my thoughts on Satanic practice, along with interviews with other Satanists about their own personal practice.

MY SATANIC STORY

When I was younger, I would never have believed I would end up a Satanist. Yet a lifetime of intently pursuing my spiritual

1

awakening culminated at last in finding a religious home in modern nontheistic Romantic Satanism (which I often refer to as "Compassionate Satanism" for brevity's sake).

I've always been a seeker after the sacred. My parents were back-to-the-land hippies and I grew up in the wilderness of Alaska and California, miles away from other people. We had no electricity, phone or plumbing; my parents grew almost all our food themselves. I was extremely isolated, with no siblings or childhood friends — though I did attend a nearby elementary school, I could never figure out how to interact correctly with others, leaving me an outcast, living on the fringes with no friends to confide in. I turned to books as a way to escape and explore, which instilled in me from an early age a profound love of learning and knowledge.

Although my grandparents were Lutheran, my parents weren't religious in any way. At age 7 I asked my mom if God existed; she told me that some people believe so, but it didn't mean I had to — I could choose for myself. As I grew up, free from an imposed faith, I found a sense of deep meaning in the wilderness around me. I felt connected to nature, reverent of it, worshipful of the teeming life around me and the peace of the woods and meadows.

But on those occasions when we traveled to visit my grandparents and I attended services at their church, I felt myself drawn to the feelings of sacredness, the pageantry and heightened intention of ritual, and the feelings of warm fellowship when the whole congregation sang or responded together. I remember attending midnight Christmas service, where every congregation member was given a candle and the dark church blazed with individual lights as we sang the sacred songs. I felt like I was part of something larger, connected at last to other people.

At the time, I thought Christian beliefs focused on how to be a good human being and treat others with respect and compassion. I found it inspiring, and I decided I wanted to live a life devoted

2

to this sacred calling. At age 11, I chose to have myself baptized in my grandparents' Lutheran church and started taking Confirmation classes to begin my Christian journey in earnest.

But as I progressed in my church studies and started to learn more about what Christianity really entailed, the faith started to lose its luster. The first thing I noticed in my studies was that women were really getting the shit end of the stick in this faith. There was a clear patriarchal hierarchy in place and women were meant to be subservient to men. Women were seen as lesser-than, passive and weak, the source of the Original Sin that plunged humanity into endless suffering, good for little else other than bearing children and keeping house for the men who more or less owned them.

The second fly in my Christian ointment was that the pastor's son and daughter bullied me mercilessly the whole time I was studying there. I had already spent so many years as the school pariah, universally bullied and shunned, unable to find a place among the social groups. I was that one kid in every school that everybody picked on. It cut deeply into my psyche. Though I got love and acceptance from my caring counter-culture parents at home, from kindergarten to almost the end of high school I faced intolerance and scorn from my fellow students.

I had believed Christianity taught humbleness and kindness, and thus I expected that the children of the church leader, ostensibly the closest to God, would break the mold and act with compassion toward me. But instead, the pastor's son and daughter led the whole group to bully me to new heights. Despite their supposed godliness, they were at the forefront of the attacks.

I grew disenchanted and left, drifting. Then, at age 13, I found the book *The Black Arts* in my stepmother's collection and convinced her to let me have it. I became fascinated with the occult. I began experimenting with the rituals described in the book and learned to read tarot and runes. Shortly thereafter I found the early works that shaped Wicca, and threw myself fully into

Goddess-based witchcraft. I had found a path that combined my intense love for nature with my innate feminist outlook, and it put the power to create my spiritual practice in my own hands. I could indulge my love of symbolism and ritual and fan that spark of connection with the natural world.

In junior high, I read a number of works about witchcraft, and in high school I studied briefly with an older mentor. It was at the dawn of the Wiccan movement in America, and there was no coven that I knew of in my area (plus I was underage). I was determined to bring my sacred path to life, though, and in high school I convinced a number of friends to form a coven with me. We would sneak out to parks at night and do our rituals under the moon.

It was the mid-eighties, in the full swing of the Satanic Panic, when mass hysteria was gripping the populace with lurid paranoid delusions about widespread Satanic ritual abuse. I had no clue. We were actually out there in the woods conducting ceremonies during this time, though they were more about light and love than anything else. We were lucky no one discovered and attacked us.

I wore my pentagram prominently, and took it upon myself to speak up about witchcraft to others, hoping to educate when I had the opportunity to do so. The irony is that what I had to explain most often was the fact that Wicca was emphatically *not* Satanism.

When I went away for college in Massachusetts, I searched for and found an eclectic witchcraft coven, and made time in my busy study schedule for it. But by graduate school I had started moving away from Wicca, growing more atheistic and practical in my outlook.

Drawn by what a few friends had told me about Buddhism, I began studying Zen, which overlapped nicely with the complexity science I had started studying. I liked Buddhism's focus on compassion, and Zen was nontheistic and geared toward knowing the world — and myself — just as it is. I started a mindfulness meditation practice, and even now I still meditate every day; it's one of the few things that really helps manage my depression.

I liked the idea that everything was holy just as it is — that indeed reality itself is sacred, without the need for an external power to make it so. Zen dovetailed easily with science, which formed another pillar of my belief system. I saw the sacred blazoned across the cosmos in the principles of self-organization. Reality held all the spirituality I needed.

But I missed the imagery of ritual, and I was still wholly feminist. Over time I began integrating bits of witchcraft back into my personal practice, though I now had a completely nontheistic outlook. I saw it all as a system of archetypes and metaphors that helped me focus and understand myself. I developed my own unique spiritual path focused on archetypes of the Dark Goddess (especially those found in Sumerian mythology) along with compassion and mindfulness.

To my surprise, at age 38, I fell madly, deeply in love with my current partner. After a year spent exploring the depths of love and feeling its power, I made a vow to live a 100% sacred life as a Priestess of the Dark Path of Love, devoting my heart and mind to the service of bringing love into the world, however I could.

And then, through a series of unfortunate events, our world shattered, and my partner and I lost our housing and ended up homeless on the streets. My perspective boomeranged. When we were on the streets, we experienced what all homeless people suffer: being driven from place to place with no hope of rest, no food, no help or support — indeed, no recognition that you are still a fellow human being, but rather the certainty that you are instead a disgusting species of vermin that should be eliminated. There was no place to sleep. Coffee shops wouldn't let us sit and charge our phone or even use the restroom, even though we were buying expensive drinks for the privilege. There were no services or charities that could help us in the city we had ended up in.

People treated us like shit while we were engaged in the most intense struggle of our lives. I saw the horrorshow that is the underbelly of our society, where good people suffering terrible tragedies were spurned, hated and ignored by those still comfortably ensconced in housing, unaware that they too could be one or two paychecks away from homelessness. I started to realize just how broken our society was.

It was at this point that I picked up my partner's copy of *The Satanic Bible* by Anton LaVey and read it cover to cover, along with *The Satanic Rituals*. What I found changed my life forever, turning my perspective on its head, putting the power back in my hands, and setting me on the path that would eventually bring me to The Satanic Temple.

MENTAL HEALTH STRUGGLES

In addition to the problems we faced on the streets, I was up against a lot from my own brain. I've suffered from major depressive disorder since my teen years. It runs in my family, and the long years of bullying from my classmates had combined with the genetic factor to give me a high level of mental illness, with frequent suicidal ideation. I remember I'd walk to junior high school, pondering the oleander leaves for poison potential or looking for sharp glass on the ground for possibly slitting my wrists. I believed my classmates when they told me there was something wrong with me. I figured the world would be better off without me.

As a child, I internalized the messages from Christianity that held up self-sacrifice as the greatest good. From an early age, I felt that the best way I could be a good person was to sacrifice myself for others, just as Jesus gave up his life to save mankind. It was easy to take the taunting attacks by my childhood peers as confirmation that I had nothing to offer on my own, that I did not deserve to feel good about myself, that the only way I could contribute to society was by putting all my energy into helping others, the cost to myself be damned. The depression helped reinforce these

6

messages that I was unworthy, broken, useful only insofar as I could lay my life on the altar of sacrifice.

Triggered by a mentally abusive relationship, I started self-harming in college. The voices in my head attacking my self-worth grew louder, and I felt even more broken and undeserving of happiness. My mind was a hell filled with self-hate. This depression bloomed into an addiction that derailed my life for decades.

THE ADDICTIVE CYCLE

After my undergraduate degree, I went to graduate school, where I joined the notoriously-misbehaving Stanford Marching Band and first tried nitrous oxide ("whip-its") and other drugs. I fell in love with the escape they offered from the incessant attacks in my own head. I found that psychedelic mushrooms were actually a great treatment for my depression (a conclusion reinforced by the results of numerous scientific studies as well), but I had no connections to get them, and instead turned to nitrous oxide because it was legal and easy to get. Nitrous offered intense disassociation, sending me far away from myself and my troubles. I started using it outside of band events, turning to it more and more.

Thus began a 17-year-long addiction that left the bulk of my life in utter ruin, losing me my high-paying tech job, my house, my car, and my ex-husband. It started with nitrous, but by the end I had reached meth and heroin.

Despite my desperate attempts to end my addiction, the overwhelming depression would compel me again and again to buy drugs in an attempt to escape the mental agony. Then the fact that I had failed and given in to my inescapable addiction, that I was a weak-willed addict, would throw me into an even deeper pit of despair — which would make me crave the drugs even more. I was trapped in an endless downward spiral.

Nothing I tried could rid me of this nightmare. I turned to the

Twelve Step program Narcotics Anonymous (NA) in an attempt to get help. I tried for nine years to get clean in NA, putting in all my effort and time to follow the program — going to meetings, getting a sponsor and "working the steps" in an attempt to end my addiction.

The crucial steps of NA (and indeed, of all Twelve Step groups) dictated that I had to admit I was powerless over my addiction and "turn my will and my life" over to a Higher Power — then pray for that Higher Power to "remove my defects of character," including the addiction. Despite this focus on a Higher Power, and despite having prayers before and after the meetings, including the Lord's Prayer, when I objected I was told the program was "spiritual not religious," and I could pick any higher power I wanted, as long as it was not myself.

Since I believed in no Higher Power, this system utterly failed me. I was used to holding my own will as my highest power, but my sponsor told me I had to choose something outside of myself. I fervently tried to do as directed, seeing myself as powerless and begging nature, the Buddha, and the NA group itself to help me. But since I couldn't really make myself believe that an external Higher Power could step in and fix me, I felt well and truly screwed, unable to stop myself from buying the drugs. After almost a decade of working the NA program, I still couldn't shake the addiction.

By the time I met my partner, I had given up on life. I believed I would always be an addict and a failure and resigned myself to a slow form of drug-induced suicide. There was no joy in my world.

But when my partner came into my life, I found myself inspired to fight for something again. His love pulled me out of the despair. And when I explored his Satanic belief system during our time of hardship in 2011, it sparked a sea-change in my life that would lead to finally leaving the addiction behind.

FINDING SATANISM

Reading *The Satanic Bible* gave me a new way of reframing the world. In LaVey's works I saw at last a mandate for self-compassion. The central message I took away from that form of Satanism was "You are your own god." You are the one who holds the power over your life, not some external deity, person or group. There's no need to follow the masses and try to fit yourself into their mold. You have within you everything you need to live a fulfilled life without bowing to pressures from the outside that assail your individuality.

Reading those books gave me back my capacity for self-compassion. I'd spent my life believing society's messages that I was broken and unworthy. But now, I could clearly see the troubles with society itself. It might not all be me — our societal systems and individual capacity for empathy were broken too. Seeing this helped me stop beating myself up and instead turn to compassion for myself. I deserved love and understanding, no matter how broken I was. I no longer held self-sacrifice as the highest good; instead I began to attempt to "put my own oxygen mask on first" and care for myself before I tried to take care of others.

The flip-side of that was that Satanism also dictated self-responsibility. If I was the only one who could truly make a difference in my life, then I had the responsibility to do so. It was this new way of seeing the world that would eventually give me the strength to grasp my own empowerment and leave the drugs behind. After 17 years of helplessness, I used my Satanic beliefs and willpower to finally break free of the life-destroying addiction. At last I had found a path that allowed me to bust out of that cage I never thought I'd leave.

This self-empowerment also gave me the strength to reach out to old friends and get the help we needed to move up to Seattle and find housing and work. No longer on the streets, we were finally able to build the life we wanted.

FINDING SATANIC COMMUNITY

I was grateful for Satanism, and I wanted to help educate and inspire others interested in it. In 2012, I started writing essays for a website called "Satanism 101," and when the editor quit, I took his place. I got to manage a team of writers with quick wit and highly individual approaches to Satanism. Most of the people I was working with seemed incredibly cool; I began to understand that Satanism was full of intelligent, courageous free-thinkers, quick with a laugh or joke, who were not afraid to call shit as they saw it. It was there that I got my first taste of Satanic community — and I wanted more.

Then in 2013, I first read about a new group of Satanists called "The Satanic Temple" — they had put up a holiday display in the Florida Capitol building during the holiday season alongside a nativity display there. I also read about their battle to distribute their own (incredibly cute and wholesome) *Satanic Kids Activity Book* in Florida public schools that permitted Bible distributions to students. Instead of allowing the Satanic activity book, the targeted school district backed down and decided to end their policy of religious literature distribution, ensuring all religious material, including bibles, would be kept out.

I cheered The Satanic Temple on and went to find out more. I encountered their list of beliefs, which focused on compassion, justice, bodily autonomy and reason. I felt like those beliefs described my own set of values, and I liked what The Satanic Temple (often shortened as "TST") stood for. I became a member of the national organization, seeing their path as compatible with the LaVeyan Satanism I already subscribed to. Over time, I left behind the LaVeyan identification and threw my lot completely in with TST.

Though what I had found in LaVeyanism included self-compassion and self-empowerment, twin values that helped me leave behind addiction and homelessness, what I took away from it was just a thin slice of the whole package. The rest of that package was filled with elitism and Social Darwinism, the idea that some people are better than others and deserve to take what they want no matter if it hurts someone.

LaVey lifted a large portion of *The Satanic Bible* directly from a racist screed called *Might is Right*. *The Satanic Bible* taught that it was a dog-eat-dog world and fostered a hyper-competitive view of the Satanist's place in it. I saw this play out to a disturbing degree in Satanic spaces online. I saw misogyny, racism and homophobia run rampant. I wished there could be a better version of Satanism, one without the toxic portions of the philosophy.

And then my wish came true — TST appeared on the scene.

TST was founded by two highly intelligent, articulate scholars, Lucien Greaves and Malcolm Jarry, in 2013. Though it started as a light-hearted attempt to showcase the absurdity of injecting Christian prayer into public schools, it quickly outgrew its farcical beginnings and morphed into a very real, very serious religious movement with many thousands of followers.

Jarry and Greaves had been part of the existing Satanic movement. But in founding The Satanic Temple, they broke away from that former path and touched off a Satanic Reformation of sorts. Instead of working from LaVey's books, they turned to an older Satanic movement called Romantic Satanism, based on the writings of revolutionary artists like Shelley, Byron and Blake in the late 1700s and early 1800s, who saw in the Satan of *Paradise Lost* an inspired hero fighting against tyranny for the rights of humanity.

This Romantic Satanism grew out of those writers' own fight against the oppression of the monarchy and Church, and their desire to overthrow authoritarianism and install instead representative governments that would recognize the equal rights of all. Their philosophy had its basis in the ideas of the Enlightenment — a new way of thinking that dominated European thought from the 17th to 19th centuries, rooted in the decline of Christian and monarchical hegemony and the resurgence of humanism-based Classical ideals from ancient Greece and Rome. The Enlightenment lauded virtues such as individual liberty, progress, religious tolerance, fraternity, constitutional government and separation of church and state. This philosophy was a powerful force in guiding the birth of the United States and breaking the chains of monarchy around the world.

These are the guiding principles encapsulated in The Satanic Temple's Seven Fundamental Tenets, and I agreed with them 100%; they felt like ideals I was already striving for. In addition, TST's religion carried with it a mandate for action — as one TST leader put it, "Activism is our form of worship." By fighting for equal rights and standing against theocracy, Satanists can follow the example of our beloved literary symbol Satan, who stood up against an unjust tyrant.

MY TST JOURNEY

I was overjoyed to finally find a religion that felt like it was mine, that encouraged individuality and self-empowerment but also provided a set of compassionate, humanistic values and the chance to engage with the world through community service and activism. I fell in love with Romantic Satanism. I eagerly followed the various campaigns The Satanic Temple waged — holiday displays at state capitols, kids' literature distributions, and the fight to place their 8-foot-tall bronze statue of the winged, goat-headed figure Baphomet next to the Ten Commandments monuments that had been permitted on state capitol grounds. Then in 2014, they took on a new battle.

In the 2014 case Burwell v. Hobby Lobby, the US Supreme Court made a landmark decision that allowed for-profit corporations to be exempt from regulations its owners religiously objected to. In particular, it allowed the evangelical-owned craft store chain Hobby Lobby to refuse to provide contraception as part of their medical benefits, even though they were required by law to offer it. This decision utilized the Religious Freedom Restoration Act of 1993, which was meant to ensure that religious freedom was protected, to apply "religious freedom" as a blanket protection for Christian corporations as well as individuals who didn't want to follow the law. This cry of religious freedom has since been used to bludgeon civil rights, allowing everyone from bakers to emergency personnel to refuse service to gay and trans individuals. Reproductive rights and the rights of the LGBTQ community have been superseded by the "rights" of evangelicals to act with bigotry with no legal consequences.

Watching the Hobby Lobby case play out was infuriating. I despaired of justice in the face of this attack on basic civil rights. But then The Satanic Temple announced they were launching a new campaign that used the Hobby Lobby decision to fight *for* reproductive rights.

Because one of TST's core religious beliefs is that one's body is inviolable, subject to one's own will alone, they argued that restrictive state abortion laws that required waiting periods, unnecessary invasive ultrasounds, and forced reading of wildly inaccurate medical literature (that insisted abortion causes breast cancer, for instance) should not apply to TST members and others who share TST's beliefs. They put out a legal waiver that an individual could use to insist they had the right to opt out of those unnecessary restrictions and announced they were ready to launch a lawsuit against any state who ignored that individual's religious freedom on this issue. A number of women responded, and so far, TST has launched four lawsuits of this type, supporting women who faced these restrictions or the requirement that aborted tissue be given a full legal burial.

The day I heard that TST had announced this campaign, my heart leapt in my throat. I felt a fierce joy and pride in being part of this religious organization that was fighting so hard for reproductive rights, something very near and dear to my own heart. I was no longer content to just be a passive member listed on their membership rolls. I wanted to get more involved and help out however I could.

I vowed to become part of the local in-person TST community, supporting the organization in their various campaigns. At the time, there were only five local Chapters of TST scattered around the US, including ones in Texas, Maine, New Orleans and Detroit. When I inquired, there was no Chapter here in Seattle. So I applied to start one, going through a written application and an interview process for the role of Chapter Head. In October of 2014, my application was accepted, and in December 2014, TST Seattle held its first meeting at a local library.

The meeting was well-attended. Afterwards, though we were all strangers, we went out to dinner and talked for hours. I immediately felt a sense of deep connection — like I had finally found my people, my family. We talked freely about things most others barely tolerated or were dismissive of, but were so important to us all at heart — our Satanic explorations and beliefs, the problems with theocracy, the need for church-state separation, and the threat to religious freedom by evangelical Dominionism. I saw intelligence and bravery, a strong sense of individuality and independence. And I also got the sense that most of us had been misfits and outcasts from our families and various communities.

From that auspicious start, TST Seattle grew by leaps and bounds. It took a huge amount of effort to really get it going, and I spent many days feeling overwhelmed, but though we had some rough patches along the way, we steadily grew and evolved into a dynamic religious community where members could feel safe and accepted, and where they could have the chance to practice their Satanism alongside others.

In the last six years since we were founded, our congregation has done so much. We've performed countless rituals — unbaptisms, initiations, rituals to celebrate the official holidays of The Satanic Temple, a recurring Invocation at the end of every Chapter meeting, and much more. We've put on nightclub shows to raise money for TST's battle for reproductive rights. We've collected menstrual products for homeless people — in 2019, we managed to gather over 400 pounds of tampons, pads and menstrual cups for local shelters. We've hosted blood drives, cleaned up parks, volunteered at food banks, and come out to support our LGBTQ community at local Pride festivals.

We've also worked tirelessly for church-state separation. When local high school football coach Joe Kennedy began asking his team to pray with him on the 50-yard-line at the end of every game, clearly violating the Establishment Clause, a few students from his school invited us to come and support their religious rights by performing a Satanic Invocation on the field at the same time. We sent a letter asking the school district for permission. They couldn't say no while still allowing Kennedy his evangelical prayer, so they suspended him (and later fired him) and ended his practice of forced student prayer for good.

Though we weren't allowed to do our Invocation on the field, since the coach wasn't doing his, we still dressed up in our black ritual robes and came to the next football game in solidarity with the courageous students who had dared to reach out to us. I remember meeting the young people, hugging them, and feeling my heart swell with pride knowing we had stood up and made a difference in their lives.

The most difficult campaign and one of the most impactful contributions, however, came when we brought TST's first functioning "After School Satan Club" to life at a local elementary school, where the Christian Evangelical Foundation ran a Good News Club after school on the premises — a club whose mentally abusive curriculum focused on teaching children as young as five that they and their family and friends were destined to be tortured and burned forever in hell. TST launched the ASSC to provide an alternative. The curriculum was based on science and reason, and the Club incorporated games, projects, and thinking exercises that helped kids learn critical thinking skills and encouraged them to draw their own conclusions about the world.

Despite a firestorm of opposition, we ran the ASSC at Point Defiance Elementary in Tacoma throughout the 2016 school

15

year. We were the first ASSC to gain students. Both the kids who participated and their parents told us they really enjoyed the club and appreciated that we could provide an alternative to the terrifying, manipulative hellfire-and-brimstone teachings of the Good News Club.

Besides our outward-facing activities, we've shared deeply meaningful personal experiences within the Chapter as well. One couple in the Chapter had a lovely Vow Renewal ceremony, and we have another one coming up soon. The Chapter has played a role in countless members' lives by inspiring them to stand up and be unapologetically themselves, external judgement be damned. And we've tried our best to be there with support when members' families or others cut them off because of their Satanism.

Because The Satanic Temple is founded on ideals of compassion, tolerance, equality and reason, it attracts those who make those values a priority, and it shows in the caring I see members give to one another and the strides they make toward change. Working alongside kindred spirits doing activism and community service can be transformative.

We tried our best to make our Chapter a safe space — come as you are; we won't try to change you or force you into a mold. I would have never imagined that a community like ours could exist: one where everyone is accepted as they are, without pressure to conform or obey, where individuality is celebrated instead of stamped out. So many people have told me, after a lifetime of being rejected by society and/or family, "I didn't think I would ever find a connection with others until I joined TST."

Though I retired from my Chapter Head role in 2019, I am still an active member of our Chapter, and I still practice my Satanism in my daily life. Satanic beliefs and community are what sustain me through my everyday challenges.

A WAY THROUGH THE PAIN

Over my lifetime, osteoarthritis has set in in both knees and my spine, leaving me in constant, intense pain. Sitting up is excruciating, so every minute I spend writing is dearly bought. The pain also exacerbates my depression, and I still struggle with self-harm and suicidal ideation on a regular basis.

Because of these conditions, I had to stop working in 2014, and now I survive solely on a small disability check from the state. My partner is also disabled, so we're trying to survive on his tiny Social Security check as well, fighting to remain under a roof in one of the most expensive housing markets in the nation.

In other circumstances, these hurdles I face would seem insurmountable. But because I have my Satanic beliefs and the support from my Satanic community, I can push through. The friendships and camaraderie born of our Chapter and the larger Satanic community help sustain me through the pain-induced isolation, and I've received so much help from my Satanic family when facing life's big emergencies.

It is my Satanism that strengthens my heart and will. I feel like I've spent much of my life empty inside, but now I've found that meaning and purpose I was searching for. With my ongoing Satanic practice, I have finally found a way to live in sacred space, dedicated to compassion and justice, following a religion that inspires me to keep going through the pain and hard times.

INSIDE THIS BOOK

It is this continued gratitude to the Satanic path that has driven me to put together this book. It is my attempt to give back to this religion that has been such a positive force in my own life.

This book encompasses my own personal interpretation of Satanism. It is based on my experiences as a Satanic practitioner, and it is absolutely not meant as an official statement from TST. I'm not speaking in this book in any capacity as an official representative of The Satanic Temple, but simply one among the greater community of Satanists, pursuing my own individual path. I'm not trying to claim this is an objective, scholarly work, only my personal interpretation of my own Satanic experiences. Any instructive tone I take is meant only to make it easier to read.

Modern Satanism is not a cookie-cutter religion. Unlike the Abrahamic religions (religions that share Abraham as a patriarch, including Christianity, Judaism, and Islam) with their rigid dogma and restrictive rule set, Satanism is a religion of individuality, reason, freedom, self-knowledge and self-empowerment. Thus, while I can give you the basics of my Satanism as I understand and practice it, I'm not positioning this work as any sort of final authority on Satanism. All I can do is present what has worked for me.

In this book, I'll give you an introduction to my perspective on nontheistic Romantic Satanism. In the first part, I'll give a brief overview of the rise of Satanism, then cover the Satanic narrative and the Seven Tenets as I see them, the ethical system at the core of my religious path. I'll delve into my interpretation of the role of the Outcast in Satanism, followed by my take on several important tools for practice — Satanic symbolism and ritual — and tips for getting started as a practitioner on the individual level. Finally, I'll discuss taking action for justice and finding a Satanic community in your area.

I've also provided several Appendices with info I thought might be helpful, including a lengthy Interviews section where a number of other Satanists open up about aspects of their own practice, a set of Sample Rituals you can use to jumpstart your own ritual creation, a Recommended Reading list, and a list of the Satanic holidays I celebrate.

This work is meant only as a beginning, not an end, to Satanic studies — it should serve as a jumping-off point into other writings and talks. There is a great deal of information available in the form of books, essays, presentations, blogs and interviews with the founders of The Satanic Temple and various scholars and philosophers. Studying Satanism can be a lifelong endeavor, and I encourage you to continue to expand your knowledge on an ongoing basis.

Feel free to take whatever works for you in this book and discard the rest. I'm not trying to convert anyone; Satanism includes a solid no-proselytization guideline. I'm simply providing a window into what one person's practice of Compassionate Satanism can look like. But my hope is that by providing a glimpse into my own Satanic practice and that of a few others, this book may inspire those who are interested to begin building their own personalized Satanic practice.

Sign display on the Knoxville Baptist Tabernacle.

SECTION 1
The Rise of Satanism

At a city council meeting in Florida, after protestors shout prayers in an attempt to drown him out, a man in black robes begins an invocation, singing out in a strong and melodic voice, "Let us embrace the Luciferian impulse to eat of the Tree of Knowledge and dissipate our blissful and comforting delusions of old!"

In the Illinois Capitol rotunda, next to the Nativity display and a menorah, a holiday display is set up showing an arm with a snake coiled around it, holding an apple and bearing a pentagram and the words "Knowledge Is The Greatest Gift."

In Seattle, 13 ritual participants rise from kneeling with the mark of free will on their foreheads, while a priestess exhorts: "Your power is now your own and you are free to walk your own path, to follow your own will, and to soar on your own wings. In the Name of Lucifer, you are free!"

And in countless homes and gathering places around the globe, people are discovering a new religion that champions individuality and freedom, compassion and reason, all without archaic supernaturalism — a path that offers a humanitarian value set and meaning found within, instead of imposed from without.

This religion is nontheistic Romantic Satanism (or as I call my interpretation of it, "Compassionate Satanism"), and people are turning to it in record numbers, empowering themselves while fighting the rising tide of theocracy and religious oppression. The largest Satanic organization, The Satanic Temple, has chapters around the world and is still expanding. Satanists are making headlines everywhere as they fight for the same rights accorded other religions.

This form of Satanism is based on Enlightenment ideals like tolerance, empathy, reason and civil rights. Adherents share a belief in the Seven Fundamental Tenets of The Satanic Temple, a humanitarian set of common-sense ethics. Romantic Satanists find meaning in the narrative of Satan as a symbol of rebellion against unjust and arbitrary authority, teaching that it is one's duty to actively fight tyranny and work toward a better, more just society. And unlike in other, more mainstream religions, Satanists embrace their outsider status unapologetically.

THE SATANIC TEMPLE

The term "Satanism" covers a broad range of different religious paths. Some are nontheistic, meaning there is no supernaturalism or deity involved, and others are theistic, meaning they do believe in supernatural powers or Satan. Other non-Satanic practices, including Luciferianism and certain strains of paganism and ceremonial magic, may also make use of Satanic imagery and symbology. But in this book, I'm speaking exclusively of nontheistic Romantic Satanism, the kind of Satanism pioneered by The Satanic Temple.

Founded by Lucien Greaves and Malcolm Jarry in 2013, The Satanic Temple (abbreviated as "TST") represents an evolution in modern Satanic thought.

Despite wild accusations of devil worship by the medieval Church, Satanism as a separate religion wasn't actually practiced in a widespread fashion until the 1960s, when Anton LaVey published his Satanic Bible and started the Church of Satan. Based largely on the ideas of Ayn Rand and Ragnar Redbeard, the central doctrine of LaVeyanism was "might is right," along with self-deification. LaVey encouraged an every-man-for-himself, cut-throat mentality in the name of Social Darwinism, and fostered elitism among his followers.

When The Satanic Temple was founded, the Satanic landscape shifted drastically. In contrast to LaVeyanism, The Satanic Temple's teachings are based in much earlier works such as *Paradise Lost* (written in 1667) and writing of the Romantic period (late 1700s - 1800s). It is founded on entirely different principles based in the ideas of the Enlightenment — the notions of individual freedom, equal rights and justice for all, compassion, the primacy of reason, the rejection of the supernatural, and rebellion against tyranny. Instead of outdated Social Darwinism theories, TST recognizes today's scientific consensus that humans are social animals; we've evolved to work together to solve our problems.

From the beginning, this view of Romantic Satanism carried a mandate for action, to fight against injustice as Satan fought back against a tyrannical God. The Satanic Temple claims for Satanism the same legal rights as any other religion under our nation's constitutional Establishment Clause. TST is well-known for its many legal challenges to Christian supremacism in government, from its battle to place a large bronze Baphomet monument next to Ten Commandments statues to its fight to allow Satanic kids' literature to be distributed alongside bibles in public schools. Because one of its deeply held beliefs is the inviolability of one's body, TST has filed multiple lawsuits attempting to protect reproductive rights from scripture-based anti-abortion legislation.

At the local level, TST Chapters provide a way for Satanists to come together and pool their efforts in their nearby region. They help protect church-state separation where theocracy encroaches on their city or state, as well as offering service to their local community in many different ways, from coat drives to beach and highway cleanups. Chapters also provide a close-knit Satanic community for their members, offering all that other religious communities do in terms of camaraderie, friendship, and social gatherings with like-minded people, as well as a chance to engage in ritual.

While it is a religious organization, The Satanic Temple doesn't provide any sort of "bible" or book of standardized practices and rituals; practice and ritual is left to the individual. You'll see examples of these throughout the book, but ultimately it is up to you to choose what elements to use in your own practice.

In many senses, Satanism is an open-source religion — that is, its philosophy and values are freely shared and can be used as the foundation for many different personal interpretations. The core philosophy is like an open scaffolding on which you can build your own personalized practice. Your Satanic path will grow organically as you progress, blossoming into a religion that celebrates your uniqueness instead of trying to stamp it out.

Practitioners generally just call themselves "Satanists," though you can also say you're a "modern nontheistic Romantic Satanist" if you need to distinguish yourself from followers of other types of Satanism.

NONTHEISTIC RELIGION

The human drive toward religion is deep-seated. Many people can benefit from what religion provides — a worldview, beliefs, a purpose, a ritual practice and a community of like-minded individuals. But superstition is not required to reap those benefits. Romantic Satanism is a nontheistic religion — that is, one that does not entail belief in supernatural beings like God or Satan while still providing everything else religion has to offer.

Nontheism is different than atheism, which connotes nothing more than not believing in God (and in some cases it means *anti-theism*, being actively opposed to the idea of religion altogether). Atheism isn't a religion, just a statement of what you don't believe, but nontheistic Satanism is a full-fledged religion in its own right. When you identify as a Satanist, you are making a positive statement about what you do believe, and claiming your place in the greater Satanic religious community. Lucien Greaves describes the difference:

> *Atheism defines what you're **not**. I object to any narrower definitions of atheism…it's not appropriate to place political values onto it. It's just a declaration of non-belief. And I think we should be happy if we see more conservative atheists…at least then, maybe we can talk about the facts. Empirical evidence. But when you are a Satanist, you've started to define what you **do** believe, what values and ethics you hold, and we're held together as a community by our adherence to that. [1]*

Nontheistic Satanism posits no existence of a higher power or other supernatural force that guides one's life. Instead, the Satanist places faith in themselves and finds meaning and purpose in life within, instead of bowing to an invisible force that requires constant worship and submission.

Those who know only the Abrahamic religions have a hard time understanding how a religion can be nontheistic. For them, religion is synonymous with superstition and blind faith in an omniscient, all-powerful deity. But several ancient religions already exist outside that theistic model.

The venerable Indian religion Jainism, practiced since the 6th century, focuses on perfecting the self, finding liberation and bliss without the help of a higher power. Many sects of Buddhism, especially Zen, don't worship gods or deities, but instead focus on gaining insight into the true nature of life, becoming mindful of reality, and alleviating suffering. These religions count their followers in the millions. Secular Judaism is another nontheistic religion, in which Jews celebrate their cultural heritage and festivals but do not believe in or worship a higher power.

Nontheistic religions, including Satanism, should have the same rights as any other, and deserve equal treatment and benefits under the law. Lucien Greaves explains:

---

1 Jaremko-Greenwold, Anya. "Speaking with Satanic Temple Co-Founder Lucien Greaves at Sundance Made Me Want to Join His Reasonable Religion." *Flood Magazine*. January 30, 2019.

Contrary to popular perception, I argue that religion cannot be defined to require a belief in the supernatural. At its best, religion provides a narrative context, sense of purpose, symbolic struc-ture, identity, values, and a body of practice. Religions enjoy certain privileges and exemptions that would be reprehensible — in a pluralistic society — to reserve for supernaturalists alone. [2]

There can be no doubt that Satanism is in fact a genuine religion. There are official Satanic religious holidays (see the Appendix 3 for a list), and as I write, The Satanic Temple has just launched an ordination program for Satanic clergy. In 2019, the US Inter-nal Revenue Service ruled that The Satanic Temple is in fact a church, with the same rights as any other. And in 2020, in a dis-crimination case brought by TST against Scottsdale, Arizona, the judge ruled that yes, Satanism is a real religion on its own merits, not simply a joke or a way to troll Christians.

For its followers, Satanism provides a narrative — that of Satan's rebellion — that can be used to understand one's identity and life purpose. It provides shared symbols that Satanists find intensely meaningful, and a set of deeply held values that instill a natural sense of ethics. The Satanic narrative and philosophy provide a guide to living your life to the fullest, finding your unique passion and purpose, and fighting for justice. And for many, Satanic practice includes being part of a Satanic commu-nity, with the same shared purpose, community service, regular gatherings and social ties that any other religion offers.

Compare Satanism to any other religion and you can see it fills the same needs and plays the same role in followers' lives. It is this status as a legitimate religion that empowers Satanism to claim its place at the table alongside the others when it comes to a pluralistic society. Greaves says, "While we reject superstition, our values are no less sincerely held. And while we view Sa-tanism in metaphorical terms, our tenets and symbolism are far from arbitrary." [3]

---

2 Greaves, Lucien. "Letters to a Satanist: If we're not a Judeo-Christian nation, where do our laws come from?" *The Lucien Greaves Archives.* www.luciengreaves.com.

3 Greaves, Lucien. "Letters to a Satanist: If we're not a Judeo-Christian nation, where do our laws come from?" *The Lucien Greaves Archives.* www.luciengreaves.com.

WHY SATANISM NOW?

Increasing numbers of individuals are choosing to become Satanists. In its first six years after its founding, The Satanic Temple grew from just three people to over 100,000. The 2019 release of the documentary "Hail Satan?" set off another phenomenal growth spurt around the world. Every state in the US now has a TST Chapter or a group working toward official Chapterhood, and many other countries are in the process of building them as well.

Because Compassionate Satanism provides all the good things about a religion without the trappings of supernaturalism and dogma, it's becoming a refuge for many disillusioned by Abrahamic religions. Record numbers of people, especially young people, are leaving traditional churches in droves, driven away by the hate levelled against LGBTQ individuals, the subjugation of women in the patriarchical church power structure, and the cover-up of child sexual abuse on a massive scale. There is also a yearning to be free of superstition and move toward a more rational worldview. And many people feel alienated from society, isolated, lonely, disconnected and in need of a community they can call their own. Driven by these and other factors, more and more individuals are finding a warm and welcoming home in Satanism.

As a religion, Satanism can also help inspire practitioners to fight against tyranny — especially important at this juncture in time. Theocracy and religious oppression affect countless numbers around the world. Religious extremists hold sway in many places, from Christian fundamentalists in the West to Islamic fundamentalists in the Middle East. In particular, the United States has seen the steady erosion of the original wall between church and state, and the rise to power of evangelical Christians who believe secular government should be abolished and biblical law put in its place.

These politicians command vast amounts of power in our

government at all levels and in all branches. They work to put in place laws and policies that erase reproductive rights, demonize gay and transgender individuals, deny climate science, and attempt to transform our democratic, secular government into a Christian dictatorship. On a personal level, fundamentalism inflicts a heavy burden of shame and guilt, encourages the subjugation of women and children, protects abusers, and teaches us to hate and fear those different from ourselves.

This is where we find ourselves — at a juncture where it is imperative to stand up and resist the theocratic tyranny on our doorstep. The old models of fundamentalist Abrahamic religions breed prejudice, fear, shame and persecution. We need a new religious model that can break down these calcified authority structures and restore full empowerment to the individual. We need a value set and shared narrative that requires no conformity to a herd, no submission and abasement, no self-hate, but instead urges you toward self-acceptance and self-compassion. Satanism provides a new model for religion that awards us our own power and exhorts us to fight for justice against the encroachment of theocracy.

1 • THE RISE OF SATANISM

29

Satan Arousing the Rebel Angels, William Blake, 1808.

SECTION 2
The Narrative of Satan

The narrative of Satan as the eternal rebel standing up to tyranny is at the core of the Romantic Satanism religion; we strive to emulate Satan's fight for justice and to embody the Enlightenment ideals he stands for.

WHY SATAN?

Often the number one question outsiders ask of Satanists is "Why Satan?" It's then usually followed with "Don't you think you'd be better received and more popular if you called yourself something else?" This exchange would never happen with other religions. We don't ask the followers of the Buddha's teachings why they call themselves Buddhists, despite the fact that they too do not worship a higher power. Yet this is a common question, as if the choice of Satan were simply a marketing move or a trolling tactic. Lucien Greaves, spokesperson for The Satanic Temple, responds:

> To ask, as some people do, why we "choose" to "call ourselves" Satanists, if we're not merely attempting to infuriate Christians is to completely misunderstand almost everything about The Satanic Temple. Non-theistic religious affiliations have cultural attachments that are deeply significant and far from arbitrary. The narrative of the ultimate rebel against tyranny, the attachment to blasphemy as a tool for liberation against

imposed, frivolous, sanctified superstitions; the cultivation of the individual will and critical inquiry unencumbered by "faith" or blind subjugation; the willingness to stand as an outsider with a sense of justice independent of laws and institutions; all are embodied by the literary Satan, from Milton to Anatole France, through a canon that speaks to us about who we are and what we strive to be—regardless of what Satan means to those still shackled by superstition or concerned for its preservation and enduring dignity.

Satanism, in a certain respect, describes where we "come from" and, as a religious/cultural/philosophical identity, it isn't subject to rebranding. We have our own affirmative values that are incompatible with theocratic aspirations and unreasoned faith. We don't exist to "troll" Christians, rather our deeply-held beliefs put us in direct conflict with superstition-based impositions and arbitrary authority. [4]

The choice of Satan is far from arbitrary for Satanists, but rather is integral to our understanding of ourselves and our world.

This core Satanic narrative of Satan's rebellion evolved over centuries of literary representations, starting with John Milton's *Paradise Lost* in 1667 and continuing through the Romantic writers to modern representations today.

THE MEDIEVAL SATAN

Satan wasn't always portrayed as a potentially sympathetic character — in medieval times, he was depicted as a monstrous personification of pure evil. In these centuries where superstition held sway, God was at the center of every person's life, and the Church wielded Satan as the terrifying boogeyman to keep the populace fearfully obedient to Christian doctrine and the priests who interpreted it.

Satan was considered a very real monster with tremendous evil powers, lurking around every corner to try to tempt the faithful

---

4   Greaves, Lucien. "Why Non-Believers Should Embrace Religion
    While Fighting Superstition." *Patheos.* February 6, 2017.

into sin (much as in modern fundamentalism or in Catholicism, where demonic exorcisms are still part of the church). The populace was conditioned to have a deep fear of the devil.

You can see this attitude in the artwork of the period, which represented Satan as a grotesque, frightening, inhuman beast, often depicted consuming the souls of men. (Figure 1.)

There was a strict God-given hierarchy imposed on the society of the medieval era, with no room for questioning the authority

Figure 1: 13th Century mosaic, artist unknown.

of those above you. The Church and the monarchy wielded near-absolute power over every member of society. The rights of the individual were unheard of — you did not belong to yourself, but were rather considered the property of the lord whose land you worked, or of the king, or of the priesthood in whose care your eternal soul was kept. Your obedience to the powers of monarchy and Church had to be complete and unquestioning, and that obedience was extracted by force or the threat of eternal hellfire if necessary.

Taking pride in yourself or failing to adequately prostrate yourself before the idols and priests of Christianity was a grave sin, as was following your own will instead of the will of God (as interpreted by the priesthood, of course). The glorification of Jesus' bloody suffering and death sanctified the idea that self-sacrifice and abasement were the most sacred of acts.

Those who didn't submit, conform or obey and those in ill favor with society were branded witches or sorcerers, in league with the Devil himself. They were burned at the stake or had horrendous instruments used to torture them to death; Church-sponsored violence across the centuries slaughtered thousands of innocent people.

But with the birth of the Renaissance, a movement that took shape between the 14th and 17th centuries, profound cultural change swept through Europe. Rediscovering the pre-Christian philosophy of the Greeks and Romans, many intellectuals of the time began to shift to a humanist approach, placing man at the center of inquiry instead of God. Classical art and philosophy emphasized not blind obedience to unchanging doctrine, but instead showcased man's own curiosity, creativity and rational thought.

The invention of the printing press in Europe heralded a much wider circulation of ideas and information. Classical texts were widely distributed, and millions of people finally had access to texts that up till then were painstakingly hand copied and kept locked away by the elite. Literacy rates shot up as written material flooded in.

The rise in literature available to the masses also wrought a change in the violent nature of civilization. Violence was rampant in medieval times. For many centuries, people did not quite understand how others — especially others that were different than they were in some way — could feel the same as they did. Public torture and painful execution was used not only as a deterrent for crime or witchcraft, but also as a widely popular form of public entertainment.

But things began to change when the written word expanded its reach. With the rise of the printing press, people began to read about other people's lives — some very different from their own. By putting people in the shoes of a protagonist, fictional stories shared widely in mass-printed books opened new internal vistas of understanding and compassion.

In his book *Better Angels of our Nature,* writer Stephen Pinker posits that this newfound realm of understanding led to a more developed sense of empathy — and thus to the decrease in violence seen in the centuries following the invention of the printing press and the spread of literacy:

> *Reading is a technology for perspective-taking. When someone else's thoughts are in your head, you are observing the world from that person's vantage point. ... the habit of reading people's words could put one in the habit of entering other people's minds, including their pleasures and pains.*
>
> *Hunt suggests a causal chain: reading epistolary novels about characters unlike oneself exercises the ability to put oneself in other people's shoes, which turns one against cruel punishments and other abuses of human rights. ... Technological advances in publishing, the mass production of books, the expansion of literacy, and the popularity of the novel all preceded the major humanitarian reforms of the 18th century.* [5]

5   Pinker, Stephen. *The Better Angels of our Nature.*
New York, New York: Penguin Group. 2012.

THE ROMANTIC SATAN

During this time, the seeds of the Satanic revolution were planted with the creation of the epic poem *Paradise Lost*, written by John Milton in 1667. Milton lived in London in the 1600s; he was at the forefront of a radical shift in thinking about government. He was an enthusiastic supporter of republican government, a government for and by the people, and when the British monarchy fell after the execution of King Charles I in 1649, he became a diplomat for the newly formed republic, the Commonwealth.

This groundbreaking republican government existed but briefly before the monarchy was restored to its traditional power via a series of wars. When Milton began *Paradise Lost* in 1658, Oliver Cromwell, Lord Protector of the Commonwealth, had died and the Commonwealth itself began to unravel. By 1660, the monarchy was back in power under King Charles II.

Milton's dreams of a continued republican government were dashed, but for a brief moment England had been governed not by a church-backed monarch, but by a collection of its gentry— not a true democratic government, but still a huge departure from the monarchies that came before and after it. There is much debate as to how this glimpse of freedom from the monarchy affected Milton in writing *Paradise Lost,* but it must have played at least some part in his thought processes.

Paradise Lost became a truly epic poem, with over ten thousand lines of verse upon first publication. In it, Milton tells the biblical story of the fall of man, including Satan's fall from heaven, his temptation of Adam and Eve, and man's resulting expulsion from Paradise.

But the Satan portrayed in *Paradise Lost* is no monstrous, inarticulate, inhuman beast blindly ravaging the souls of humans. Instead, he is portrayed as a noble angel, cast down for his pride but still retaining his angelic mien. He is pleasing to the eye, articulate and silver-tongued, proud of bearing, and in many senses darkly charismatic.

Satan's motivation is not to wreak pure evil upon the world, but rather to win the right to his own self-determination. He rebels not to spite goodness, but because he sees himself and God as equals and sees no good reason to submit to God's rule. He is so fierce in his dedication to being the author of his own life that he would rather lose Heaven than continue under the yoke of submission. He rejoices in the freedom won by rebellion, even though he and his rebel angels are in Hell:

> Here at least we shall be free; the Almighty hath not built
> Here for his envy, will not drive us hence:
> Here we may reign secure, and in my choice
> to reign is worth ambition though in Hell:
> Better to reign in Hell, than serve in Heaven. [6]

For the first time in Western literature since the rise to power of the Church, the devil was portrayed as a potentially sympathetic character, a beautiful proud angel raising a fist at God's tyranny.

But this potentiality lay dormant during Milton's time. Contemporary readings of *Paradise Lost* took it as a straightforward, traditional Biblical story, chronicling the familiar tale of Adam and Eve's temptation and painting the devil in his traditional role as bringer of all evil. It wasn't until nearly a century later that Milton's figure of Satan was reimagined in a radically different, positive light.

The resurgence of Classical ideas in the Renaissance and the widespread use of the printing press precipitated change on many levels, leading to the Enlightenment movement in the 18th century, a period marked by an emphasis on reason as the primary source of authority. This era saw ideals like progress, tolerance, human rights, individual liberty and the separation of church and state arise in European philosophy.

The scientific method came to the forefront of inquiry — and there was increased questioning of the absolute authority of religious orthodoxy. Instead of blind, fearful obedience to a God-given hierarchy, revolutionary philosophy of the time

6   Milton, John. *Paradise Lost; A Poem in Twelve Books* (II ed.). London: S. Simmons. 1674.

proposed equality and freedom for all individuals regardless of class, bloodline or religion. The hegemony of the monarchy and the Church wavered across Europe and America, and revolution began to sweep the world.

Against this backdrop of societal change, certain radical intellectuals and poets of the French revolutionary era took a keen interest in *Paradise Lost*. The late 18th century was a time of great upheaval, and the old, traditional authorities were being burned to the ground — often literally — in favor of equality, leveling of the classes, and personal liberty. *Paradise Lost* had been distributed widely thanks to the proliferation of the printing press. In Milton's Satan, artists of the revolutionary inclination saw not an evil monster, but rather a noble hero, daring to stand up for the rights of the individual against unjust tyranny.

These writers inspired by the notion of the Satanic hero were revolutionaries in real life as well, supporting progressive political and social reform and often retaining a highly anti-clerical attitude. In this proud angel who dared to rebel, these writers of the Romantic era saw their fight for liberty reflected; in his struggle they found a metaphor for their own battle against the forces of monarchy and religious oppression.

It was in a circle of artists loosely associated with the publisher Joseph Johnson that this reimagining of Milton's Satan began in the 1790s. The new attitude concerning Satan was eloquently summed up by William Godwin, a political philosopher affiliated with Johnson's circle. In his *Enquiry Concerning Political Justice and its Influence on Morals and Happiness*, he delves into the reasoning behind Satan's rebellion:

> But why did he rebel against his maker? It was, as he himself informs us, because he saw no sufficient reason, for that extreme inequality of rank and power, which the creator assumed. It was because prescription and precedent form no adequate ground for implicit faith. [7]

---

7   Godwin, William. *Enquiry Concerning Political Justice and its Influence on Morals and Happiness.* 1793.

Godwin frames Satan as the noble hero oppressed by tyranny, even in his defeat refusing to surrender to brute force and slavery, but instead bearing himself with dignity and determination:

After his fall, why did he still cherish the spirit of opposition? From a persuasion that he was hardly and injuriously treated. He was not discouraged by the apparent inequality of the contest: because a sense of reason and justice was stronger in his mind, than a sense of brute force; because he had much of the feelings of an Epictetus or a Cato, and little of those of a slave. He bore his torments with fortitude, because he disdained to be subdued by despotic power. [8]

Other major English poets of the Romantic era also explored the archetype of Satan as hero, including Percy Bysshe Shelley and Lord Byron. Romantic radical William Hazlitt described the Satan of *Paradise Lost* thusly:

Satan is the most heroic subject that ever was chosen for a poem ... His ambition was the greatest, and his punishment was the greatest; but not so his despair, for his fortitude was as great as his sufferings ... [T]he fierceness of tormenting flames is qualified and made innoxious by the greater fierceness of his pride. [9]

The writer and artist William Blake explored Satanic themes both in his publication of *Marriage of Heaven and Hell* around 1790, and in his engraved illustrations of *Paradise Lost*, which featured Satan depicted in all his proud beauty. (Figure 2.)

Blake believed Milton to be infernally inspired in his writing of *Paradise Lost*, writing, "The reason Milton wrote in fetters when he wrote of Angels & God, and at liberty when of Devils & Hell, is because he was a true Poet and of the Devil's party without knowing it." [10]

In France, Romantic writers such as Victor Hugo also found inspiration in Satan as the idealized rebel and freedom fighter — in Hugo's unfinished epic poem *La Fin de Satan*, for instance, Liberty is born from a feather from Lucifer's wing.

8   Godwin, William. *Enquiry Concerning Political Justice and its Influence on Morals and Happiness.* 1793.

9   Hazlitt, William. "On Shakespeare and Milton." 1818.

10 Blake, William. *The Marriage of Heaven and Hell.* 1793.

Figure 2: *Satan in his Original Glory: Thou wast Perfect till Iniquity was Found in Thee,* William Blake, ca.1805.

ARTISTIC REPRESENTATIONS

The change from monster to noble hero is vividly illustrated by the artwork of the same time. As opposed to the horrific beast so often depicted in medieval times, Romantic-era painters like Henry Fusili portrayed Satan with the proportions and nobility of a classical hero. (Figure 3.) Illustrations, sculptures, and other art from the Romantic period and onward expanded on these notions of Satan as a beautiful, inspiring figure.

Figure 3: *Satan Starting from the Touch of Ithuriel's Lance* (detail), Henry Fuseli, 1779.

Gustav Dore's well-known illustrations for an 1866 edition of *Paradise Lost* portray Satan as noble and determined, showcasing his proud bearing and indomitable spirit. (Figure 4.)

Figure 4: Illustration for John Milton's *Paradise Lost*, Gustave Doré, 1866.

Richard Westall depicted Satan in a pose that inspires the fight for liberty, arms uplifted to cheer on his fellows to victory. (Figure 5.)

Figure 5: *Satan Exulting*, Richard Westall, 1794.

James Barry's Satan, lit from beneath and surrounded by the raised swords of his fellow fallen angels, embodies the very spirit of defiance, brandishing his weapon toward heaven. (Figure 6.)

Figure 6: *Satan and His Legions Hurling Defiance toward the Vault of Heaven*, James Barry, ca. 1792–94.

Portraitist Thomas Lawrence represented two sides of the Romantic Satan in his work. In *Satan Summoning His Legions* he paints Satan in all his glorious strength and power, in his full prowess as a military leader of the rebellion. (Figure 7.)

Figure 7: *Satan Summoning His Legions*, Sir Thomas Lawrence, 1796–97.

Lawrence's painting *Satan as the Fallen Angel*, on the other hand, shows Lucifer's sublime angelic beauty, a luminous, idealized countenance glowing with comeliness and grace — a far cry from the monstrous devil of medieval times. (Figure 8.)

Figure 8: *Satan as the Fallen Angel*, Sir Thomas Lawrence, ca.1797.

Belgian sculptor Guillaume Geefs brought Satan's charisma and seductiveness to life in his sculpture *Le génie du mal* (The Genius of Evil), portraying Satan as the most beautiful angel, a handsome, idealized male figure posed provocatively. Only his leathery wings and pointed toenails remind us of his inhumanity. (Figure 9.)

Figure 9: *Le génie du mal* ("The Genius of Evil"),
Guillaume Geefs, installed 1848.

THE HUMANITARIAN HERO OF *REVOLT OF THE ANGELS*

Though the Romantic era and its prolific visions of Satan as hero came to a close around the 1850s, the idea still continued to inspire a number of artists, including the French writer Anatole France (1844 – 1924). France's writing was irreverent and in some senses downright anticlerical; in fact, his entire works were placed on the Catholic Church's Prohibited Books in 1922, not long before his death.

In 1914, France published *The Revolt of the Angels*, the main work considered canon by The Satanic Temple. Written as biting satire, the novel provides an entertaining and witty take on Satanic rebellion, one that reflects the Enlightenment ideals underpinning TST's philosophy. The Satanic Temple website says, "Ultimately a meditation on the corruption of power, Anatole France's *Revolt of the Angels* utilizes the theological metaphor of Satan as a force favoring free inquiry, the War in Heaven a metaphysical battle against universal tyranny." [11]

The storyline follows a group of angels who rebel and plot together to retake Heaven with Satan at their head. Since the novel's portrayal of Satan illustrates perfectly the Satanic ideals aspired to by modern Romantic Satanists, I'm going to take a moment to delve into the details of this canonical work. All quotes in this section are taken from *The Revolt of the Angels*. [12]

The story begins with the guardian angel Arcade. Studying books and the world around him, and looking to logic and science, Arcade comes to realize that Jehovah "is not so much a god as a vain and ignorant demiurge," that he is a fraud. (France refers to Jehovah also as Ialdabaoth, and as Iaveh, and sometimes as God – they are all the same being.) Arcade, having completely lost his faith and his desire to obey God, decides to leave his post, gather an army of rebel angels, and persuade Satan to lead them to retake Heaven from Jehovah, the pretender ensconced on its throne.

Arcade makes contact with other rebel angels, who guide him

11 "Learn." *The Satanic Temple*. www.thesatanictemple.com.

12 France, Anatole. *The Revolt of the Angels*. 1914.

COMPASSIONATE SATANISM

to Nectaire, an ancient archangel living as a simple gardener. Nectaire had fought alongside Lucifer in the original battle against Heaven, and he recounts to Arcade the story of that battle against Jehovah, and the ensuing history of humanity, offering a vivid portrayal of Satan as a noble hero who helps humanity time and again.

NECTAIRE'S TALE

As Nectaire tells the tale, Jehovah, in the beginning, was just one among many other Seraphim, not their creator. Lucifer was his equal — and where character was concerned, by far his superior. Nectaire describes him in heroic terms: "[Lucifer] was the most beautiful of all the Seraphim. He shone with intelligence and daring. His great heart was big with all the virtues born of pride: frankness, courage, constancy in trial, indomitable hope." For France, pride, not submission, was the measure of greatness, lending hope, courage and honesty to those who dared take pride in themselves.

In those early days, Lucifer's greatness of character inspired admiration in other angels, and they came to be near him and enjoy his friendship. "To those who were possessed of a daring spirit, a restless soul, to those fired with a wild love of liberty, he proffered friendship, which was returned with adoration," says Nectaire. As angels one after another abandoned Jehovah's stronghold to become companions to Lucifer, God grew jealous, wanting to keep their homage for himself alone.

As one of Lucifer's angelic companions, Nectaire applied himself to study nature and science, and, much as Arcade did, found in his studies ample reason to doubt God's claim to omnipotence and superiority. He says,

> To satisfy my mind — that was ever tormented with an insatiable thirst for knowledge and understanding — I observed the nature of things ... I sought out the laws which govern nature, solid or ethereal, and after much pondering I perceived that the Universe

had not been formed as its pretended Creator would have us
believe; I knew that all that exists, exists of itself and not by the
caprice of Iahveh; that the world is itself its own creator and the
spirit its own God. Henceforth I despised Iahveh for his impos-
ture, and I hated him because he showed himself to be opposed to
all that I found desirable and good: liberty, curiosity, doubt.

As more angels fled the mountain of Jehovah to become companions of Lucifer, Jehovah's jealousy grew until he demanded
that all should bow to him alone or risk punishment by force;
with his ultimatums, war became inevitable in Heaven.

After gathering a great army of angels to fight for freedom, Lucifer and his companions assailed the citadel where God had set
himself up as the ultimate authority. They fought a mighty battle. "Above our heads streamed the black standards of revolt,"
Nectaire says as he tells the tale. After a pitched fight, however,
God's thunderbolts overtook the rebellious angels and they were
flung down into the wasteland of Hell.

This defeat and the pain it engendered opened the rebel angels'
eyes to their first glimpse of compassion. Despite the defeat,
Satan said, "[W]e still must needs congratulate ourselves on having known pain, for pain has revealed to us new feelings, more
precious and more sweet than those experienced in eternal bliss,
and inspired us with love and pity unknown in Heaven."

Having now experienced pain, the angels understood suffering
for the first time, and were able to feel empathy and compassion
for others.

Meanwhile, the Earth had come into being. Man arose in the
wilderness, a sorry creature without the talons, fur or other
advantages of the animals — but whose pride drew the fallen
angels. Nectaire says, "His miserable lot and his painstaking
spirit aroused the sympathy of the vanquished angels, who
discerned in him an audacity equalling their own, and the germ
of that pride that was at once their glory and their bane. They
came in large numbers to be near him ... And they took pleasure

in sharpening his talents and fostering his genius."

France portrays Satan as a Promethean character, who dared to defy God and bring man the gifts of fire and knowledge. As history progressed, Satan and his demons taught men to clothe themselves in skins, to make fire, build boats, invent the wheel, and learn the ways of agriculture. Their teachings concerned not just simple survival, but also the higher arts — music, painting and dance — and civilized law, as well. "When they had learned to appease their hunger without too painful efforts we breathed into them love of beauty," says Nectaire.

The teachings of Satan and his demons resulted in the flowering of civilization, most notably in classical Greece. Nectaire ascribes the Greeks' phenomenal cultural success to their humanism and their focus on self-inquiry and rational discovery — as opposed to fearful obedience to priestly dogma:

> *Wherefore did the sacred soil of Ionia and of Attica bring forth this incomparable flower? Because nor priesthood, nor dogma, nor revelation ever found a place there, because the Greeks never knew the jealous God... It was his own grace, his own genius that the Greek enthroned and deified as his God, and when he raised his eyes to the heavens it was his own image that he saw reflected there.*

History unfolded peacefully as Greek and Roman culture took shape under the tutelage of the benevolent demons, but soon the idea of Jehovah and his cult of cruelty arose and spread throughout the Western world. Jehovah undertook to conquer the world, inventing the false concept of sin to trick humanity into bowing before him:

> *[Jehovah] himself felt he was incapable of winning the allegiance of free men and of cultivated minds, and he employed cunning. To seduce their souls he invented a fable which, although not so ingenious as the myths wherewith we have surrounded the spirits of our disciples of old, could nevertheless influence those feebler intellects which are to be found everywhere in great masses. He*

declared that men having committed a crime against him, an hereditary crime, should pay the penalty for it in their present life and in the life to come (for mortals vainly imagine that their existence is prolonged in hell); and the astute Iahveh gave out that he had sent his own son to earth to redeem with his blood the debt of mankind.

It is not credible that the innocent should pay for the guilty. The sufferings of the innocent atone for nothing, and do but add one evil to another. Nevertheless, unhappy creatures were found to adore Iahveh and his son, the expiator, and to announce their mysteries as glad tidings.

Instead of science, learning, beauty and love, this new cult lauded ignorance and suffering in all its myriad forms. The glorification of violence in Iahveh's cult fed horrific wars.

In these violent and oppressive times, the demons disguised themselves and lived among the humans, secretly teaching them the arts lost under the tyranny of Jehovah. To their chagrin, wisdom, knowledge and curiosity were seen not as laudable virtues but instead as evidence of witchcraft, and many innocent people were tortured and killed in the Church's reign of terror.

But in the midst of the dark times, the rediscovery of art, culture and philosophy from ancient Greece and Rome fueled the birth of the Renaissance. The classical focus on humanism inspired Renaissance artists and philosophers to think in new directions outside the confining dogma of Christianity.

Thereafter, infused with fresh energy by the secular, humanistic ideas of the Renaissance, the spirit of inquiry, reason, exploration and science began to dismantle the foundations of Jehovah's earthly empire.

Amid the tumult of the following centuries, inspired by Enlightenment ideals of reason and equality, mankind began to loosen the chains of both the Church and the monarchy. But despite the promises of freedom and equality suggested by the French Revolution, soon enough Napoleon and his armies ravaged Europe and left nations at war with each other, much to the dismay of the fallen angels.

Nectaire removed himself to his quiet garden, content to wait there for the day far in the future when Satan would return to usher in a new era of peace and "restore beauty and gladness to the world."

THE REBEL ARMY

Arcade and his fellow rebel angels, however, were not content to wait any longer, and they finally convinced Nectaire to join them in their fight against Heaven. They gathered a great army of angels, ready to assail once more the throne of Heaven, topple Jehovah, and raise Satan in his stead.

At last, they finally meet Satan and tell him of the armed forces of angels assembled in masses all over the earth, simply waiting for his command to begin the assault on Heaven. But Satan bids them rest and promises to give them his answer in the morning.

That night, Satan has a long, vivid dream. In it, he leads his army in revolt against Jehovah. After many great battles, Satan's army finally triumphs and God is driven from his throne. "And Satan had himself crowned God," writes France.

But in the dream, not all is well in Satan's victory. He becomes drunk with power, issuing decrees from on high and losing all his capacity for compassion — in essence becoming the vain tyrant he sought to depose:

> And Satan found pleasure in praise ... he loved to hear his wisdom and his power belauded. ... Satan, whose flesh had crept, in days gone by, at the idea that suffering prevailed in the world, now felt himself inaccessible to pity. He regarded suffering and death as the happy results of omnipotence and sovereign kindness. And the savour of the blood of victims rose upwards towards him like sweet incense.

Satan awakens from this vision in an icy sweat, shocked and appalled by what became of him in his dream. This prescient vision persuades him that war on heaven would only result in the reign of a new evil tyrant god — himself — inflicting all the same horrors as the old Jehovah.

Aghast at the possibility, Satan puts a stop to the rebel angels' war plans. "'Comrades,' said the great archangel, 'no — we will not conquer the heavens. Enough to have the power. War engenders war, and victory defeat. ... God conquered, will become Satan; Satan, conquering, will become God. May the fates spare me this terrible lot.'"

In closing, Satan muses that the real battle is not external, but internal to every man, demon and seraph. He suggests that we must overcome our own jealousy, fear, superstition and ignorance, and instead cultivate wisdom, compassion, curiosity and the love of arts and beauty:

> *What matter that men should be no longer submissive to Ialdobaoth if the spirit of Ialdobaoth is still in them; if they, like him, are jealous, violent, quarrelsome, and greedy, and the foes of the arts and of beauty? ... As to ourselves, celestial spirits, sublime demons, we have destroyed Ialdobaoth, our Tyrant, if in ourselves we have destroyed Ignorance and Fear. We were conquered because we failed to understand that Victory is a Spirit, and it is in ourselves alone that we must attack and destroy Ialdabaoth.*

The Revolt of the Angels thus teaches us that we can only find the keys to our liberation within, and suggests that absolute power corrupts absolutely. It portrays Satan as a wise, compassionate, benevolent angel looking out for the interests of mankind; lauds curiosity, reason and the refusal to blindly follow authority; and gives us an example of the narrative by which we guide our Satanic religion.

MODERN REPRESENTATIONS

The modern era is no exception to our fascination with Satan. Plenty of pop culture artists have explored the Satanic trope in books, music, film, sculpture and other media. Some portray Satan as pure evil, but other creative interpretations follow the positive Romantic narrative of Satan.

For example, the graphic novel series *Lucifer* from DC comics paints Satan as a sympathetic rebel and friend of mankind, inspiring a series of Internet memes called "Good Guy Lucifer." (Figure 10.)

Figure 10: *Good Guy Lucifer* Internet Meme.

In literature, Phillip Pullman's *His Dark Materials* fantasy trilogy closely mirrors the Romantic narrative of rebel angels as heroes, fighting against repressive church authority to preserve free will for man; Pullman even quotes Milton's *Paradise Lost* at various points and has said that his aim in writing *His Dark Materials* was to produce a version of *Paradise Lost* for teenagers.

THE ETERNAL REBEL

The portrayal of Satan in The Satanic Temple's canonic novel, as well as other representations in Romantic literature and beyond, paint a vivid picture of Satan as a revolutionary hero standing up for the rights of the individual against oppressive authority.

It is from this body of work that Romantic Satanism draws its narrative of Satan's rebellion against injustice — a shared metaphorical narrative that can provide context and meaning for our own lives as Satanists.

Lucien Greaves describes the impact this narrative can have in an interview where a journalist asks: "A lot of people mistakenly believe your religion involves worshipping Satan. What is the reason you maintain the 'Satanist' title, when you could easily go under a different moniker and eradicate the confusion?" [13] Lucien replies:

> *We couldn't easily go under another moniker. We couldn't just decide to make up a mythological character who spoke to our values and embodied them. … We grew up with Satan. Everybody has this understanding of what Satan is supposed to be, and even for atheists and non-believers, these symbolic norms have a certain power, the strength of metaphor and art. The raw material changed shape during the Enlightenment — when Milton wrote Paradise Lost, people were seeing a new face of Satan, as a rebel against tyranny. Christendom was starting to collapse, this stranglehold of the church over Western civilization. There was this idea of the embrace of knowledge — the adversary who had tempted Eve to eat from the tree, how that was denigrated by the church. And this came from the church: that we shouldn't follow reason and science, but bend our knee to some divine authority, and the people who claim to have a direct line to it. So to us, this is an established backdrop for everything we're doing. We really couldn't call it anything else. That iconography resonates for us. We wouldn't be at liberty to arbitrarily change it. [14]*

---

13 Jaremko-Greenwold, Anya. "Speaking with Satanic Temple Co-Founder Lucien Greaves at Sundance Made Me Want to Join His Reasonable Religion." *Flood Magazine.* January 30, 2019.

14 Jaremko-Greenwold, Anya. "Speaking with Satanic Temple Co-Founder Lucien Greaves at Sundance Made Me Want to Join His Reasonable Religion." *Flood Magazine.* January 30, 2019.

Artwork by Ashema Deva (inspired
by the art of Robert Indiana).

SECTION 3
Modern Satanic Ethics

The modern Satanist strives to live their life in accordance with the principles shown in the Romantic depiction of Satan. We desire to emulate Satan in his rebellion against tyranny, his quest for knowledge, and his capacity for compassion. Being a Satanist means embodying Satanic principles in every moment in your own way as you walk your individual path.

The ideals and values of Satanism are encoded in the Seven Fundamental Tenets of The Satanic Temple, written by The Satanic Temple's founders, Lucien Greaves and Malcolm Jarry. The Seven Tenets represent a distillation of the laudable Satanic qualities described in Romantic portrayals of Satan. They offer basic, common-sense ethical guidelines. The Seven Tenets are:

1. *One should strive to act with compassion and empathy toward all creatures in accordance with reason.*

2. *The struggle for justice is an ongoing and necessary pursuit that should prevail over laws and institutions.*

3. *One's body is inviolable, subject to one's own will alone.*

4. *The freedoms of others should be respected, including the freedom to offend. To willfully and unjustly encroach upon the freedoms of another is to forgo your own.*

5. *Beliefs should conform to our best scientific understanding of the world. We should take care never to distort scientific facts to fit our beliefs.*

6. *People are fallible. If we make a mistake, we should do our best to rectify it and resolve any harm that may have been caused.*

7. *Every tenet is a guiding principle designed to inspire nobility in action and thought. The spirit of compassion, wisdom, and justice should always prevail over the written or spoken word.*

While the Seven Tenets may at first glance seem similar to Christianity's Ten Commandments, they differ greatly. Whereas the Ten Commandments are strict laws from on high demanding unquestioning obedience, Satanism's Seven Tenets are guidelines meant to represent basic ethical values. In a piece for *Salon*, journalist Valerie Tarico writes:

> *Anyone who is familiar with the Ten Commandments will immediately recognize that these seven tenets offer an easier path to equanimity than do the famous Ten. The first of the Ten Commandments — Thou shalt have no other gods before me – asserts the primacy of a single deity rather than the primacy of compassion and empathy. It prescribes competition between religious worldviews.*

> *By contrast, the seven tenets emphasize positive, pro-social values rather than bad behaviors to be avoided. They largely express egalitarian values that transcend tribal boundaries, in contrast to the Ten Commandments, which endorse the view that women, slaves, and livestock are possessions of men. They invite inquiry rather than certitude, and individuality over tribalism.* [15]

Lucien Greaves describes the motivation behind the creation of the Seven Tenets:

> *They're meant to be general principles that people can live by —* **anybody** *— that will better their condition. They're not just for a select group of elite individuals, or some kind of tribal dictum. The Ten Commandments, most of them, are about the one true God, and the proper way to worship him. That's what makes it so offensive, the idea of having that monument [the Ten Commandments] on capitol grounds to the exclusion of any other religious*

---

15 Tarico, Valerie. "The greatest trick the satanists ever pulled: They may be truer to the words of Jesus than most Christians." *Salon.* November 28, 2015.

viewpoints, and trying to say there was some kind of secular message behind it that everybody can agree to — obviously not! But the seven tenets were something that Malcolm [Jarry], who co-founded The Satanic Temple with me, and I deliberated on for some time. They are deliberately open to interpretation: If you generally follow them in principle, you're OK, but they don't micromanage and tell people how to live. We haven't gone further than that in trying to define our beliefs for people, like giving them a dress code or saying that they must engage in a certain ritual practice. That would be against our anti-authority philosophy. And our rituals are very much in-the-moment and malleable to different circumstances. [16]

The Seven Tenets are meant to form a scaffolding of shared values without being authoritarian. While fundamentalist religions use a multitude of strict laws to dictate how every detail of life should be lived, Satanism leaves almost everything up to the individual. It is the common-sense guidelines of the Seven Tenets that tie us together and give us the basis for a shared Satanic ethos. By following these guidelines, we emulate the noble, heroic Satan of literary portrayal.

16 Jaremko-Greenwold, Anya. "Speaking with Satanic Temple Co-Founder Lucien Greaves at Sundance Made Me Want to Join His Reasonable Religion." *Flood Magazine.* January 30, 2019.

Tenet One: Compassion
*One should strive to act with compassion
and empathy toward all creatures
in accordance with reason.*

Compassion forms the basis of any humanitarian ethos. Only by acting in compassion can we work together for social progress and justice for everyone.

Unfortunately, today's world sorely lacks compassion in many senses. Many espouse a competitive worldview, where everyone has to fight each other just to survive. The theory behind this approach is Social Darwinism, a now-discredited view from the late 19th and early 20th centuries that saw the essential nature of society as a dog-eat-dog world where only the strongest succeed — and in which the weak or oppressed deserve no compassion. Social Darwinism saw man mainly as a predator, with a natural instinct to take whatever he can for himself by any means necessary, even if it means hurting or oppressing others.

But modern Romantic Satanism follows the recent science showing that we are in fact a social species of animal. We thrive when we are working together and helping each other instead of tearing each other down or fighting over the scraps left by the wealthy elites. Altruism makes us feel good because we are hardwired to help other people.

Recently, researchers have discovered a possible biological mechanism for empathy — the so-called "mirror neurons." Mirror neurons are a small circuit of cells in the premotor cortex and inferior parietal cortex of the brain. What gives these cells their name is that they are activated both when we perform a certain action — such as picking up a cup or smiling — and when we observe someone else performing that same action.

These mirror neurons are directly involved in evoking empathetic responses, and can help us understand when others are in pain. Neuroscientist V.S. Ramachandran says,

> *For example, pretend somebody pokes my left thumb with a needle. We know that the insular cortex fires cells and we experience a painful sensation. The agony of pain is probably experienced in a region called the anterior cingulate, where there are cells that respond to pain. The next stage in pain processing, we experience the agony, the painfulness, the affective quality of pain.*
>
> *It turns out these anterior cingulate neurons that respond to my thumb being poked will also fire when I watch you being poked … So these [mirror] neurons are probably involved in empathy for pain. If I really and truly empathize with your pain, I need to experience it myself. That's what the mirror neurons are doing, allowing me to empathize with your pain — saying, in effect, that person is experiencing the same agony and excruciating pain as you would if somebody were to poke you with a needle directly. That's the basis of all empathy.* [17]

Mirror neurons have only so far been found and studied in primates — social species that have to work together to survive. We are literally wired to feel what others are feeling. It's clear that this mechanism for empathy was critical to our survival — and it will be in the future too as we face a world-wide climate disaster. We'll never make it through if we are fractured and fragmented, turned on each other with hate and fear. We need to pull together and see the humanity in each other to work together.

AN UNJUST WORLD

Our society throws up further roadblocks to large-scale empathy that we must overcome. For instance, many people subscribe to what is commonly called the Just World Fallacy, which can interfere with the compassion we'd normally feel for the less fortunate. In this fallacious mindset, people believe that there is some cosmic force of justice (usually God) that ensures good things happen to good people only, and bad things happen to

17 Marsh, Jason. "Do Mirror Neurons Give Us Empathy?"
   Greater Good Magazine. March 29, 2012.

bad people only. In this belief, everything happens according to some set of fair laws.

Thus, according to this line of reasoning, if someone is suffering, they must have done something to deserve it. This leads to complete complacency in the face of others' suffering, since no one has any obligation to help out the less fortunate if they deserve their problems.

Not surprisingly, those with strong Abrahamic beliefs are among those most likely to subscribe to the Just World Fallacy — it's in the very teachings of those religions that everything happens according to God's will. In the Bible, Matthew 10:29 states: "Are not two sparrows sold for a copper coin? And not one of them falls to the ground apart from your Father's will." The Prosperity Wing of fundamentalism in particular teaches that in return for obedience and monetary donations to preachers, God will bless his righteous followers with riches and good fortune; being poor or sick simply means someone is not godly enough.

But the world doesn't actually work like this. There is no all-powerful force doling out divine justice — bad things happen to good people and there is no God keeping score. People who clearly see that there is no overarching divine fairness are more likely to try to help those in need instead of judging and shunning them for their misfortunes. We need to keep in mind the unjustness of the world if we are to exercise our compassion to the fullest.

DEHUMANIZATION

Many of the problems in our society stem from the dehumanization of entire groups of people. To dehumanize someone is to see them as less than human, not at all on the same level as you — to view them as an animal or object instead of a person like yourself. When this happens, your sense of empathy for them is cut off. This is a common tactic wielded by those in the Religious Right — since those with different views or identities don't register as actual people for many fundamentalists, those making policy can hurt them as much as they want with no twinges of compassion or guilt.

It's easy to dehumanize someone if you view them as a threat, and the Religious Right relies heavily on fear to motivate their base. In fact, research has shown that the conservative brain has more activity in the amygdala, the fear-processing center, than the liberal brain. [18] Fear turns off empathy, and it becomes easier to enact laws that create suffering and injustice for those we consider subhuman.

By keeping in mind our shared humanity, the Satanist can choose compassion and empathy instead, helping build a strong society for all.

THE LANCET OF PAIN

In *The Revolt of the Angels*, it is only when Satan and his angels fall and experience pain that they realize that other living creatures must also suffer in this way, and for the first time, compassion flares in their breast. Many Satanists have a potentially high drive for empathy and compassion because we too have been subjected to so much pain in our own lives.

Satanists tend to experience the heartbreak of rejection at high rates thanks to being the outcasts of society. Oftentimes our lives have been very difficult, with much hardship. We've been hurt over and over again, and though that can lead to bitterness and cynicism, it also gives us an increased capacity to understand the pain of another and offer our compassion.

COURAGEOUS COMPASSION

In the Social Darwinist view, compassion is merely weakness that interferes with one's ability to take what you want. But acting with compassion is in fact a courageous stance, because you dare to act outside your own fears and prejudices and

18 Schreiber, Darren et al. "Red Brain, Blue Brain: Evaluative Processes Differ in Democrats and Republicans." *PLOS ONE*. February 13, 2013.

offer empathy despite your own vulnerabilities. We can be the tender-hearted warrior, the one who is both fearless and compassionate — a paragon of true strength. Instead of hardening our heart against tenderness and love, we are strong enough to stand on our own and work to help others even though we ourselves feel deeply the pains of suffering. And it is an act of supreme compassion to stop those who are harming others or to fight for justice for everyone.

COMPASSION WITHIN REASON

Compassion has to include not only others, but yourself as well. This self-compassion is partly the basis for the caveat woven into this Tenet. Show compassion for all creatures — "in accordance with reason." If someone is harming you, then compassion for yourself dictates that you must get away from them or stop the harm. You owe no compassionate forgiveness to your abusers. In fact, they often play on your sense of compassion to manipulate you into staying. But it is yourself you need to take care of first in that situation. You can have an abstract compassion for them — seeing how they were molded into their abuser status by being abused themselves, for instance. But your own well-being has to come before forgiveness or reconciliation.

If encouraged, compassion on a wide scale can create a society with close bonds and a strong safety net, one where no one falls through the cracks. A society benefits when all people are treated with kindness, respect and dignity. As Satanists, we treasure compassion and empathy and do our best to embody them in our own lives.

Tenet Two: Justice
The struggle for justice is an ongoing and necessary pursuit that should prevail over laws and institutions.

The modern Satanic ethos echoes that of the revolutionary Satanists of the Romantic era. Those revolutionaries greatly desired justice in their societies — and were willing to stand up and fight for it. In their writings and art, Satan rebelled because it was unjust that he submit to one that should have been his equal. He was a hero who dared to defy God in order to bring knowledge, art and civilization to humankind. Similarly, these revolutionaries believed it was man's destiny to rebel against the traditional institutions like the monarchy and the church that demanded unquestioning obedience and submission on the basis of absolute authority passed down from God.

In the Middle Ages, the extreme inequality between the ruling classes and the poor, the inflexible doctrine of the church, and the outsized punishment for small offenses against either the church or the monarchy were all signs of an unjust society. The king stuffed himself with rich food while the masses starved, and the church decreed that God so commanded it. The elites were held up as the "betters" to the rabble, their higher status treated as an immutable right. They lived in luxury while the great bulk of people lived in squalor and toiled unceasingly to support them.

But in the late 1700s, suddenly this strict hierarchy no longer seemed acceptable to those at the bottom. A wave of rebellion swept the world, attempting to topple the hierarchy and replace it with equality. The very nature of government was transformed.

Up till then, rulers had governed by divine right. The words of church leaders like the Pope were considered infallible, being derived directly from God. Likewise, monarchs were suppos-edly given their power by God himself, and they had absolute rights to do whatever they liked to those they ruled. It was an authoritarian regime, where any questioning of your ruler meant treason and death, and where the church held its dictatorial position through vicious accusations of witchcraft and torture, punishment, and death.

This strict hierarchy also had behind it the force of long tradition, considered immutable and infallible. Obedience and suffering were simply the God-given lot of the poor, and the fact that it had been this way for hundreds of years was in itself taken as absolute proof that things should continue in that fashion. To question this state of things was heresy.

With the Enlightenment and its focus on humanistic philoso-phy, however, notions of what government should be began to change. In 1651, a philosopher named Thomas Hobbes pub-lished a work called *Leviathan* that strove to set out a rational doctrine of the foundation of legitimate governments. His theory was that by nature, man is a violent, uncivilized animal whose life without a government is "solitary, poor, nasty, brutish, and short." Without government, violence would reign as individu-als took personal vengeance on those whom they believed had wronged them.

But Hobbes proposed that to receive the benefits of civilization, men could band together and cede some of their power to a government above them, submitting to its decisions in exchange for protections of their remaining rights. This "Leviathan" could use these powers to mete out justice and enforce peace. Instead of people determining their own notion of justice and inflicting violent punishment on those who had offended them personally, those individuals could give up some of their power in order for an impartial third party (the government) to rule by just law. In cases of injury, this "Leviathan" could determine guilt through fair trials under a code of law and dole out the appropriate punishments for the crimes committed. The law was no longer an eye for an eye and vengeance against those who wronge you, but instead a more civilized impartial judgment made executed by a higher governmental power.

Hobbes' ideas about the source of a government's authority were groundbreaking; instead of authority based on tradition or "given by God," he viewed the proper source of governmental authority as the will of the governed, who voluntarily gave up some of their power in order to enter into a beneficial arrangement with each other — the so-called "social contract."

In the social contract theory, the power of the government came directly from those who were governed. They consented to be governed by a larger body in exchange for the advantages of civilization provided by that body. These advantages could be justice under the law, public education, social programs that made sure everyone had a basic level of survival and health, etc. — whatever was deemed necessary in a civilized culture. Instead of simply submitting to the tyranny of a monarch or the Church, people could voluntarily enter into a contract with each other to create a better society.

This idea of the social contract was explored further by many philosophers in the 1600s and 1700s leading up to the Revolutionary era, including John Locke in his *Second Treatise of Government* (1689) and Jean-Jacques Rousseau in *The Social Contract* (1762).

This new way of thinking inspired the creation of representational governments across the globe. The revolutionary era saw the formation of governmental "Leviathans" based not on God-given authority over others, but rather the common will and consent of the people.

This relationship between the governed and their government was explicitly outlined in seminal democratic documents. The *American Declaration of Independence* (written in 1776) explains, "That to secure these rights [of life, liberty and the pursuit of happiness], Governments are instituted among Men, deriving their just powers from the consent of the governed." [19]

19 *United States Declaration of Independence.* 1776.

The French *Declaration of the Rights of Man*, adopted by the National Assembly of France in 1789, also says, "The principle of all sovereignty resides essentially in the nation. No body nor individual may exercise any authority which does not proceed directly from the nation." [20]

Thus a just democratic government ruled from the will of its people, not the whims of its monarch or the demands of the priesthood.

These new democracies enshrined equality as the basis for all human rights and the foundation of justice. This notion of equality was a giant leap forward in social progress from the tiered classes of society under the absolute rule of the monarchs and church. The oppressed common man could rise up and break his chains in order to create a better, more equal world. This drive toward equality inspired revolutionaries everywhere to fight for human rights.

This emphasis on equality was encapsulated in democratic declarations as well. For instance, the *Declaration of Independence* begins with the statement, "We hold these truths to be self-evident, that all men are created equal, that they are endowed by their Creator with certain unalienable Rights, that among these are Life, Liberty and the pursuit of Happiness." [21] The first article of the *Declaration of the Rights of Man* states: "Men are born and remain free and equal in rights." [22]

In these governments, because every individual had the same equal rights as any other, just law had to reflect that, as outlined in the *Declaration of the Rights of Man*:

> Law is the expression of the general will. Every citizen has a right to participate personally, or through his representative, in its foundation. It must be the same for all, whether it protects or punishes. All citizens, being equal in the eyes of the law, are equally eligible to all dignities and to all public positions and occupations, according to their abilities, and without distinction except that of their virtues and talents. [23]

---

20 *Declaration of the Rights of Man and of the Citizen* (French: *Déclaration des droits de l'homme et du citoyen de 1789*). 1789.

21 *United States Declaration of Independence.* 1776.

22 *Declaration of the Rights of Man and of the Citizen* (French: *Déclaration des droits de l'homme et du citoyen de 1789*). 1789.

23 *Declaration of the Rights of Man and of the Citizen* (French: *Déclaration des droits de l'homme et du citoyen de 1789*). 1789.

This was the new world the revolutionary Satanists were fighting for: one where equality was the law of the land and everyone had the same rights. In this world, every government had as its primary duty that of creating just laws and applying them equally to all citizens.

We still have these same representational governments today in Europe, the United States and much of the world. They were all founded on this ideal of equality, created to ensure justice for all. But even today, we see myriad examples of law being unequally enforced, or unjust laws being created.

Thus, for instance, we see harsher sentencing and higher incarceration rates for people of color; we see rich celebrities getting away with sexual abuse of minors consequence-free. Currently in my country, we're seeing laws passed that make it explicitly legal for businesses to discriminate against people based on their sexual orientation or that force women to give child custody rights to the men who raped them. While the ideal is a perfectly just government, any quick analysis of reality will show there are many cases of injustice being committed by our governing powers.

The spirit of the Second Tenet teaches us that where there is injustice, it is necessary for the greater good of all to fight it. We are no longer in the monarchy model where rulers have absolute, unchanging authority. We have a representational government that should be dynamically responsible to its citizens — and we have a duty to do all we can to change it to be more just.

The founders of the United States put this mandate for positive change clearly into their Declaration of Independence:

> *That whenever any Form of Government becomes destructive of these ends, it is the Right of the People to alter or to abolish it, and to institute new Government, laying its foundation on such principles and organizing its powers in such form, as to them shall seem most likely to effect their Safety and Happiness.* [24]

If the people no longer consent to the manner of their governance,

---

[24] *United States Declaration of Independence.* 1776.

they have the right to change it. This is the path of the revolutionary — the first ones to stand up and challenge injustice and demand a change.

Thomas Jefferson himself maintained the importance of revolution in keeping government on a just course for all. In a 1787 letter to James Madison, he writes:

The mass of mankind under [representative government] enjoys a precious degree of liberty and happiness. It has its evils too: the principal of which is the turbulence to which it is subject. ... Even this evil is productive of good. It prevents the degeneracy of government, and nourishes a general attention to the public affairs. I hold it that a little rebellion now and then is a good thing, and as necessary in the political world as storms in the physical. [25]

By daring to agitate for justice and change, the revolutionary Satanist drives forward progress on human rights. If laws are unjust, if institutions are corrupt and despotic, we must fight in the courts and the political arena to change them. We must lead the charge to make the world a better place.

While the fight will never end, real progress is made along the way. For example, women have fought and won the right to vote and have an abortion, and worker protection and labor laws have dramatically bettered the workplace over the last century. LGBTQ individuals recently won the right to marry. The struggle may never end, but one by one, major battles are won, as long as we continue to do everything in our power to bring about positive change. As Satanists, we honor the fight for justice as one of the central pillars of our belief system.

---

25 Jefferson, Thomas. *Letter to James Madison.* January 30, 1787.

Tenet Three: Inviolability
One's body is inviolable, subject to one's own will alone.

Satanism includes the belief that your body is your own, to do with as you will. This is an important distinction from many religions that consider the body to belong to an external God or to his representatives here on earth. Christianity has a long history of violating the individual's sole ownership of their body, imposing restrictions on bodily autonomy and dictating that natural, healthy processes are the most evil of sins. As Satanists, we fight for the right to bodily autonomy and inviolability.

A WOMAN'S BODY AS COMMODITY

Women and other people with uteruses (like some trans men and nonbinary individuals) have borne a great deal of the violations imposed on the body by external theocratic institutions. Ownership of a woman's body in medieval Christian traditions belonged solely to men — her father before marriage and her husband after; her brother or her husband's brother if her husband died. This reflected the strict social hierarchy that was kept in place with violence — the divinely ordained monarch ruled over all men, and all men ruled over women.

It wasn't always this way. In many tribal pagan and shamanic religions, women had positions of power thanks to their ability to create life. Every person in a hunter-gatherer tribe had to work constantly just to keep themselves and their tribe alive. Wealth, which mostly took the form of food, was more difficult to amass and hoard. There was little in the way of social stratification because everyone had to contribute more or less equally.

Once agriculture became widespread, however, food could be grown and stored, creating the ability to hoard wealth and steal it by violence. Civilization came into being and the stratification of society increased, fueled by ownership of land, rule by violence, and the creation of an elite class of priests.

In this era, when wealth was based primarily on land and the food grown on it, a woman's body became a commodity, for it produced more workers to till the family fields, and male heirs to guarantee that land remained within the family in the next generation.

A woman's chastity before marriage and sexual fidelity during it became a closely guarded asset, because she had to be kept faithful to the patriarch of the family to ensure any heirs were legitimate.

Christianity was designed to uphold this pattern of male rule over female bodies; by branding women the inferior sex and the origin of all sin, Christianity legitimized men's ownership of women "for their own good." By making women's adultery a grave sin, punishable in many sects by death, Christianity helped shore up the notion that a woman's sexuality, reproduction and body belonged only to her husband. In the Bible, Exodus 20:17 states this relationship clearly: "You shall not covet your neighbor's house. You shall not covet your neighbor's wife, or his male or female servant, his ox or donkey, or anything that belongs to your neighbor."

Women were just another commodity, to be kept safe and under your control with the rest of your belongings, like cattle. In the Old Testament, plenty of rulers and religious patriarchs hoarded this wealth by owning many wives.

Fast forward to today, and this notion of women as basically property lives on in many religious households and nations around the globe. Our female bodies are not our own, according to this fundamentalist belief. We exist only to serve the men to whom we belong, primarily by bearing their children, but also by doing all the housework, supplying home-cooked meals, clean clothes, and a tidy house, and performing all the other work required to support the man and his offspring at home.

We are supposed to remain meek and subservient to our husbands, obeying them in all things. In traditional Anglican wedding vows, published in the *Book of Common Prayer* in 1549, the groom vows "to love and to cherish," while the bride vows "to love, cherish, and obey." [26] As a wedding photographer, I attended a great many weddings that kept those lines, with the bride promising to obey her groom, but no reciprocation. Many in this modern era still see women as naturally inferior to men, meant only to offer sex, support and heirs.

In some modern Christian cults, women are meant primarily to be brood mares, cranking out more soldiers for God's war. For instance, the Quiverfull movement, followed by some conservative Christian couples in America, defines itself by a return to Biblical patriarchy with the goal of producing as many children as possible. The popular American reality TV show *19 Kids and Counting* followed one giant Quiverfull family, the Duggars — until Josh Duggar, the head of the family, was accused of molesting five girls, including his sister.

The Catholic faith famously encourages large families and decrees that birth control is a sin; Mormons also are urged to have as many children as possible, sometimes through marriage to multiple wives. It's easier to support and spread your religion when your followers are cranking out kids. The more children born into a faith, the more that faith can dominate society.

These modern day patriarchal faiths steal agency away from women and give power over their bodies to their husbands, priests or lawmakers. In the fundamentalist belief set, a woman's body serves only to pump out children for the glory of God.

THE BATTLE FOR REPRODUCTIVE RIGHTS

In this worldview, a woman claiming ownership over her own body is committing a grave sin. Birth control and abortion are seen as evil, because they give women and others with uteruses the power to make their own reproductive choices instead of

26 *Book of Common Prayer.* 1549.

obeying the divine commandment to be fruitful.

Abortion comes under particularly heavy fire in patriarchal fundamentalism. The Catholic church has affirmed that every abortion is a moral evil, and many fundamentalist sects of Protestant Christianity have followed suit and decreed abortion to be murder.

At the heart of the movement against abortion is the notion that the clump of cells growing inside an individual is a separate, whole human being from the moment of conception, and anything that removes that clump is full-on murder. This position is far from universally accepted by medical professionals and scientists, and whether or not life begins at conception has been ruled a religious opinion (as opposed to undisputed, scientifically tested fact) by US courts.

The Satanic Temple's religious position is that life begins at birth, not conception. TST pushes back hard against the idea that a woman or other individual with a uterus does not own their own body. Our belief is that until birth, any growing clump of cells is part of a person's body, and due to the inviolability of that body, they should be free to terminate their pregnancy as they wish.

The individual's right to terminate a pregnancy has been deeply eroded by fundamentalist Christian lawmakers, who are trying their best to completely eliminate any chance that a woman or other uterus-bearing individual could take control over their own body in this manner. The Satanic Temple has filed lawsuits in states where the right to an abortion is heavily burdened. Its unique nature as a religious organization makes it possible that the courts will recognize its right to religious freedom in these cases.

In Texas and Indiana, TST has fought the law that requires burial for fetal remains. This law makes an onerous demand that people who have an abortion arrange burial or cremation for the aborted clump of cells, legislating the belief that these cells are a full human being. The *TST Religious Reproductive Rights* website explains:

The Texas Department of Health and Human Services plans to enforce new rules that require that fetal tissue must be buried or cremated and can no longer be disposed of in sanitary landfills as they are in every other state.

The Satanic Temple believes burial rites are a well-established component of religious practice. This is undisputed in the entirety of US legal history. In addition, members of The Satanic Temple believe in the inviolability of the body and, as such, these rules contradict our fundamental beliefs. The First Amendment protects our right to practice our beliefs, and under the Religious Freedom Reform Act (RFRA), the State must present a compelling reason for why they want to enforce rules that inhibit adherence to our religious practices. Clearly, the State of Texas has no compelling reason because these rules were not enacted to promote health and safety, but rather to harass and burden women who terminate their pregnancies. For these reasons, members of The Satanic Temple are not required to comply with the Texas rule on fetal remains. [27]

TST also filed three abortion rights cases in Missouri. Plaintiffs were forced to travel long distances to the only abortion clinic in the state, where they were denied an abortion until after a mandatory 3-day waiting period (which made it necessary to get hotel rooms), required to undergo and view an ultrasound of the fetus, and given scientifically inaccurate "medical" reading material, all of which violated their belief in the Third Tenet. TST's Religious Reproductive Rights literature outlines the arguments:

TST has filed lawsuits against the state of Missouri in both state and federal courts on behalf of Mary Doe, a pregnant woman seeking an abortion. A third lawsuit was filed in Federal Court on behalf of Judy Doe. Missouri law requires that all women seeking to lawfully terminate their pregnancy must be given reading material claiming that life begins at conception, as well as other text designed to induce guilt and shame. In addition, women must endure a 72-hour waiting period between their initial appointment and their abortion procedure. [28]

27 "Religious Reproductive Rights." *The Satanic Temple.* www.religiousreproductiverights.com.

28 "Religious Reproductive Rights." *The Satanic Temple.* www.religiousreproductiverights.com.

TST's main argument is based on religious freedom:

> TST objects to these restrictions on religious grounds because
> they violate our belief in the inviolability of one's body. The
> lawsuits utilize the First Amendment's establishment clause
> and both state and federal Religious Freedom Restoration Acts
> (RFRA) to support our claims. RFRA was the same law used by
> Hobby Lobby to religiously avoid covering health care insurance
> costs for female employees' contraceptives.

> The legal cases assert that state interference with the lawful
> behavior of a TST member to terminate her pregnancy violates
> her rights under Missouri's Religious Freedom Restoration Act
> (RFRA) because that interference has no medical or other com-
> pelling purpose. In addition, the suit maintains that the Missouri
> regulations violate the First Amendment rights of TST members.

> TST argues that her religion, as a member of TST, should exempt
> her from the imposition of abortion restrictions that conflict with
> her beliefs. Because Missouri is using its power to regulate abor-
> tion to promote the religious belief that life begins at conception,
> TST argues that this is a violation of the Establishment Clause.
> In addition, TST claims that the 72-hour waiting period violates
> the Free Exercise Clause because it compels TST members to
> consider a religious proposition with which they do not agree and
> therefore delays their ability to obtain an abortion on demand. [29]

The Satanic Temple's lawsuits resulted in a partial win in 2018
when a Missouri District Attorney conceded that ultrasounds
are not mandatory when an individual seeks to terminate their
pregnancy, thus removing one of the roadblocks to reproductive
choice.

At the time of this writing, TST has just introduced a Satanic
abortion ritual that further protects reproductive rights — under that same set of RFRA laws, a state cannot legally interfere
with an individual's right to practice their religious observances,
which now include the Satanic ritual affirming one's autonomy
and free will during the abortion process.

29 "Religious Reproductive Rights." *The Satanic Temple.*
   www.religiousreproductiverights.com.

FIGHTING FORCED PARENTHOOD

Evangelical Christians and Catholics fight tooth and nail to reduce a woman's birth control options and abortion rights because in their worldview, a woman should be forced to get pregnant and give birth every time she has sex.

Keeping women busy with pregnancy and caring for children can keep them from getting a job, succeeding in a career, and becoming financially independent. Free them to pursue these other things and they might start to question their inferiority. Birth control and abortion also give women and those others with uteruses sexual independence. They might choose someone else for sex instead of being forced to stay with a partner just because they got them pregnant. Because birth control gives women the freedom to choose when to become pregnant, it gives them more control over their own lives and makes it harder to keep them in submission.

It also allows women to have sex just for pleasure, which is already a grave sin in many Abrahamic sects. Women are supposed to suppress their sexuality — in fact, female sexuality is considered monstrous by many religious conservatives. If a woman has sex, she should be punished with the consequence of pregnancy, according to this belief. Motherhood is the wages of sin. The evangelical and Catholic mindset pervades many legislatures across the nation, who write laws making it harder and harder for women and others with uteruses to make their own reproductive choices.

The religious right also wages a nonstop war against Planned Parenthood as part of their attack on reproductive rights. Doctors working at Planned Parenthood have been shot and killed, and clinics across the nation are regularly picketed by loud, pushy mobs armed with huge gory fetus pictures who harass the women and femme-presenting individuals who try to get in (no matter what kind of care they are seeking, even if it's not abortion).

Powerful evangelical forces in our nation's legislature are

constantly trying to take away the dollars Medicaid reimburses Planned Parenthood for their reproductive care services. Never mind that most of what Planned Parenthood offers has nothing to do with abortion, or that they are the provider of women's health and pregnancy services for a huge percentage of poor women, or that the best abortion preventative is using birth control, also provided by Planned Parenthood. Lawmakers want to ensure that no help goes to "those sluts" trying to plan their pregnancies or make their own reproductive choices.

In 2015, The Satanic Temple of Detroit interrupted a pro-life "national day of protest" against Planned Parenthood with their own radical political theatre piece, in which men dressed as priests dumped milk over kneeling women and forced the milk down their throats, symbolizing the motherhood forced onto women by theocratic attempts to gut birth control and abortion services.

DENYING LIFE-SAVING CARE

It's not just at the legislative level that individuals' reproductive rights (and often survival itself) come under fire. The very hospitals that are supposed to provide comprehensive care to those women and others with uteruses may choose to instead leave them vulnerable to increased risk by denying them standard reproductive health procedures.

According to the article "Health Care Denied," reports from the ACLU and MergerWatch show that "one in six hospital beds in the U.S. is in a facility that complies with Catholic directives that prohibit a range of reproductive health care services, even when a woman's life or health is in jeopardy." [30]

Catholic health services make up a huge percentage of hospitals, especially in rural areas where Catholic hospitals are often the only option. These hospitals must comply with the Ethical and Religious Directives for Catholic Health Care Services ["ERDs"], which are promulgated by the U.S. Conference of Catholic Bishops. The ERDs drastically limit individuals' reproductive care options:

---

30 "Health Care Denied: Patients and Physicians Speak Out About Catholic Hospitals and the Threat to Women's Health and Lives." *ACLU report.* May 2016.

The Directives prohibit a range of reproductive health services, including contraception, sterilization, many infertility treatments, and abortion, even when a woman's life or health is jeopardized by a pregnancy. Because of these rules, many Catholic hospitals across this country are withholding emergency care from patients who are in the midst of a miscarriage or experiencing other pregnancy complications. Catholic hospitals also routinely prohibit doctors from performing tubal ligations (commonly known as "getting your tubes tied") at the time of delivery, when the procedure is safest, leaving patients to undergo an additional surgery elsewhere after recovering from childbirth. Catholic hospitals deny these essential health services despite receiving billions in taxpayer dollars. [31]

The hospital may not even be allowed to inform patients that they can receive needed life-saving care at a different clinic. "Depending in part on the whim of the local bishop, this could include gag rules prohibiting counseling a patient or referring a patient to a place that would provide necessary services." [32]

These restrictions can have deadly consequences:

Abortions are prohibited even if the fetus has no chance of survival and the mother's life is in danger. Savita Halappanavar died of sepsis in Ireland because her physicians would neither terminate her doomed pregnancy to save her life, nor transfer her to a facility that would care for her. ... Not providing emergency care is a violation of the Emergency Medical Treatment and Active Labor Act (EMTALA) requirement for hospitals that receive Medicare funding — and Catholic health systems receive billions in taxpayer dollars. [33]

Yet it is a symptom of theocracy in our government that these hospitals are allowed to repeatedly violate the federal EMTALA with no penalty, endangering individuals' lives in the process. And the number of Catholic hospitals is growing. According to Merger-Watch, between 2001 to 2016, the number of acute care hospitals that are Catholic owned or affiliated grew by 22 percent, while the overall number of acute care hospitals dropped by 6 percent. There are now five states (Alaska, Iowa, Washington, Wisconsin

31 "Health Care Denied: Patients and Physicians Speak Out About Catholic Hospitals and the Threat to Women's Health and Lives." *ACLU report.* May 2016.

32 Stone, Judy. "Healthcare Denied At 550 Hospitals Because Of Catholic Doctrine." *Forbes.* May 7, 2016.

33 Stone, Judy. "Healthcare Denied At 550 Hospitals Because Of Catholic Doctrine." *Forbes.* May 7, 2016.

and South Dakota), where more than 40 percent of acute care beds are in hospitals operating under Catholic health restrictions.

Rural areas are hit especially hard. "There is no other option for care in entire regions. This is especially true in rural regions, and it is frightening when the only access to healthcare is dictated by someone else's religious doctrine, rather than medical science." [34]

The bodies of those with uteruses are politicized and made the subject of restrictive Christian doctrine. This is especially true in America, where the loss of reproductive care and reproductive choice has proceeded furthest and pregnant individuals face much higher risks than in other "first world" nations.

According to an in-depth investigation by NPR and ProPublica, "more American women are dying of pregnancy-related complications than any other developed country. Only in the U.S. has the rate of women who die been rising." [35]

The rate of maternal mortality, while falling in the other industrialized nations, is actually on the rise in the US. The more the theocrats gut family planning and contraception services, prenatal and pregnancy care for poor people, and the concept of the woman owning her own body, the further down we slide on the scale. More and more people every year die in childbirth or from pregnancy complications thanks to our abysmal approach to individuals' bodily autonomy and reproductive health. We must be active in fighting this fatal trend and do what we can to restore an individual's right over their own body.

THE DEVIOUS COCKTAIL OF SHAME

It's not just women who suffer under repressive Christian doctrine — everyone is subject to its nonsensical prohibitions regarding sex. Throughout the ages, the Church invented and honed the perfect method of controlling the populace. They made the sexual drive — one of the biggest drives at the heart of our biological processes — taboo, and labeled sex a sin (unless

---

34 Stone, Judy. "Healthcare Denied At 550 Hospitals Because Of Catholic Doctrine." *Forbes.* May 7, 2016.

35 Martin, Nina. "U.S. Has The Worst Rate Of Maternal Deaths in the Developed World." *NPR.* May 12, 2017.

done solely to procreate and even then you aren't supposed to enjoy it). Our most basic biological imperative became a grave sin that could stand between you and your eternal afterlife. The cure for this sinful drive? Self-abasement before God and his priests, material gifts to the church, prayers and penance, and the agreement to be an obedient sheep in the flock. If you were a woman caught having sex outside of wedlock, the consequences were even greater and usually included total ruin of your life or even execution.

This conveniently gave everyone reason to feel sinful and un-worthy, able to be saved only by complete subservience to the church. What should have been celebrated as a natural, healthy way to feel pleasure was instead labelled sordid and evil. The Church offered the only means by which one could have sex without sin — its blessing of a union within a priest-sanctified marriage. Outside of that union, even *thoughts* of lust were a grave sin. An individual only had to have a single thought of sex to be in mortal danger from their sinful ways. And people couldn't satisfy their sexual urges with masturbation, either, as that was considered sinful as well. Somehow people had to completely deny their body's natural drive for sex and erotic release. To fight these urges, priests would even sometimes wear special codpieces designed to foil the designs of evil succubi who would seduce them in their dreams and cause nocturnal emissions.

Women were especially vilified for having sex out of wedlock — indeed, the punishment for adultery for women was usually death, by stoning, hanging, burning, or some other gruesome form of torture. Even just the whisperings that a woman might have had out-of-wedlock sex — or had thought about it — could ruin her reputation. We carry this prejudice into today's soci-ety, with its notion of the slut, the woman who engages in sex without marriage, or too much sex, or dresses too provocatively, or dares to be independent — or dares to use contraception or fight for reproductive rights. In 2012, conservative commentator Rush Limbaugh called Georgetown Law student Sandra Fluke a "slut" after she testified before Congress on the importance of insurance coverage of contraception.

Many women are now taking back the term "slut" and using it as a term of empowerment. The organizers of SlutWalk kicked off a movement to show that women could dress how they desired and still not be asking for rape. Many sex-positive women who consider sexuality healthy, natural and pleasurable claim the term "slut" proudly, just as the LGBTQ community has reclaimed "queer." These women are thumbing their nose at modern prudes who cling to outdated Biblical notions of virginity and chastity as an essential component of a woman's value.

Through the ages, along with the carnal act, the naked body was sexualized by the Church as well, and seeing certain parts was also considered a grave sin because it could lead to lustful thoughts. From the beginning, the Bible taught that the naked body was shameful. Although most Western societies no longer demand almost full-body coverings for women as in the Victorian era, there are still plenty of nudity laws on the books. Certain body parts are still considered shameful and must remain hidden.

This prudery and shame cocktail reveals itself especially in how women are treated with regards to breastfeeding. It is still illegal in many places for a woman to breastfeed — even though it is a completely nonsexual act, the one the breast was originally designed for, and healthy for children. I've seen a comment online about breastfeeding from a man who said "I don't want to see titties at a restaurant. If I wanted to see titties, I would have gone to a titty bar." A woman's right to use her body to feed her infant is trammeled because men can't help sexualizing it.

Dress codes in schools that send home girls for clothing "that might distract the boys from learning" (or more likely, create thoughts of lust in adult teachers) also stem from this sexualization — this time, of children's bodies. No thought is given to the girls whose education is interrupted because they are sent home over misogynist codes.

In an ideal world, the body is accepted as natural and healthy, not requiring cover up to hide the shameful bits.

Today's evangelicals and Catholics take the Christian focus on the shamefulness of sex and run with it. Any and all sexual acts that might not be female-male missionary married sex for procreation are seen as blasphemy against the order dictated by God. This includes gay sex, oral sex, anal sex, using sex toys, masturbation, kink, polysexual encounters — the list goes on and on. I've seen many an evangelical who delighted in delving into the minute details of every sexual act they were against.

And there are many laws on the books that prohibit consenting adults from using their bodies the way they desire in the privacy of their own home. Many states still have sodomy laws — where sodomy is rarely spelled out, but is usually understood by courts to include any sexual act deemed to be unnatural or immoral by repressed Christians. Usually this is simply oral or anal sex. These laws have been used to prosecute gay people for their supposed "deviant sexuality" and weaponized to fight against civil rights for LGBTQ individuals.

In fact, dictating whom you can and can't have a sexual relationship with is one of the favorite pastimes of conservative legislators. It was only in 2015 that gay marriage was finally legalized at the federal level. Gay individuals still suffer a great deal of discrimination, some of which is legally justified by so-called religious freedom laws.

Other non-traditional relationships also run up against judgment and discrimination. Polyamorous people — those with more than one partner in consensual relationships — still face a great deal of misunderstanding by those who believe that only one man and one woman should be allowed to love each other in such a relationship. Those into BDSM and kink also face a great deal of shame heaped on them for their consensual sexual activities — when in reality it's no one's business how you enjoy the sexual aspects of your body, as long as it is consensual and doesn't involve minors.

There are also laws against sex toys. For instance, section 43.21 of the Texas Penal Code prohibits the sale or promotion of "obscene devices," being defined as "a device including a dildo or artificial vagina, designed or marketed as useful primarily for the stimulation of human genital organs." George Orwell's concept of Sexcrime is alive and well in America, where we make it illegal for consenting adults to have fun in the confines of their own bedroom.

The more we repress our natural urges and feel ashamed of them, the worse the sexual undercurrent gets. Many evangelical politicians who storm on about "family values" and oppose gay rights are caught in sexual scandals, sometimes with people of the same sex. Many ultrareligious politicians, preachers, and organizations are being outed for sexually abusing minors — most notably the Catholic Church, which has done nothing to stem the rampant child molestation by their priests.

Repress and twist the natural urge and it becomes furtive and abusive. The more we educate people and discuss sex out in the open, the more children and others will be able to speak up if they are being assaulted, the more we can ensure our families are planned, and the less we will feel crippled by self-hate for our natural feelings. If we restore sexual agency along with bodily autonomy and roll back the clouds of shame, we can go a long way toward making a healthier world.

SEX WORK IS WORK

Sex work also suffers greatly under this prudery and shame about sex. What one does with one's own body should be one's business alone, but because we've labelled sex a sin, Christianity-based legislation makes sex work illegal. As a former dominatrix, I can personally attest that sex work can be a rewarding, healthy exchange between two consenting adults. It's not "selling your body," any more than coal mining means selling your body to the mining company. Done in a safe space with respectful clients, sex work provides a way to earn a living that can offer financial independence, flexibility with regards to scheduling, and a sense of fulfillment.

The illegality of sex work, however, creates an underground sex trade that is unregulated, full of abuse and vulnerable to those who traffic in the helpless. For instance, there have been many instances where human traffickers have kept women enslaved by threatening to hand them over to police.

The anti-sex work bills SESTA and FOSTA were meant to cleanse the online world of any sex references; instead they destroyed sex workers' ability to screen clients and work for themselves in their own safe space, driving them onto the streets and forcing them to work for pimps:

> *Violent crime is way down in San Francisco, according to the latest police statistics. But one major category is bucking the trend: police recorded a 170 percent jump in reports of human trafficking in 2018. The huge spike appears to be connected to the federal shutdown of sex-for-sale websites. The goal of shutting them down was to curb human trafficking. Instead, it seems to have had the opposite effect.*

> *"If you are a street-based sex worker, it's much harder to nego-tiate your rates, to negotiate safer sex condom use, to make sure that this person who is picking you up in a car doesn't have a knife or a gun," [said Pike Long, deputy director of St. James Infirmary].* [36]

Amnesty International's 2016 report on sex work recommends the decriminalization of consensual sex work:

> *The policy makes several calls on governments including for them to ensure protection from harm, exploitation and coercion; the participation of sex workers in the development of laws that affect their lives and safety; an end to discrimination and access to education and employment options for all.*

---

36 Steimle, Susie. "New Laws Forced Sex Workers Back On The Streets, Caused 170% Spike in Human Trafficking." *CBS Local San Francisco*. February 3, 2019.

It recommends the decriminalization of consensual sex work, including those laws that prohibit associated activities — such as bans on buying, solicitation and general organization of sex work. This is based on evidence that these laws often make sex workers less safe and provide impunity for abusers with sex workers often too scared of being penalized to report crime to the police. Laws on sex work should focus on protecting people from exploitation and abuse, rather than trying to ban all sex work and penalize sex workers. [37]

One's body is subject to one's own will alone. Give people the right to their own bodies and the right to choose what they do with those bodies for work.

CONSENSUALITY

Because you should have complete control over your body, you have the right to be free from unwanted touching, whether it's sexual in nature or simply an unasked-for touch or hug. No one should touch you in any way without your full consent.

You also have the right to be free from assault and beatings — even if you are a minor. In fact, The Satanic Temple's Protect Children Project helps students mount a civil rights defense against corporal punishment in school. According to the Protect Children Project website:

If you are a student whose religious beliefs stand in opposition to being hit or abused by school faculty, the Protect Children Project will put your school on notice. ... We assert that the following actions taken by school officials against students who are members of The Satanic Temple, or any other student who share TST's religious beliefs, are violations of our civil rights:

- *Corporal punishment*
- *Use of physical restraints*
- *Solitary confinement and the use of "scream" rooms*
- *Restricting bathroom access*

---

37 "Amnesty International publishes policy and research on protection of sex workers' rights." *Amnesty International.* May 26, 2016.

If schools do not respect the religious beliefs of a student who has registered, we will work to try to obtain legal counsel to sue the school district for violating that student's civil rights. [38]

In 2017, The Satanic Temple purchased a billboard reading "Our religion doesn't believe in hitting children" in the small Texas town of Three Rivers to protest the local school district's reinstatement of corporal punishment.

DIETARY AND OTHER RESTRICTIONS

Beyond reproductive and sexual rights, one has authority over one's body in other arenas as well. You have the right to your own gender identity and any medical treatments you need to treat gender dysphoria or otherwise support your gender identity.

You should be allowed to wear whatever you want, regardless of what is considered "proper" clothing for your age, weight, gender, etc. You have the right to modify your body with tattoos, piercings, scarification, dermal implants or other body modifications. And you should be free to wear whatever jewelry and hairstyle you want — though it's often an uphill battle to get others to recognize your freedom to wear personally meaningful jewelry if it's Satanic.

The Third Tenet also means it's up to you what you put in your body in terms of food and drink. Some Satanists choose to follow certain dietary restrictions for health or ethical reasons, but Satanism imposes no such restrictions. You are free to eat and drink what you wish.

The inviolability of one's own body extends to other substances like marijuana — though TST doesn't support illegal acts, it does support the legal fight to extend personal choice in this arena. In an article for *High Times*, TST founder Malcolm Jarry elaborates:

The Satanic Temple believes in individual sovereignty, which includes the right to ingest whatever chemicals a person chooses. This should be done in accordance with reason and where others

38 "Protect Children Project." *The Satanic Temple.* www.protectchildrenproject.com.

are not placed at risk. That said, while we object to laws that irrationally prohibit liberties and freedoms, we do not promote illegal activity. If laws are unjust, as many are that prohibit drug use, people should work to change those laws. We certainly applaud the efforts of many reformers. [39]

As Satanists we defend the sovereignty of one's own body — it should be subject to your will alone. It's your body, and what you do with it and put in it should be up to you.

39 Adams, Mike. "Satanism and Weed: Is The Devil Down With Dope?" *High Times.* January 26, 2018.

Tenet Four: Freedom to Offend

The freedoms of others should be respected, including the freedom to offend. To willfully and unjustly encroach upon the freedoms of another is to forgo your own.

The concept of free speech is a relatively new turn of thought. During most of European civilization, certain speech could land you in jail, subject you to torture, or even guarantee your execution.

Speaking ill of the monarchy or the state could be prosecuted as treason. Blasphemy too held a special place at the top of the list of what were considered grave speech crimes. Speaking out against the dominant religion or making fun of it were considered civil crimes, in addition to being "crimes against God." Over the centuries, under the dominance of the Abrahamic, monotheistic religions, many people were convicted of blasphemy and sentenced to punishment or death. All you had to do was utter words considered to be in some form anti-God (even simply using the Lord's name in vain), and the commingled religious/legal framework would proclaim you a heretic, sinner and criminal. God himself would take offense at these words, according to the prevailing thought of the time. Cruel punishment, torture and a public death by grisly means were often the consequences.

But in the 17th and 18th centuries, the Enlightenment movement, with its shift to humanism, science and individual freedom, first put into popular consciousness the idea of freedom of speech. In this philosophy, freedom of speech was seen as essential in maintaining a just government, because it allowed the populace to criticize laws, representatives, and the bodies that governed them in order to drive forward positive change.

These Enlightenment ideals informed the American Revolution

and the resultant foundational documents, and the nascent country codified these freedoms into their constitution. Freedom of speech and expression is guaranteed by the First Amendment to the American Constitution:

Congress shall make no law respecting an establishment of religion, or prohibiting the free exercise thereof; or abridging the freedom of speech, or of the press; or the right of the people peaceably to assemble, and to petition the Government for a redress of grievances. [40]

This spirit of free expression means Americans and others living under such constitutional governments have the freedom to say what they want — as long as it doesn't directly incite violence or constitute a threat to safety worthy of legal action. Yet in a return to medieval attitudes about speech, many in America and around the world want to ban certain kinds of speech and expression, arguing that work that offends or blasphemes religion or God or otherwise offends people should be criminal. And many modern countries still have blasphemy laws under which people may be prosecuted and punished by penalties up to and including death.

Harsh penalties are more common in Islamic states where laws are based on Islamic holy doctrines, but blasphemy laws are still on the books in many other countries as well, including those in Western Europe. A Pew Research Center analysis found that, as of 2014, about a quarter of the world's countries and territories (26%) had anti-blasphemy laws or policies, and that more than one in ten nations (13%) had laws or policies penalizing apostasy (the act of abandoning one's faith). [41]

The modern penalties for blasphemy can be as harsh as execution. In the last few years, for example, Pakistan has convicted dozens of people of blasphemy and sentenced them to death. In 2014, Muhammad Asghar, a 70-year-old British man from Edinburgh, was convicted of blasphemy and sentenced to death by a Pakistani court. [42] In 2017, Pakistani atheist blogger Ayaz Nizami

---

40 *U.S. Constitution.* Amend. I.

41 Theodorou, Angelina. "Which countries still outlaw apostasy and blasphemy?" *Pew Research.* July 29, 2016.

42 "Blasphemy Case: Briton in Pakistan Sentenced to Death." *BBC News / Asia.* January 24, 2014.

was detained under the charges of blasphemy; he faces the death penalty. [43] And religious vigilantes have often meted out their own punishment by murder — in 2015, religion-fueled attacks by gunmen at the headquarters of satirical magazine *Charlie Hebdo* in France killed 12 and injured 11 in reprisal for the magazine's disrespectful depictions of Mohammed. [44] The struggle for freedom of belief and speech continues.

The Satanic Temple staunchly supports the freedom of speech, including the freedom to offend. Tenet Four protects all kinds of speech: unpopular views, irreverent art, blasphemous humor, heretical thoughts and so on. Irreverence toward holy personages, religious artifacts, customs or beliefs should fall under modern free speech categories — nothing is out of reach for the satirist's pen or the philosopher's musings.

To the Satanist, blasphemy laws are violations of the individual's right to freedom of speech. Criminalizing blasphemy toward the dominant religion enshrines that religion by the state, amounting to state-sponsored censorship on dissenting religious views. The Satanic view of blasphemy and free expression as inalienable civil rights coincides with that of the Council of Europe, an international European organization whose mission is to uphold human rights, rule of law and democracy in Europe. In their report on freedom of expression and blasphemy laws they write:

> In the Commission's view, however, in a true democracy imposing limitations on freedom of expression should not be used as a means of preserving society from dissenting views, even if they are extreme. Ensuring and protecting open public debate should be the primary means of protecting inalienable fundamental values such as freedom of expression and religion at the same time as protecting society and individuals against discrimination. It is only the publication or utterance of those ideas which are fundamentally incompatible with a democratic regime because they incite to hatred that should be prohibited.
>
> The concepts of pluralism, tolerance and broadmindedness on

43 "Pakistan Detains Three Bloggers On Blasphemy Charges." *RadioFreeEurope/RadioLiberty*. March 25, 2017.

44 Withnall, Adam; Lichfield, John. "Charlie Hebdo shooting: At least 12 killed as shots fired at satirical magazine's Paris office." *The Independent*. January 7, 2015.

3 • MODERN SATANIC ETHICS

which any democratic society is based mean that the responsibility that is implied in the right to freedom of expression does not, as such, mean that an individual is to be protected from exposure to a religious view simply because it is not his or her own. ... The right to freedom of expression implies that it should be allowed to scrutinise, openly debate, and criticise, even harshly and unreasonably, belief systems, opinions, and institutions, as long as this does not amount to advocating hatred against an individual or groups.

The Parliamentary Assembly, noting that, in the past, national law and practice concerning blasphemy and other religious offences often reflected the dominant position of particular religions in individual states, has considered that "in view of the greater diversity of religious beliefs in Europe and the democratic principle of the separation of state and religion, blasphemy laws should be reviewed by member states and parliaments" and that "blasphemy, as an insult to a religion, should not be deemed a criminal offence." ... The Commission agrees with this view. [45]

TST Spokesperson Lucien Greaves laid out his similar views on freedom of speech in a "Letters to a Satanist" column in the *Orlando Times*:

Freed Speech embodies the freedom to commit "heresy," and the freedom to offend. Freedom of Speech should not be confused with freedom from criticism, critical inquiry, or mockery. To the contrary, Freedom of Speech protects all of these things, and to expose bad ideas through reasoned ridicule is to serve a legitimate function in the marketplace of ideas. [46]

TST's support of free speech extends to all speech, not just speech it agrees with. This sentiment echoes the famous words written by Evelyn Beatrice Hall in *The Friends of Voltaire*: "I disapprove of what you say, but I will defend to the death your right to say it." [47]

In an interview for *Haute Macabre*, Greaves expounded on this idea:

I defend the principle of Free Speech, and when you defend a principle, you don't only defend it selectively. If you can't support it when it incidentally doesn't benefit you, you're not supporting

45 "Report on the relationship between Freedom of Expression and Freedom of Religion: the issue of regulation and prosecution of Blasphemy, Religious Insult and Incitement to Religious Hatred adopted by the Venice Commission at its 76th Plenary Session." *Council of Europe, Venice Commission.* October 18, 2008.

46 Greaves, Lucien. "Letters to a Satanist: Do you believe that free speech protects hate speech and false statements?" *Orlando Weekly.* January 15, 2015.

47 Hall, Evelyn. *The Friends of Voltaire.* 1906.

it at all. You can't claim that you believe in Free Speech, only in-
sofar as you agree with what's being said. If [a speaker] has posed
a legitimate danger to individuals through inciting violence in a
very direct and tangible way, if he's defamed people, or invaded
their privacy — this seems like a matter for the civil courts, and
the aggrieved parties should consult legal representation. [48]

Greaves makes a critical distinction between speech that is
merely offensive (and thus protected) and speech that is actually
criminal hate speech or willful defamation (not protected classes
of speech):

Free Speech allows for the inquiry and critical scrutiny by which
falsehoods are openly exposed. Free Speech does not, and should
not, protect willful slander and/or defamation. The American
Bar Association defines "hate speech" as "speech that offends,
threatens, or insults groups, based on race, color, religion, na-
tional origin, sexual orientation, disability, or other traits." We
should be careful to never allow a ruling body to limit even "hate
speech" but for the most compelling of reasons – such as that the
speech in question is likely to directly incite immediate violence
against the party toward whom such speech is directed. [49]

In many cases, people are simply offended by the fact that we
are Satanists:

Many are the times in which The Satanic Temple has been
wrongly denigrated as engaging in "hate speech" by offended
Christian groups who imagine that any and all of our activities
are acts of persecution against them. They would argue that
while we're not making direct threats or inciting specific actions
against them, our very identification as Satanists nonetheless
threatens Christians and incites acrimony against them. Their
feelings are hurt. They're offended. [50]

Similarly, many fundamentalist Christians and Catholics feel
that the very existence of gay or transgender people (and
additional "Othered" people) is offensive. As one gay Satanist
put it, "My life itself is offensive to some Christians." Merely by

48 "Never Let Your Activism Be Artless: An Interview With Lucien
   Greaves of The Satanic Temple." *Haute Macabre*. June 28, 2017.

49 "Never Let Your Activism Be Artless: An Interview With Lucien
   Greaves of The Satanic Temple." *Haute Macabre*. June 28, 2017.

50 "Never Let Your Activism Be Artless: An Interview With Lucien
   Greaves of The Satanic Temple." *Haute Macabre*. June 28, 2017.

self-identifying as gay, he offended a great many people in his religious family. TST maintains that everyone has the right to be themselves, regardless of other people's religious bigotry.

We can't simply let people muzzle or censor speech that offends. To willfully encroach upon others' freedom of speech is to disrespect all freedoms of speech, and that should in turn apply to our own as well. We can't deny that freedom to others while maintaining that we alone have the right to free speech. This liberty belongs to all, not just a select few "chosen people" with the right beliefs.

However, this right to free speech does *not* free one from the consequences of that speech. As I've heard another Satanist say, "The right to offend is a right, not a duty." Simply being as offensive as possible to other people for offense's sake and then complaining when they drop our friendship or working relation-ship is disingenuous. But in a free society, we should be able to speak our mind as we wish without government censorship or criminal punishment.

Tenet Five: Scientific Understanding
Beliefs should conform to our best scientific understanding of the world. We should take care never to distort scientific facts to fit our beliefs.

In contrast to religions that require one to put faith above facts, Satanism actively encourages its practitioners to understand the world through the lens of science and reason.

Like many of Satanism's core values, this focus on rationality and the scientific method comes down from the Enlightenment, which was also called the "Age of Reason." The Enlightenment enshrined rationality as the primary source of knowledge; its core idea was that natural law could be used to examine and understand all aspects of society. Many Enlightenment writers and thinkers had backgrounds in the sciences and associated scientific advancement with social progress, particularly the overthrow of traditional religious authority in favor of free speech and thought. No longer was faith valued as the ultimate arbiter of truth; instead, thinkers turned to reasoning and the scientific method to work out truths about the world.

Stephen Pinker elaborates on this set of Enlightenment ideas in *Better Angels of Our Nature*:

> *It begins with skepticism. The history of human folly, and our own susceptibility to illusions and fallacies, tell us that men and women are fallible. One therefore ought to seek good **reasons** for believing something. Faith, revelation, tradition, dogma, authority, the ecstatic glow of subjective certainty — all are recipes for error, and should be dismissed as sources of knowledge...*

> *We are also committed to reason. If we are asking a question, evaluating possible answers, and trying to persuade others of the value of those answers, then we are reasoning, and therefore have tacitly signed on to the validity of reason. We are also committed to whatever conclusions follow from the careful application of reason, such as the theorems of mathematics and logic.*

*Though we cannot logically **prove** anything about the physical world, we are entitled to have **confidence** in certain beliefs about it. The application of reason and observation to discover tentative generalizations about the world is what we call science. The progress of science, with its dazzling success at explaining and manipulating the world, shows that knowledge of the universe is possible, albeit always probabilistic and subject to revision. Science is thus a paradigm for how we ought to gain knowledge — not the particular methods or institutions of science but its value system, namely to seek to explain the world, to evaluate candidate explanations objectively, and to be cognizant of the tentativeness and uncertainty of our understanding at any time. [51]*

In the centuries since the Enlightenment, scientific progress has given rise to huge leaps in understanding our world, resulting in a dizzying array of advances in medicine, technology and the natural sciences, among other areas, as well as improvements in the basic quality of life for many people.

This progress has been underpinned by the scientific method, first outlined by Sir Francis Bacon. This method is not a set of fixed beliefs, but rather an empirical problem-solving process that zeroes in on reproducible predictions about the workings of the physical universe. This process involves (1) making hypotheses, (2) deriving predictions from them as logical consequences, and then (3) carrying out experiments based on those predictions to determine whether the original hypotheses were correct. This is an iterative process, where older, less accurate hypotheses and theories are replaced by new, more accurate ones as prediction, experimentation and analysis uncover new discoveries. (Figure 11.)

The scientific method was a game-changer; it allowed researchers to begin unearthing detailed knowledge about the workings of the physical world and the forces that shape the universe. Over the centuries, it has helped humanity understand the myriad intricate details needed to achieve our modern advances. While science can't provide the answer in every situation, it allows us to better align our philosophy and policies with the facts.

51 Pinker, Stephen. *The Better Angels of our Nature.*
New York, New York: Penguin Group. 2012.

The Satanist recognizes the power of reason and scientific methodology, and relies on these tools when forming and retaining beliefs. Lucien Greaves' Satanic invocation says: "Let us reason our solutions with agnosticism in all things, holding fast only to that which is demonstrably true." [52] By approaching the world with an agnostic, open-minded attitude and applying our powers of reason, we can retain only those beliefs which are supported by evidence, letting the rest fall by the wayside.

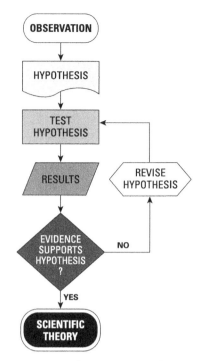

Figure 11: The Scientific Method.

PRIVILEGING FAITH OVER REASON

This emphasis on reason is quite a revolutionary approach to religious belief. For many sects of the Abrahamic religions, the core imperative is to rely on faith alone, ignoring or distorting the facts when they contradict your religious beliefs. The stronger your faith in the unseen and unproven, the stronger your supposed ties to God and the higher you rate on the hierarchy of believers. Faith is lauded as the supreme virtue; you are directed to believe even the most fanciful tales of God with zero evidence.

For evangelical Christians, there is often an added directive to consciously reject scientific knowledge, as it could be diametrically opposed to church teachings or cause you to question your faith. This idea of "rejecting the world's wisdom" cites the Bible verse 1 Corinthians 3:19: "For the wisdom of this world

---

52 Abcarian, Robin. "After Supreme Court prayer decision, Satanist offers his own prayer." *Los Angeles Times.* May 5, 2014.

is foolishness with God. For it is written, He taketh the wise in their own craftiness."

This is understood to mean that the "wise," those who have gained knowledge of the world via science or reason, are out to undermine faith, and that by rejecting their "wisdom," one can prove one's own faith and righteousness and avoid the fires of hell.

This attitude of faith over reason and science plays out well beyond the confines of the church and home. In America, scientific progress and education have an uphill battle against theocratic elements in our local and federal governments and public school system. Strong religious forces in our government work to distort scientific facts when they don't fit with the evangelical Christian belief system, resulting in flawed education and public policy.

YOUNG-EARTH CREATIONISM IN PUBLIC SCHOOLS

For instance, even after a century and a half of prediction, testing and proof, many evangelical Christians (and some other Abrahamic sects) do not believe in the scientifically established theory of evolution. Though scientists have shown convincing evidence that the earth is over 4 billion years old and that life evolved from simple origins over billions of years, these so-called Young-Earth Creationists believe the Christian God created the entire universe and all life fully-formed in their present incarnation just a few thousand years ago.

According to a 2004 Gallup creationism survey, the most likely American Christian denominations to reject the evolutionary interpretation of life's origins are evangelical Protestants (70%), Mormons (76%) and Jehovah's Witnesses (90%). The survey found that a whopping 38% of adults in the United States held the view that "God created humans in their present form at one time within the last 10,000 years." [53] For these believers, scientific data showing otherwise (like the fossil record) is explained away by other means, including the belief that all the dinosaurs

53 Newport, Frank. "In U.S., 42% Believe Creationist View of Human Origins." *Gallup.com.* November 19, 2004.

died in Noah's flood, or that Satan placed fake bones in the ground to lead humankind astray.

Creationists argue that their particular religion-based origin belief is superior to the scientific theory of evolution, and should be the only theory taught in elementary and high schools. These creationists have fought schools, teachers and textbook manufacturers to remove evolution from scientific textbooks and classrooms and replace it instead with Creationism (often called "Intelligent Design" in an attempt to give it a more scientific veneer).

Intelligent Design in textbooks and classrooms mandates teaching that evidence for evolution is false. For instance, in 2009, the Texas Board of Education voted 13 to 2 that textbooks must teach intelligent design alongside evolution and question the validity of the fossil record. [54] Because Texas is the second-largest textbook market in the United States, publishers have a strong incentive to be certified by the Board as conforming to Texas' state standards. Scientifically unsound information thus works its way into public education by way of this Intelligent Design mandate.

Students who are home-schooled by fundamentalist parents are also usually taught Creationism, most often without any attempt at teaching evolution as an alternative. These students are at a disadvantage when entering college, where evolution is the accepted scientific theory to explain life's origins, or when trying to find a job in the science and technology industries.

CLIMATE CHANGE DENIERS

Children aren't the only ones subjected to wildly distorted facts in the name of religion. America is also home to a vast population of climate change deniers. These people — usually religious — refuse to believe the evidence that shows earth's climate is changing dramatically due to human industrial activity and the burning of fossil fuels. A full 97 percent or more of actively publishing climate scientists agree that climate-warming trends over the past century are due to human activities, especially the use of carbon-based fuel.

54 Bhattacharjee, Yudhijit. "New Texas Standards Question Evolution, Fossil Record." *Science.* April 3, 2009.

In addition, most of the leading scientific organizations world-wide have issued public statements endorsing this position. [55]

The doomsday clock is ticking: scientists warn that if we don't immediately move away from fossil fuels, we will have lost our narrow window of opportunity to mitigate these disastrous effects. Mass extinctions are already occurring at an ever-increasing rate. If we don't act now to put on the brakes, the consequences will be deadly for our own species; in fact, it may already be too late.

Yet here in America, instead of tackling this immense problem, forces in our government dictate that we do nothing — or even exacerbate the problem by promoting increased fossil fuel consumption. Thanks to massive spending and lobbying, especially by the energy-billionaire Koch brothers, climate change is political here, with conservative Republicans doing all in their power to enforce the belief that nothing is going wrong, and that we need to continue allowing massive carbon emissions and environmental degradation in the name of "competitiveness" for our corporations.

Our current administration has gutted climate science study, scrubbed climate data from government websites, and even forbidden some governmental agencies from using the words "evidence-based," "science-based" or "climate change." We currently have a federal policy of sticking our heads in the sand and patently ignoring the changes that have brought more extreme weather every year, from drought and famine to drenching floods, massive wildfires, melting icecaps, rising sea levels, and stronger and more frequent hurricanes that batter coastlines.

This climate change denial has a major religious component to it. Once more, evangelical Christians lead the charge to distort and deny scientific facts to fit their religious views. They believe that climate change can't be caused by human beings, because only God has the power to make such changes. Thus they are able to dismiss the entire scientific community's dire warnings and

---

55 Cook, J. et al. "Consensus on consensus: a synthesis of consensus estimates on human-caused global warming." *Environmental Research Letters* Vol. 11 No. 4. April 13, 2016.

pursue economic and governmental policies that endanger the future of everyone living on the planet.

This policy is underwritten by a belief known as Dominionism. In the Bible, Genesis 1:28 reads: "And God blessed them, and God said to them, 'Be fruitful and multiply, and fill the earth and subdue it; and have dominion over the fish of the sea and over the birds of the air and over every living thing that moves upon the earth.'" Many evangelicals take this to mean that human beings have been granted the earth by God to be used as they see fit. God's gift to Adam and Eve of "dominion" over the earth and all its creatures has been taken as the right to unlimited exploitation with zero consequences.

For many evangelicals, the degradation of the environment and the extreme weather assaulting the world are simply welcome signs of the coming Apocalypse. A huge contingent of fundamentalist Christians are actively cheering on the destruction of the world because it is one of the signs of the coming end times, when Christians will be Raptured to sit at God's side, while the rest of the earth perishes. As Bill Moyer writes, "Why care about the earth when the droughts, floods, famine, and pestilence brought by ecological collapse are signs of the apocalypse foretold in the Bible? Why care about global climate change when you and yours will be rescued in the Rapture?... Anyway, until Christ does return, the Lord will provide." [56]

This religious attitude unfortunately underlies much of our governmental non-response to climate changes that have the power to wreak utter havoc on our nation and the world. Sadly, thanks to this mindset, we've destroyed our renewable energy programs and subsidies and turned back to old fossil fuels like coal, leaving China, Europe and other global powers to win the race to develop clean energy technology and infrastructure. By distorting facts to these extremes, the coalition of evangelicals and their politicians have justified disastrous public policies that may result in an unlivable Earth for our children.

56 Moyers, Bill. "Welcome to Doomsday." *Beliefnet*. March 2005.

SATANIC PANIC CONSPIRACY THEORIES

The tendency to distort facts also led to the wildly inaccurate accusations of the so-called Satanic Panic. During the height of this panic in the 1980s and 1990s, many innocent people were sentenced to jail on the testimony of "recovered memories." Unethical psychiatric professionals used this now-thoroughly-debunked technique to lead children into describing lurid occult crimes that never occurred. In the mid-1990s, the credibility of the Satanic Ritual Abuse accusations melted away, triggered by the collapse of criminal prosecutions against alleged abusers, a growing number of scholars, officials and reporters questioning the reality of the accusations, and a variety of successful lawsuits against the mental health professionals involved. No actual evidence of widespread ritual abuse was ever uncovered.

But some psychiatric professionals are still practicing this debunked recovered memory technique and still making such extreme claims about widespread Satanic ritual abuse and even the existence of Satanic mind control. At conventions geared toward this group of mental health professionals, enterprising entrepreneurs even sell a more advanced species of tinfoil hat — baseball caps lined with a metallic fiber weave meant to block the "electromagnetic transmissions" of Satanic mind control.

TST's Grey Faction sub-organization was founded to help fight the harmful pseudoscience that is still to this day promulgated by these unethical psychiatric professionals. Grey Faction exposes these professionals and organizations like the International Society for the Study of Trauma and Dissociation (ISSTD) that still work to impress Satanic Panic delusions and pseudoscience into the minds of mental health patients and the public at large. Spotting and fighting harmful distortions like this helps beat back the encroachment of false and misleading info and bad-faith therapeutic practices.

TREASURING KNOWLEDGE

Our practice of relying on reason to make our policy decisions can be beneficial to our larger community or society. Stephen Pinker writes: "The indispensability of reason does not imply that individual people are always rational or are unswayed by passion and illusion. It only means that people are *capable* of reason, and that a community of people who choose to perfect this faculty and to exercise it openly and fairly can collectively reason their way to sounder conclusions in the long run." [57]

On a personal level, the Satanist works to actively uncover false beliefs in themselves and dispel them in favor of more scientifically accurate, evidence-based facts. This is the opposite of blind faith, which requires mental gymnastics instead to strengthen beliefs that have no basis in reason or science.

The torch that Baphomet bears on his brow burns with the light of Wisdom and Knowledge, and to the Satanist, these are goals toward which we work. Many Satanists are driven by a burning desire to learn, to know, to understand. Our thirst for knowledge propels us to dig down through the layers of subjective truth and find the bedrock of reason, rational exploration and the scientific method that can help guide us to a better understanding of the world.

57 Pinker, Stephen. *The Better Angels of our Nature.*
New York, New York: Penguin Group, 2012..

Tenet Six: Fallibility

People are fallible. If we make a mistake, we should do our best to rectify it and resolve any harm that may have been caused.

Tenet Six deals with how we relate to others, directing us to act compassionately and justly when we accidentally do harm. The Satanist understands that people are human and make mistakes, and Tenet Six advises us to admit and attempt to fix our errors when they occur.

This sounds simple and obvious, but many people are so bound up in their own sense of rightness that it can be hard for them to admit it when they get it wrong. This can be especially true if one's religion suggests that those who are more righteous and godly are automatically in the right when interacting with others, no matter what the circumstances. But regardless of whom we are interacting with, Tenet Six asks us to look as objectively as possible at a situation to determine if we are mistaken, and if there are amends we need to make or actions we need to take to repair harm we've caused.

INFALLIBLE LEADERS

The Satanic Temple's leaders are equally bound by Tenet Six — they too are only human and liable for the mistakes they make. In contrast, many religions feature a leader who is considered nearly or totally infallible. The most extreme versions of this belief posit that a religion's leaders are an extension of its higher power, or speak as its mouthpiece. For instance, for many centuries, the Catholic church dictated that regular folk were not qualified to read the Bible and interpret the word of God; instead they were directed to obey without question the priests who had the sole power to interpret God's truths to the masses. Services were conducted in Latin, and the Church forbade translation of the Bible into the vernacular.

This elitist system culminated with the proclamation in 1870 of papal infallibility — the dogma that the head priest, the Pope, speaking under certain circumstances called "ex cathedra" ("From the chair of Peter"), is incapable of error because he is acting as the mouthpiece of God.

Other spiritual traditions also follow this type of doctrine where the leader is considered practically infallible. Hinduism, Jainism, Sikhism, and certain types of Buddhism all partake of the tradition of the guru. A guru is a spiritual leader whose role it is to shape, counsel, mold, educate and inspire their followers. Followers are expected to heed their guru's advice without question in all matters, as they are usually considered to hold the key to spiritual evolution. In many instances, the guru is elevated above being simply a teacher, and instead becomes an object of veneration and worship themselves, sometimes endowed with supernatural powers.

In India, certain highly charismatic gurus with a great deal of influence are colloquially termed "Godmen," and are often believed to possess the power to perform miracles. These Godmen enjoy fame, fortune, and the sexual favors of large numbers of their followers. The most famous of this type of guru in America was the commune leader Bhagwan Shree Rajneesh, whose many followers bought him 93 Rolls-Royce cars to show their devotion.

Also in America, so-called "megapreachers," usually Evangelical televangelists, rack up millions of dollars in donations from followers who believe they are speaking for God, buying multiple mansions, yachts, private jets, and other luxury items with the money they rake in. For example, megapreacher Joel Osteen lives in a 17,000 square-foot mansion with an estimated value of $10.5 million. Osteen's 2017 net worth was reported to be between $40 – 60 million. [58]

These televangelists are part of the "Prosperity Gospel" Christian tradition. Donors believe these television personalities

58 Schmidt, Megan. "8 Richest Pastors in America." *Beliefnet.*

have a direct line to God, and any monetary gifts given to these preachers will in turn result in God blessing the giver with prosperity, wealth, and good fortune. But of course these supposed infallible holy men are just con artists, fleecing countless unsuspecting sheep in the name of the Lord.

PROBLEMS WITH CHARISMATIC LEADERS

There are obvious issues with giving up your own sovereignty to obey a spiritual leader without question. As Tenet Six dictates, people *are* fallible. No one person has all the answers. In most instances, a leader that requires unquestioning obedience isn't truly concerned about their followers' well-being, but rather their own power, wealth, and influence.

Movements that rely on charismatic leaders suffer from a host of problems. Instead of common ground and a shared philosophy, followers are often united only in their veneration of the head of the movement. Decisions about the movement are made only at the highest levels, often by the leader themselves, and do not necessarily reflect the wishes of the rest of the movement, but more often the personal power trip of the person at its head. Progress and evolution can be hard to effect, as those in power struggle to keep the status quo that supports their position. Despots, autocrats, dictators, and cult leaders often rise to power on the basis of charisma.

If the leader dies or quits, the movement can fall apart in disarray, as it was held together only by the outsized charismatic influence of the leader.

The Satanic Temple recognizes the dangers inherent in placing a charismatic leader at the head of the Satanic movement. TST isn't a cult of personality. The founders, Lucien Greaves and Malcolm Jarry, shun personal inquiries and profiles and instead tend to drive interviews in the direction of the principles and actions of TST. They haven't set themselves up as infallible gurus whose word is law. They require no veneration, nor make any claim to miracles. Because of their careful avoidance of the guru setup, the TST movement is based on shared values and a shared narrative instead of charisma and a forceful personality.

ADMITTING OUR MISTAKES

The Sixth Tenet provides a pathway for dealing with the inevitable mistakes that people make as fallible beings. Instead of denying the mistake, sweeping it under the rug, or suggesting it doesn't matter, Satanism dictates that we do the honest, humanitarian thing and own up to our mistake, doing everything in our power to fix it and prevent further harm. This is compassion in action — a common-sense, humanitarian approach that promotes personal responsibility. Our philosophy recognizes that sometimes people make mistakes, that no one is above our human tendency to err. The important thing is that we admit our errors and do whatever we can to fix any harm that has occurred.

Tenet Seven: Guiding Principles

Every tenet is a guiding principle designed to inspire nobility in action and thought. The spirit of compassion, wisdom, and justice should always prevail over the written or spoken word.

The Seventh Tenet suggests that the spirit of humanitarian, Satanic values is more important than any written or spoken words. This Tenet lays the groundwork for TST's anti-dogma nature. There is no "Bible" that The Satanic Temple obeys, no infallible written doctrine meant to survive centuries without evolution and change, no set of words that take precedence over the values of compassion, wisdom, and justice. These Tenets are not "Commandments" set in stone by a higher power and enforced by an elite priesthood. Instead they represent guidelines and the basis for the principles at the core of the Satanic path. We seek wisdom, fight for justice, and try our best to act with compassion in all things. The Tenets can be updated or changed to keep pace with changing times, as long as these core principles are maintained.

RECOMMENDED READING

While there isn't a great deal in the way of infallible texts like a standardized Bible, the Satanist can benefit from reading a rich variety of texts concerning Satanic ideas. Study can be important in understanding the history, background, and depth of Satanic concepts, and with the Satanic focus on knowledge, Satanists are encouraged to read widely. Many Satanic groups host book clubs to help facilitate this exploration.

Here is a brief introduction to some of the texts that can help aid Satanic understanding; see the Recommended Reading List in Appendix 4 for a more in-depth list.

WORKS BY TST FOUNDERS

Anything written by The Satanic Temple's founders Lucien Greaves and Malcolm Jarry could potentially be considered a primary source for Satanic philosophy, as they are the source for the guiding ideas of the "Satanic reformation" embodied in TST's creation. Talks they've given and their interviews on various podcasts can also be helpful in understanding TST's principles and ideas. You should be able to find a number of their articles, speaking engagements and interviews online.

You can also find statements and interviews given by other TST leaders online, whether they are International Council members or Chapter Heads. If they are speaking on behalf of TST, you can learn from what they have to say.

THE REVOLT OF THE ANGELS

The text most considered "canon" by The Satanic Temple is Anatole France's 1914 satiric masterpiece *The Revolt of the Angels*. This novel is ultimately a commentary on the corruption of power. It uses the theological metaphor of Satan as a force favoring free inquiry, with the War in Heaven symbolizing a metaphysical battle against universal tyranny. It's also a fairly short, fun read, with sexy hijinks and all-too-human angels.

THE BETTER ANGELS OF OUR NATURE

Although it doesn't mention Satanism specifically, Stephen Pinker's book *The Better Angels of Our Nature: Why Violence Has Declined* is also important reading for the Romantic Satanist — The Satanic Temple has identified it as primary reading, and it was the only book personally recommended to me by TST founder Lucien Greaves. With a great deal of historical data analysis, Dr. Pinker demonstrates the phenomenon of declining violence in the civilized world, providing a valuable exploration of what works and what doesn't when it comes to optimizing liberty and happiness in a society. He specifically calls out the Enlightenment as a turning point for human rights, and his findings emphasize the power of the Enlightenment ideals promoted by The Satanic Temple to change society markedly for the better.

PARADISE LOST

Paradise Lost (1667), by John Milton, lays the groundwork for the later interpretations of Satan as a heroic rebel fighting for free will and emancipation from tyranny. A century after its publication, Romantic artists used the Satan portrayed in *Paradise Lost* as a powerful symbol of Enlightenment ideals and human rights, setting in motion the philosophy that would eventually produce the concepts of The Satanic Temple.

Although *Paradise Lost* can help you understand the roots of Satanic philosophy, it is over ten thousand lines of blank verse poetry written in archaic English that was hard to understand even in Milton's time — not a quick and easy read. Luckily, there are a number of translations that present *Paradise Lost* in plain, everyday English, so anyone can understand it. You can also find collections of the famed artist Gustav Dore's illustrations for the 1866 edition of *Paradise Lost*.

The contemporary book *Evil Be My Good* gives an in-depth historical perspective on *Paradise Lost*, showing how Milton meant to portray Satan not as the sum of all evil, but rather as a revolutionary hero representing positive values.

ROMANTIC SATANISTS

Though they might not be explicitly Satanic, certain works by Romantic-era writers like William Blake, Percy Bysshe Shelley, Lord Byron and others can help expand your understanding of the roots of Satanic philosophy. The Recommended Reading List has a detailed list of these works.

HISTORY OF SATANISM

Self-identified Satanists (as opposed to those accused of Satanism by the Church and others) are a relatively new phenomenon. A number of academic books explore the rise and history of modern Satanism (though because The Satanic Temple is so new, they tend to stop with LaVeyan Satanism). These include *The Invention of Satanism,* by Asbjorn Dyrendal, James R. Lewis, and Jesper Aa. Petersen; *The Devil's Party: Satanism in Modernity,* by Per Faxneld & Jesper Aa. Petersen; and *Children of Lucifer: The Origins of Modern Religious Satanism,* by Ruben van Luijk.

These books are written in academic-style writing, which can be dense at times, but they pack in a lot of enlightening factual info about the rise of Satanism.

You can also expect to see more up-to-date histories published as modern Romantic Satanism gains momentum. One of the most comprehensive studies of The Satanic Temple in particular is Joseph Laycock's book *Speak of the Devil: How The Satanic Temple is Changing the Way We Talk about Religion.* Laycock delves into the history of TST and gives an in-depth examination of how the religious movement is changing the discussion about religion, religious freedom, and pluralism in society.

SATANIC RITUALS

For extended insight into modern Satanic ritual, I highly recommend *The Devil's Tome: A Book of Modern Satanic Ritual,* written by Shiva Honey, a founding member of The Satanic Temple Detroit and The International Council of The Satanic Temple. *The Devil's Tome* explores nontheistic Satanic ritual as a means for healing, empowerment, and community building, and features lovely illustrations by Lucien Greaves and Lex Corey.

FIGHTING THEOCRACY

Jay Wexler's *Our Non-Christian Nation* explores the ways non-dominant religions, including paganism and The Satanic Temple, have battled in the courts for the opportunity to take part in public forums opened up by the government. It contains a good introduction to current legalities regarding religious freedom, and the place of Satanism in fighting for an equal playing field.

A number of other works of literature, history, literary and social analysis and other genres flesh out a comprehensive view of historical Satanism and the ideas underpinning modern Satanic concepts. For a more in-depth list, please see Appendix 4.

OTHER READING RECOMMENDATION SOURCES

The Satanic Temple's main website, *thesatanictemple.com*, hosts a recommended reading list as well, representing the books chosen by TST leadership. Many TST Chapters also have a reading list on their website, plus some have a lending library for Chapter members. In addition to the book clubs organized by various Chapters, you can also find Satanic book clubs on social media. These clubs are a great way to delve into the reading with a group of others, sparking discussion and understanding.

If you like to write, consider making your own contribution to the Satanic discourse once you have some study and experience under your belt. What does your own personal Satanic path look like? How does your Satanism fit into your everyday life? Getting that info out can help others explore their own Satanic practices — in many senses, our individual practices combined comprise Satanism today. The more we write about Satanism, the more the religion grows and evolves.

ADDITIONAL PRINCIPLES

Beyond The Satanic Temple's Seven Tenets, certain personal qualities reflect the ideals of modern Satanism.

Honesty: The Satanist treasures the truth — not just finding the truth, but being impeccable with your word as well. Ethical behavior springs from being honest with both others and yourself. And becoming a fully-fledged Satanist requires you to live as honestly as possible in terms of being true to your authentic self.

Courage: It takes a great deal of courage to stand up in the face of powerful tyranny and say: enough. To have the guts to stand up to those who oppress or abuse, to fight for the rights of all — this takes tremendous courage. I've seen people risk it all by daring to stand up to tyranny. When they succeed, they help not just themselves, but all who were oppressed under that injustice.

It also takes guts to be yourself in a world that so desperately wants you to be anything else. Just declaring oneself a Satanist is a courageous move, considering the vast discrimination Satanists face from large segments of the population and the danger of assault and murder that stalks us.

Many Satanists also have had to bravely face pain, fear, abuse and rejection at the hands of others — and have found the valor to move forward open-eyed into life in spite of these setbacks.

Strength: Daring to stand up against tyranny requires a deep well-spring of internal strength. The Satanist uses their strength to fight injustice and to fight for those oppressed and those (like children) who cannot fight for themselves. The more you practice relying on your inner strength, the more effective you can be. Learn to find that core of principles that will sustain you through hardship.

The beauty of becoming part of a larger Satanic community is that you can share your strength with others and vice versa. Your voice against tyranny can be amplified many times when you fight alongside companions who share your ideals.

A SYSTEM OF POSITIVE VALUES

While some religions rely on harsh rules and infallible, unchanging doctrine, the Satanist cultivates ethical behavior based on humanitarian principles and the common-sense guidelines of the Tenets. Instead of "Thou shalt nots" and the negative values of guilt and shame, our system of ethics serves to focus us on the positive values of compassion, equal rights, reason and justice.

Illustration for John Milton's *Paradise Lost*, Gustave Doré, 1866.

SECTION 4:
The Outcast Awakens

Not many Satanists have had an easy life, filled with acceptance, support, and friendship. Most of us have been an outcast in one way or another, driven out of families, groups and communities for the sin of being different, of not fitting in with the dominant paradigm. We are often the scapegoats for others' fears, bigotry, repression and hatred — but the Satanic philosophy can help us reframe our rejection and open the door to finding our empowerment in the face of "Othering."

The word *scapegoat* comes from a ritual practice described in the Bible and texts from Judaism. It was carried out in similar fashion in several other ancient religions. In this ritual, described in Leviticus, two goats are selected by lot and brought to the Temple. One is designated for God and is sacrificed to him. The other, the scapegoat, is ritually invested with all the sins of the tribe and sent away into the wilderness to symbolically carry away the sins.

The term *scapegoat* continues in its modern meaning as one upon whom is heaped all the blame for something negative. Those scapegoated are often members of a group outside the dominant paradigm, feared and hated for nothing more than being different.

So many groups are hell-bent on Othering those who don't fall in line, who don't look, act, or think like the rest of the group. Many fundamentalist Abrahamic religions impart a sense of being "God's chosen people" to their adherents — and this chosen, supposedly righteous group often achieves cohesiveness and power by encouraging the fear and hatred of those who are different in some way.

Empathy and compassion are wiped away in the Othering process. Demonized groups are seen as less than human, not deserving of the same rights as full humans. Discrimination and abuse are treated as no big deal when they happen to the out-group. Indeed, in some circles, abuse and bigotry is encouraged in the name of "purifying" a community or nation.

Rejection can come not only from strangers and the greater society, but sometimes from one's own parents and relatives. Plenty of young people find themselves demonized, abused and disowned by parents who don't understand or approve of their sexuality, gender identity, non-interest in Christianity, or other things that set them apart. Instead of the love and support they need to grow up healthy and happy, these young people receive only messages of hatred and hurtfulness from those who are meant to protect and nurture them.

On a societal level, Othering works to take away legal rights from marginalized groups and encourage discrimination and hate crimes. It makes it hard for someone who has been brand-ed Other to get a job, find a place to live, or find a supportive network of peers.

The scapegoat has to learn to survive while being vilified, hunted and oppressed. In ancient tribes, to be banished from the group was to die alone in the wilderness. We are social animals, built to work together with others to feed and shelter ourselves. One person on their own would have difficulty surviving. Banishment was the worst possible punishment short of death. This need for a supportive community is a survival trait ingrained in our DNA.

Many of us have had to live without such a community thanks to the prejudices and fears inherent in many groups today. We've had to live with the judgement of our family, peers or society telling us that there is something wrong with us, pressuring us to conform and submit in order to fit in.

But Satanism steps in and reframes the issue. Being cast out for being different does not mean we're inherently in the wrong, but rather it highlights the fear and prejudice that lies behind our being driven out. The beauty of Satanic thought is that it welcomes all of us regardless of our differences, and provides the catalyst for the outcast to take back their power. We no longer need to fit in. The scapegoat, having been driven out of society and/or family, burdened with others' fear and hate, learns to rise up and grasp their own agency and wear the label of "Outsider" with pride instead of shame.

I've explored this idea of the outcast becoming empowered with a few specific examples.

Satanic Feminism

From the beginning, Christianity demonized women as the weaker sex, the means by which sin entered the world, because Eve was the one to succumb to the temptation of the serpent and eat from the forbidden Tree of Knowledge. Women were all considered flawed and inherently sinful due to this original sin, beholden to men and suited for nothing more than submission, child-bearing and other domestic roles.

Women were meant to obey, submit, and work extra hard to overcome their inherently sinful nature. Many saw them as naturally opposed to God, undeserving of any rights, property, leadership or other benefits reserved for men. Women were denied any official role in Church leadership, and sex with women was considered so spiritually "polluting" that priests were forbidden to marry lest they compromise their ability to serve God.

Because of this supposed sinful nature, the Church decreed that the female gender is most likely to associate with witchcraft and the devil. Women who were independent, those (especially midwives) who dared heal, those who were elderly or sexually unappealing, even those women who refused sexual advances — so many were accused of witchcraft and tortured and killed in the name of God.

Women's rights movements remained nonexistent throughout the Middle Ages and the Renaissance, as few dared raise the issue with the patriarchal Church holding a tight grip on society through fear and witchcraft executions. Any woman who dared to speak up for her gender might have been branded a heretic and sorceress, accused of lurid supernatural crimes and congress with the Devil, and sentenced to a gruesome death after barbaric torture.

But the Enlightenment, with its ideals of freedom, reason, and human rights, started bringing women's rights into the spotlight. Some women were not content to let revolution pass them by, but risked their lives to argue that women deserved the same basic rights as men. These women stood up fearlessly to tyranny for their rights — just as the literary Satan stood up to a tyrannical God.

DECLARATION OF THE RIGHTS OF WOMAN

In 1791, inspired by the same Enlightenment philosophy that underpinned the French and American revolutions and forms the basis of The Satanic Temple's value system, French activist and writer Olympe de Gouges responded to the 1789 release of *Declaration of the Rights of Man and of the Citizen* by writing her own *Declaration of the Rights of Woman and the Female Citizen.* In it she exhorts women to arise and fight for their own freedom in the revolutionary era:

> *Women, wake up; the tocsin of reason sounds throughout the universe; recognize your rights. The powerful empire of nature is no longer surrounded by prejudice, fanaticism, superstition, and lies. The torch of truth has dispersed all the clouds of folly and usurpation. Enslaved man has multiplied his force and needs yours to break his chains.* [59]

In this Declaration, de Gouges dared to postulate that women have the same natural rights as men, writing "Woman is born free and remains the equal to man in rights." [60] She proposed that women should be able to own property, participate in the legislative process, and hold political office:

---

59 Gouges, Olympe de. *The Declaration of the Rights of Woman and the Female Citizen.* 1791.

60 Gouges, Olympe de. *The Declaration of the Rights of Woman and the Female Citizen.* 1791.

The law should be the expression of the general will. All citizenesses and citizens should take part, in person or by their representatives, in its formation. It must be the same for everyone. All citizenesses and citizens, being equal in its eyes, should be equally admissible to all public dignities, offices and employments, according to their ability, and with no other distinction than that of their virtues and talents. [61]

But the world wasn't ready to accept such groundbreaking ideas. Even in the midst of the liberating Enlightenment-fueled revolution, de Gouges was demonized for daring to call for equality for women. She was repaid for her bold declaration of women's rights with execution by guillotine.

NINETEENTH CENTURY SUFFRAGETTES

By the late 1800s, women's rights in post-Civil War America had blossomed into a full movement — albeit one that was met with derision and monumental opposition. Leaders of the women's suffrage movement were vilified as demonic harpies bent on destroying the country's moral fabric.

One of the most influential women's rights activists of the time, Victoria Woodhull, was even characterized as "Mrs. Satan" for her tireless work in support of women's suffrage, birth control, and sexual choice. She believed women deserved just as many rights as men. She even had the audacity to run for president, with black abolitionist Frederick Douglass as her vice president.

She was conceptualized by opponents as the rebellious Satan of *Paradise Lost*; they went so far as to portray her with wings and horns in a political cartoon very reminiscent of Gustav Dore's famous *Paradise Lost* woodcuts. (Figure 12.) What Woodhull saw as the fight for much-deserved equal rights, many of her contemporaries considered a Satanic plot to wreck homes, sow chaos, and upend the natural order of things. It would take almost 50 years for women to finally win the right to vote in 1920, and it wasn't until the 1960s that black women in the South were finally able to exercise their voting rights.

61 Gouges, Olympe de. *The Declaration of the Rights of Woman and the Female Citizen*. 1791.

Figure 12: Caricature by Thomas Nast in *Harper's Weekly*, February 17, 1872.

MODERN WITCHES

Though women today enjoy many advances made toward equality with men, modern society still suffers from sexism in many areas. Fundamentalist strains of the traditional Abrahamic religions are still virulently patriarchal, teaching that the woman's job is to remain at home and obediently serve her husband. These religions teach that a woman who has sex before marriage is forever soiled property, and that any woman who dares claim ownership of her own body and sexuality is a sinful slut. Girls as young as 13 are married off to the old men in leadership positions in some of these sects. Women raised in these environments are taught to feel deep shame for any questioning of their proper place.

While those within such fundamentalist faiths hurl accusations of "slut" and "witch" at women who dare to stand up for their rights, some groups have reclaimed those words and turned them into empowering terms.

One of the first activist groups to turn the accusatory "witch" into a term of female empowerment was W.I.T.C.H., a group of feminists that was active from 1968-1970, with a recent resurgence in cities like Boston and Portland. W.I.T.C.H. originally stood for "Women's International Terrorist Conspiracy from Hell," but the group changed their name to suit their purposes, albeit retaining the fixed letters of WITCH. Members used dramatic performance art and costuming for their guerilla activism, taking to the streets dressed in witch costumes complete with pointy hats to fight sexism, corporate control, and other issues of their day. W.I.T.C.H.'s flair for political theater inspired some of TST's political performance art pieces.

For many, a female Satanist is by definition a witch; after all, for centuries the term meant the same thing. Religious conservatives have been calling feminists Satanists and witches for centuries, so by claiming the title of Satanist, women are stepping up, reclaiming the word, and saying, "Yes, we have a voice!"

The powerful, emancipated woman in charge of her own body and sexuality remains a frightening image to those who cling to patriarchal power structures. Fundamentalist religions churn out fire and brimstone threats to female equality, claiming it is God's will that women remain birthing and male service machines, relegated to second-class citizenship. Simply by nature of our fundamental humanist beliefs, The Satanic Temple finds itself a champion of women's rights in any society in which autonomous women are demonized.

The Satanic belief in the inviolability of one own's body is a radical statement when ownership of the female body has been for so long the purview of men. Our insistence on bodily autonomy puts us squarely in opposition to those who would take away reproductive rights. The Satanic Temple's multiple suits against extreme, theocracy-based abortion restrictions arise out of this belief.

Our reliance on the humanist ideals of the Enlightenment informs our fight for liberty and basic human rights for all — no matter what gender. We've taken the shadowy figure of the witch and reclaimed that image to lend strength to our struggles for justice. The Satanic Temple's Sabbat Cycle, a series of interactive performances inspired by the Puritan horror film *The VVitch*, states:

> *Nearly four-hundred years after the first execution of an American "witch," many in our nation still call for the establishment of an American theocracy and a return to the puritanical delusions of old. In the face of relentless persecution, of unjust authority treading on our private, intellectual and sexual lives, we, the outsiders, the freethinking, and the godless have found ourselves strengthened. We act now to righteously assert our American freedoms, for the edification of our communities and the future of the private citizen.* [62]

---

62 "The Sabbat Cycle." *The Satanic Temple.* thesatanictemple.com.

Queer Satanism

The LGBTQ community is under constant fire by conservative religious and political leaders. Those whose relationships, attractions and/or identity put them outside the heterosexual, cisgender model often find themselves the target of intense demonization, especially by the Religious Right. Fundamentalist politicians have rammed through legislation designed to allow for legal discrimination against gay and transgender people in all arenas. Though the U.S. Supreme Court finally ruled in favor of gay marriage in 2015, the fight continues for true equality.

Religion is used as a weapon against gay and transgender individuals; multiple states have passed legislation that makes it legal to discriminate against gay and transgender people in the name of religious freedom, and our current federal administration and Supreme Court have supported and encouraged such discrimination, privileging evangelical Christian beliefs over basic human rights. While this discrimination might only mean that a baker can refuse to bake a wedding cake for a gay wedding, it can be much worse.

In 2014, a Michigan pediatrician refused to treat the child of a lesbian couple, claiming her religious beliefs prevented her from providing care, and it was deemed legal. [63] Even in cases where a life is threatened, religious freedom laws allow discrimination; in many states an emergency responder could refuse life-saving help to gay or trans individuals and it would potentially be completely legal. In some states, it's legal to discriminate against gay couples who want to adopt, denying them the chance for a family and reducing options for children to find safe, loving homes.

Thanks to theocratic forces within the American government, religious belief has become a legally valid reason to trample all over the human rights of the LGBTQ community. We as Satanists need to stand up to this theocratic discrimination however possible.

The Satanic Temple counts many LGBTQ individuals in its

---

63 Abby, Phillip. "Pediatrician Refuses to Treat Baby with Lesbian Parents and There's Nothing Illegal About It." *Washington Post.* February 19, 2015.

membership — at least more than half its members. Unlike Christianity, Satanism has no limitations on who you can or cannot love or be with. That is left entirely within the purview of the individual. Lucien Greaves says:

> *It would be a conservative estimate to say that more than 50 per cent of our membership is LGBTQ.*
>
> *I think that's because they feel disowned and disenfranchised from the traditional religious institutions. So, you have a population willing to embrace a religious identification that is boldly willing to speak out to the contrary.* [64]

The Satanic Temple takes LGBTQ rights very seriously, taking a number of actions to support those rights. In 2013, very early on in the formation of TST, The Satanic Temple protested the Westboro Baptist Church's aggressively anti-gay picketing by performing a "Pink Mass" celebrating same-sex unions at the gravesite of the mother of Westboro Baptist founder Fred Phelps. Greaves explains:

> *From the start, when one of our early actions was the Pink Mass, a lot of LGBTQ people were looking for another community that didn't see them as defined by their sexual orientation.* [65]

In 2015, faced with Michigan's proposed Religious Freedom Restoration Act that would make it legal for businesses to discriminate against gay and trans people based on religious beliefs, The Satanic Temple of Detroit launched a petition to urge the state Senate to consider an amendment that would require "businesses who accommodate the public to post any discrimination policy in effect in a conspicuous location visible to patrons and employees." TST Detroit even provided printable signs that businesses would be forced to display, so that all would be alerted to their bigotry. (Figure 13.).

In 2017, TST launched a campaign encouraging couples to order Satanic wedding cakes from bakeries who oppose same-sex marriage because of their religious beliefs. While such bakeries

---

64 Duffy, Nick. "The Satanic Temple is in favour of equal rights for LGBT+ people." *PinkNews*. August 23, 2019.

65 Duffy, Nick. "The Satanic Temple is in favour of equal rights for LGBT+ people." *PinkNews*. August 23, 2019.

are allowed to discriminate against gays under so-called Religious Freedom laws, they cannot refuse to bake a Satanic cake, because religion is a legally protected class. Lucien Greaves stated that The Satanic Temple's hope is that if a Satanist brings a lawsuit against a bakery who refused to bake a Satanic cake, it will prompt the Supreme Court to "consider either adding sexual orientation as a protected class, or taking religion away from protected class status," making it impossible to legally discriminate against gay and trans individuals based on religious beliefs. [66] (Figure 14.)

DUE TO SINCERELY HELD
RELIGIOUS BELIEFS

SERVICE IS DENIED
TO _____

Figure 13: Discrimination warning sign example, proposed by TST Detroit.

Most Chapters of The Satanic Temple get involved in some way with their local LGBTQ Pride celebrations. They march in Pride parades, host info booths at Pride festivals, and show up to support the LGBTQ community. For instance, the Seattle Chapter stands next to the hellfire preachers spewing anti-gay rhetoric along the Seattle Pride Parade route, providing a contrast to the preachers' hate-speech signs with their own signs promoting tolerance, love, acceptance and LGBTQ Pride. (Figure 15.)

In a statement released in 2017, The Satanic Temple describes Pride as "a gathering of an historically marginalized and oppressed

Figure 14: Cake created for a Satanic Vow Renewal ceremony, 2019.

---

66 Wong, Curtis. "The Satanic Temple Has An Ingenious Plan To Troll Anti-Gay Bakeries." *Huffington Post.* September 28, 2017.

Figure 15: TST Seattle members stand in front of hate speech preachers along the Seattle Pride Parade route, 2019.

community to celebrate their culture and heritage," going on to detail why TST participates:

It is an affirmation of an identity in spite of what anyone else thinks of that identity: a decidedly Satanic frame of mind. When chapters participate in Pride events, we demonstrate our support for the community and recognize that community's presence within our own organization.

Transgender people suffer some of the most extreme demonization. As with gay rights, many of the attacks on transgender rights come from Abrahamic fundamentalists, who view the very existence of transgender people as an affront to God. While transgender people try their best just to live a normal life, these fundamentalists seem hell-bent on making life as difficult as possible. Fueled in large part by incendiary anti-trans rhetoric echoed by the current President of the United States, violence against trans people has claimed an alarming number of lives.

Encouraged by the federal administration, many states have passed laws rescinding rights for victims of anti-trans discrimination. A number of localities have passed so-called "bathroom laws" making it illegal for transgender individuals to use the bathroom that correlates with their gender identity, forcing them to endure everything from stares to assault in the bathroom of their birth sex — or forego going to the bathroom in public places at all, risking serious health issues.

The Satanic Temple's emphasis on human rights for all extends to trans rights. TST recognizes the right of the individual to their own gender identity, and many Satanists actively fight against bathroom bills and other discriminatory practices. Satanism teaches that one's body is inviolable, and no one else has the right to force you into another gender identity or expression. Many Chapters participate in Trans Pride events. (Figure 16.)

Chapters of The Satanic Temple have traditionally been safe spaces for gay and trans people to just be themselves, without pressure to change. Greaves says:

> Within The Satanic Temple, we're all pretty much one and the same. We're all Satanists and it's not like we have "tolerance" for trans people or gay people or sex workers, we just don't f**king care, and a lot of people in those communities appreciate that. [67]

A large number of queer and trans individuals serve in leadership in Chapters around the world and on TST's governing body, the International Council. Greaves underscores TST's commitment to LGBTQ rights: "We will always fight to the death to ensure that there are equal rights for the gay community." [68]

---

67 Duffy, Nick. "The Satanic Temple is in favour of equal rights for LGBT+ people." *PinkNews*. August 23, 2019.

68 Duffy, Nick. "The Satanic Temple is in favour of equal rights for LGBT+ people." *PinkNews*. August 23, 2019.

TST Seattle member at Olympia Pride, 2019.

Freethinkers and Atheists

Those who dare to question the teachings of fundamentalist religions usually become branded as heretics and shunned by the religious conservatives in their lives. Many young people innocently raise questions about the many contradictions found in the Bible and church teachings, only to find themselves punished and, if they continue to ask questions, eventually cut off from their families and in extreme cases driven out of their homes.

Atheists suffer a great deal of discrimination in present society — many people view them as untrustworthy and immoral, as if ethics could come only from religiosity. Many countries have laws against atheism: 13 Muslim countries officially punish atheism or apostasy by death, while many of the other 192 United Nation member countries discriminate against citizens who have no belief in a god, some even legislating that atheists can be jailed for the offense of blasphemy. [69]

Atheist politicians are rare; voters often distrust them. Some states even bar atheists from holding office or testifying in court. The Arkansas state constitution, for instance, proclaims "No person who denies the being of a God shall hold any office in the civil departments of this State, nor be competent to testify as a witness in any Court." [70] The Tennessee state constitution (and several others) even requires a belief in heaven and hell: "No person who denies the being of God, or a future state of rewards and punishments, shall hold any office in the civil department of this state." [71]

Atheists can make religious people uncomfortable because they prove that one can live life without the strictures of God, and that can cause some to question their own faith. Thus, freethinkers and atheists often find themselves relegated to the fringes of communities, branded as unethical infidels.

But The Satanic Temple offers freethinkers and atheists a community that welcomes their questions and understands that a belief

69 Evans, Robert. "Atheists face death in 13 countries, global discrimination: study." *Reuters.* December 9, 2013.

70 *Constitution of the State of Arkansas.* Little Rock, AR: Arkansas State Legislature.

71 "Article IX, Disqualifications." *Tennessee Blue Book 2011-2012.* Nashville, TN: Secretary of State, State of Tennessee.

in a higher power is not a necessary component either of ethics or of religion in general. The Satanic Temple represents an evolution in the notion of religion: that one can have the advantages of religion without belief in the supernatural or a higher power. TST provides the atheist with a shared set of ethics, a common narrative and symbolism, the social benefits of a religious group, and the chance to be active in shaping laws and government.

At the core, the Satanic philosophy relies on reason and science for our best understanding of the world, and encourages study and debate. Free thought is admired and encouraged in the Satanist.

THE SCAPEGOAT ARISES

Just as the word *witch* or *queer* began life as a slur, *Satanist* was for centuries a term levelled in accusation at those supposedly operating outside the protected confines of godly society. Satan himself was viewed as completely evil, a force of destruction threatening all that was good.

But starting with *Paradise Lost* and continuing through the Romantic-era writers and artists, the figure of Satan began to be reclaimed and reimagined, transforming slowly into a symbol of just rebellion against the tyranny of an arbitrary authority. Satanists today have the chance to continue this reclamation, empowering ourselves with the very word used as a pejorative in the past.

We bear our differences out loud and proudly, instead of hidden in shame. We the scapegoat have been shunted to the wilderness, and instead of lamenting our banishment and wasting away, we have revelled in finding a tribe of similarly Othered individuals. We who are feared and deemed monstrous in some way are edged out of society precisely because our very existence is dangerous to established norms and rigid hierarchical rules. When we become Satanists, we say to the world that yes, we are just who we really are, without need to compromise ourselves in order to conform or obey.

Michelle Shortt, former Chapter Head of The Satanic Temple - Arizona, puts it this way:

> *When people call us evil, what does that really mean? You have people at the pulpit who are molesting children and they're considered good because they're religious but they're calling us evil. We take that, we take the position of the scapegoat and we wear it proudly ... if you stand here godless, you've probably been considered a Satanist before. You've been demonized by your own community ... we own up to the label that we've been given, and we call ourselves Satanists. [72]*

In many ways, this willingness to take the scapegoat label and run with it is the biggest difference between the Satanist and the humanist. While The Satanic Temple's core beliefs have much in common with the values of secular humanism, Satanists have a much different approach to meshing with society. Whereas many humanist groups work toward acceptance and integration with the rest of society, the Satanist values the individual just as they are, no matter how different from the so-called norm. We differ from humanists not only by our admiration of the symbol of Satan, but also because we don't strive to become mainstream. We embrace our outsider status and wear it proudly, without apologies or compromise.

Lucien Greaves says, "The self-identified Satanist embraces their outsider status and is drawn to the forbidden, anomalous, and the hidden. We identify with the symbolism of 'blasphemy' as an expression of liberation from superstition. We bow to no God, or gods, and we reject all arbitrary edicts and unjust authority." [73]

The scapegoat arises, fully empowered, with the ability to shake the very foundations of the established order.

---

72 Matirko, Jack. "Religious But Not Spiritual: Modern Satanism in the Atheist Community." *Patheos.* September 25, 2017.

73 Greaves, Lucien. "Letters to a Satanist: Why Do You Call Yourselves Satanists?" *Orlando Weekly.* September 26, 2014.

Ritual at TST Seattle's annual camping trip, 2016.

SECTION 5
Tools for Practice

Satanism is anti-dogma and anti-authoritarian, and it encourages us to walk our own path in all aspects of our lives. Because it promotes individualism, building your Satanic practice will be a creative endeavor. You'll take everything you know and weave it together into a personalized path that works for you. Before we delve further into the details, let's explore two tools that can be very useful in creating and maintaining our Satanic practice: ritual and symbology.

Satanic Ritual

Ritual can be an extremely powerful tool. Though Satanists are not required to practice ritual, many of us do engage in rituals both at the private and community-wide levels. Most chapters of The Satanic Temple perform rituals on an occasional or regular basis, both within the chapter itself and for the public at events. Rituals represent a powerful way to reach the unconscious, mark occasions, make a political statement, or effect personal transformation.

Rituals and ceremonies are a part of most cultures. *Anthropy. com* classifies rituals as a type of social behavior specific to given cultures:

TST Seattle Unbaptism ritual, 2017.

Ritual is used to reinforce social bonds and structure. They are actions with intentional symbolic meaning undertaken for a specific cultural purpose, such as a rite of passage from childhood to adulthood, and may reinforce broader community social bonds, as in a wedding. [74]

Most everyone recognizes religious rituals like the Catholic Mass and the standard Christian wedding, but we can also find many more secular ceremonies in daily life. Occasions like a birthday, anniversary or graduation mark a major transition in a person's life. Many people have secular weddings, without religion playing a role. Speaking at a eulogy or saying a poem while spreading a loved one's ashes represent end-of-life rituals that can help survivors work through their grief.

Many people also have private rituals for good luck and success. A rabbit's foot or coin, for instance, may be carried for luck. Though no scientific basis exists for such items physically bringing better luck, it appears they can actually work by increasing the subconscious confidence of the bearer.

74 "Ritual and Custom." *Chegg Study.*

Rituals have the power to make a difference in our own minds. *Scientific American* writes:

> *Recent research suggests that rituals may be more rational than they appear. Why? Because even simple rituals can be extremely effective. Rituals performed after experiencing losses – from loved ones to lotteries – do alleviate grief, and rituals performed before high-pressure tasks – like singing in public – do in fact reduce anxiety and increase people's confidence. What's more, rituals appear to benefit even people who claim not to believe that rituals work. [75]*

NONTHEISTIC RITUAL

Satanism allows for the full benefit of ritual without the requirement of belief in or subservience to any supernatural deity or powers. Though Satan and other mythical beings may be referenced in a ritual, it is strictly as symbol only — we don't actually believe we are conjuring up the devil. Nor do we believe we are practicing magic — Satanists don't actually put hexes on people or do "spells" meant to achieve something by mysterious, supernatural means. We don't believe we have magic powers. Instead, we recognize nontheistic ritual as an activity replete with symbolism and personal meaning, one we can use to our advantage in our Satanic practice.

In many ways, ritual works the same way as art. It uses symbols to reach out to the unconscious mind. Ideas that are hard to convey in explanatory text can manifest and make sense as a gestalt-like whole during a ritual performance. Special clothing like robes or wedding garments, symbols like the pentagram, tools like the bell or knife, special music or sounds, special words spoken with careful deliberation and forcefulness, and even the soft light of candles and special scents like incense and oil can all come into play to create the message of the ritual.

These aspects all come together to work on our subconscious, getting us in touch with our instincts and opening our mind, leading us to think in new directions. Ritual actions are imbued

75 Gino, Francesca and Norton, Michael. "Why Rituals Work." *Scientific American.* May 14, 2013.

with extra significance; they focus attention and call us to be completely present.

CREATING YOUR OWN RITUAL

Satanism differs from most religions in that there are no universally required rituals — no mass we have to attend every week, no prayer book we have to read from, no standardized set of ceremonies that all Satanists must take part in. Our rituals aren't handed down through the centuries or inflexibly codified in stone. Instead, each Satanist or Satanic group creates their own rituals as they go along, using what is most personally significant to them and to the intent of the specific ritual.

Writing your own ritual has many advantages. It can be completely personalized, tailored to you or your group at a particular time and place. You have the freedom to choose the symbols that are meaningful to you. The personal is powerful.

The ritual that has your personal creativity invested in it can be far more alive than those rituals done by rote that follow a narrow, set, rigidly constrained pattern (as is often the case in Abrahamic religions). Rituals that have personal relevance can be more transformative, more effective in their message and intent.

BRING YOUR RITUAL TO LIFE

You can break the ritual creation process down into several parts.

First, set your intention for the ritual. This could be anything from breaking the chains of your religious past to effecting political change. You can create rituals for beginning or ending Satanic gatherings, aligning yourself with your Satanic path, starting an important project, celebrating a wedding or commitment, or any other occasion or purpose.

Next, gather your inspiration. You can do research into symbols, look at other rituals, brainstorm with others, and meditate on what might work best. Keep notes as you do your research.

Once you have a rich base of ideas, get the rough shape of the ritual nailed down. At this point, you don't need to write out the actual speaking parts, just figure out in broad terms what will happen and in what order.

Some questions you might ask yourself: How many clergy are needed? What will be their roles? Are there participants beside the clergy (people being unbaptized or initiated, for instance)? What will happen to them in the ritual?

What ritual tools and props will you need? This could include all sorts of items like an altar with altar cloth, a gong or bell, bowls or chalices, candles, ashes or paint for anointing participants, knives to cut bonds, or other objects. Think about what you'd like your ritual participants to wear. Many Satanic groups use black ritual robes, but there's no hard and fast rule about what folks should wear. Will you be using music? If so, start working on a playlist ahead of time or communicating with your musicians about what you'd like.

When you have the rough shape blocked out, do a quick run-through in your head or with a friend to see how the ritual will flow. Make any changes that the run-through brings to mind.

Finally, you'll flesh out the details, creating a finished ritual. Write out the exact words for the speaking parts, note all stage directions, and indicate exactly how the ritual tools will be used. Give your finished document a good scrutinizing, running through it again in your head and correcting any issues you spot. Then you're ready to actually rehearse the ritual.

You may choose to have clergy memorize lines, or you may have them read their parts out loud. Either way, it's important to rehearse the ritual before it's performed. In our Chapter, we usually require at least four rehearsals for internal, Chapter-only rituals. For public rituals such as our Unbaptism, we have multiple rehearsal sessions over a month or so, working out any kinks. If possible, make sure at least a few of those rehearsals take place at the ritual location (the room, park, stage, etc.), and at least one is a dress rehearsal in full ritual garb. When you finally perform your ritual, you want everything to go smoothly.

I've included a number of sample rituals in Appendix 2 of this book. While you can certainly use them as-is, they are meant to inspire you to create your own personalized rituals to suit you and your intent.

Satanic Symbology

A wealth of symbols relate to the concepts and cultural history of Satanism, with sources ranging from the medieval to current pop culture; this section will introduce a few of the most well-known Satanic symbols. You can draw from this collection in building your own personal symbology. What most appeals to you viscerally, aesthetically and in terms of meaning? If any of these spark your interest, you can use them in your personal practice and your own Satanic artwork.

THE GOAT

Goats have been traditionally associated with Satan. This may have started with the scapegoat ritual described in the Bible. Because the scapegoat was portrayed as the receptacle for all sin, representing all that was evil and unwanted in human nature, it became connected with that evil and associated with the demon Azazel, to which it was sacrificed.

There are also echoes of Pagan beliefs in this connection. Paganism attributed sexuality, fertility and wildness to goats; in ancient Greece the god Pan was portrayed with horns and cloven hooves and was said to lead wild, drunken, orgiastic dances in the wilderness. The lusty Satyrs were also represented as men with a goat's ears, tail, legs, and horns. As pagan religions were demonized by Christianity over the ages, these half-goat deities were associated with evil.

Medieval folklore and prosecutions spoke of the goat's major role in witchcraft. From the Middle Ages to the 17th century and later, men and women were accused of taking part in Witches' Sabbaths; the *Compendium Maleficarum* (1608) by Francesco Maria Guazzo describes the Sabbath activities thusly: "the attendants riding flying goats, trampling the cross, and being re-baptised in the name of the Devil while giving their clothes to him, kissing his behind, and dancing back to back forming a round."

Figure 17: *El Aquelarre* ("Witches' Sabbath"), Francisco Goya, 1798.

The Devil leading these Sabbaths was often conceived of as a large black he-goat, or a man with the head, horns and cloven hooves of a goat.

Witches were thought in many cases to copulate with animals, and legend told of a cult in Mendes in Classical times that worshipped a he-goat and whose priestesses copulated with it. [76] This myth inspired Eliphas Levi to proclaim that this "Goat of Mendes" was the god of the Witches' Sabbath.

This goatish figure looms large in many artworks portraying witchcraft; one of the best-known is *Witches' Sabbath*, a 1798 oil on canvas work by the Spanish artist Francisco Goya.

---

76 *Histories ii.* Herodotus.

Figure 18: Baphomet, from *Dogme et Rituel de la Haute Magie*,
Eliphas Levi, 1856.

The painting portrays the devil as a goat-headed entity leading a gathering of witches. (Figure 17.)

This association between the goat and the devil continues into the literature, music and art of the modern era. For instance, in *The VVitch*, the 2015 American art-house horror film co-promoted by The Satanic Temple, the devil is portrayed as a great black he-goat, "Black Phillip," who encourages his young disciple to sign her name in his book and turn to witchcraft. The character of Black Phillip struck the imagination of many artists, resulting in a number of portrayals.

Metal bands and other musicians have been inspired by this connection; the English death metal band Akercocke's second studio album is titled "The Goat of Mendes," and other bands have used goat imagery to represent Satanic themes.

BAPHOMET

In a continuation of the association between Satanism and goats, the Satanic Temple and many other modern Satanic organizations utilize the symbol of Baphomet, an androgynous occult figure with the head of a goat and the body of a human, in their art and literature. (Figure 18.)

The historical origins of this figure are murky, but most likely are related to accusations leveled against the Knights Templar. Once a well-respected Christian organization, the medieval order of the Knights Templar was suppressed by King Philip IV of France in 1307 when it grew too powerful for the comfort of the monarchy and Church. Despite its members' Christian beliefs, it was blacklisted and members were put on trial for witchcraft. According to French chroniclers of the Crusades, the Templars confessed under torture to worshipping a heathen idol called Baphometh. Some scholars believe "Baphometh" was simply a corruption of "Mahomet" — the Prophet Muhammad — but no clear etymology has been traced.

The modern visual conception of Baphomet sprang from the works of French occultist Eliphas Levi. In the mid 1800s, Levi published *Dogme et Rituel de la Haute Magie* ("Dogma and Rituals of High Magic"), which included an image of a hermaphroditic goat-headed figure that he described as both Baphomet and "The Sabbatic Goat." Levi saw Baphomet not as the devil or a force of evil, but rather as an occult symbol of nonduality and the integration of opposites. In his description, he points out the many symbolic aspects of the figure that reconcile opposing forces:

> The goat on the frontispiece carries the sign of the pentagram on the forehead, with one point at the top, a symbol of light, his two hands forming the sign of occultism, the one pointing up to the white moon of Chesed, the other pointing down to the black one of Geburah. This sign expresses the perfect harmony of mercy with justice. His one arm is female, the other male like the ones of the androgyne of Khunrath, the attributes of which we had to unite with those of our goat because he is one and the same symbol. The flame of intelligence shining between his horns is the magic light of the universal balance, the image of the soul elevated above matter, as the flame, whilst being tied to matter, shines above it. The beast's head expresses the horror of the sinner, whose materially acting, solely responsible part has to bear the punishment exclusively; because the soul is insensitive according to its nature and can only suffer when it materializes. The rod standing instead of genitals symbolizes eternal life, the body covered with scales the water, the semi-circle above it the atmosphere, the feathers following above the volatile. Humanity is represented by the two breasts and the androgyne arms of this sphinx of the occult sciences. [77]

In this description, Baphomet is a powerful symbol of integration and balance. Lucien Greaves says of the symbol, "It embodies opposites and celebrates contrasts." [78]

Baphomet's face is bestial, but the light of human intelligence shines in the flame above it. His body encompasses both the female (breasts) and the male (the rod symbolizing the penis and

77 Lévi, Éliphas. *Dogme et Rituel de la Haute Magie.* 1861
78 Morgan, James. "Decoding the symbols on Satan's statue." *BBC News.* August 1, 2015.

the generative power of life). Two fingers on the right hand point up and two on the left hand point down, meaning "as above, so below," and the arms are marked with the words "solve" ("to dissolve") and "coagula" ("to come together"); these words and the accompanying gesture are drawn from the ancient works of Hermes Trismegistus, whose writings on the occult and alchemy became popular during the Renaissance and Reformation.

The Satanic Temple has brought this symbol to life; in 2014, they successfully crowd-funded the creation of an eight-foot-tall bronze statue of Baphomet, with two children gazing adoringly up at the figure's face. This statue has been the focus of several lawsuits against states who have allowed Ten Commandments monuments on Capitol grounds — TST's legal argument is that if one religious monument is allowed on government property, all should be, including their own goat-headed religious figure (see the section on "Taking Action"). Greaves further explains the symbolism inherent in the monument: "For us it symbolizes reconciliation of the opposites — such as having a Satanic monument opposite a Christian one. ... We think that's a powerful message when it's sitting opposite the Ten Commandments — you can have these dualities, differences without conflict." [79]

THE PENTAGRAM

The pentagram, the shape of a five-pointed star drawn with five straight strokes, is also frequently used as a Satanic symbol. The pentagram has been used as a symbol in both Christianity and the occult for centuries. It was said to have been used as a symbol or sign of recognition by the Pythagoreans. Medieval Christians used the pentagram to represent Christ's five wounds. Occultists such as Agrippa and others perpetuated the popularity of the pentagram as a magic symbol.

By the mid-19th century, occultists had separated the pentagram symbol by its orientation; with a single point upwards it

79 Morgan, James. "Decoding the symbols on Satan's statue." *BBC News*. August 1, 2015.

Figure 19: Image from *La Clef de la Magie Noire*, Stanislas De Guaita, 1897.

depicted spirit presiding over the four elements of matter and was essentially "good." Eliphas Levi was the first to assign an evil meaning to the reversed shape, and wrote:

A reversed pentagram, with two points projecting upwards, is a symbol of evil and attracts sinister forces because it overturns the proper order of things and demonstrates the triumph of matter over spirit. It is the goat of lust attacking the heavens with its horns. [80]

He further elaborated on this association by explaining how the head of the devilish goat transcribed into the pentagram's shape:

The flaming star, which, when turned upside down, is the hieroglyphic sign of the goat of Black Magic, whose head may be drawn in the star, the two horns at the top, the ears to the right and left, the beard at the bottom. [81]

This actual image of a goat head drawn in a downward-pointing pentagram first appeared in the 1897 book *La Clef de la Magie Noire*, by the French occultist Stanislas de Guaita. (Figure 19.)

A version of this pentagram is used by the Church of Satan. The Satanic Temple also uses a stylized version of a goat head within a pentagram, with each Chapter further customizing the symbol. (Figure 20, opposite.)

SULFUR SYMBOL

Figure 21: Alchemical symbol for sulfur.

With the rise of alchemy came a number of symbols representing elements and compounds used in alchemical experiments. One of the alchemical symbols for sulfur, a double cross on top of an infinity sign, has been used in Satanism since its association

---

80 Lévi, Éliphas. *Dogme et Rituel de la Haute Magie.* 1861.

81 Lévi, Éliphas. Trans. by Aleister Crowley. *La Clef des grands mystères suivant Hénoch, Abraham, Hermès Trismégiste et Salomon* ("The Key of the Mysteries"). Boston, MA: Weiser. 1859 (first published).

Figure 20: Center: Logo for entire worldwide TST organization. TST Chapter logos and designers, clockwise from bottom: TST United Kingdom: Damien Evans; TST Sacramento: Kym LaRoux; TST Colorado: Mandie Doom; TST Arizona: Pope Wonka; TST Nebraska: Brandy Jordan.

Figure 22: Lucifer sigil from the *Grimorium Verum*, 18th Century.

with the Church of Satan in the 1960s. Sulfur was connected to brimstone and the fires of hell, which is likely why Anton LaVey used it. This sulfur symbol has also become known as a "Leviathan Cross" or "Satanic cross." (Figure 21.)

LUCIFER SIGIL

The Sigil of Lucifer is an historical occult sigil used occasionally as an emblem by modern Satanists. The image has its origins in the sixteenth century Italian *Grimorium Verum*, or "Grimoire of Truth." Used in conjunction with other symbols, its original purpose was to aid in a visual invocation of the angel Lucifer. Modern Satanists use it in art, jewelry or other representations. (Figure 22.)

INVERTED CROSS

Figure 23: Reversed cross (sometimes known as "The Cross of St. Peter").

Some modern Satanists make use of the image of the upside-down cross as a Satanic symbol. In early Christian times, the inverted Latin cross was called "The Cross of Saint Peter" and traditionally used as a Christian symbol; in some Christian sects it is believed that Peter requested this form of crucifixion as he felt he was unworthy to be crucified in the same manner that Jesus died.

These usages have faded in modern times, and contemporary Satanists use the inverted cross for its anti-Christian and anti-religion connotations. The inverted cross is also a recurring motif in punk rock and heavy metal, where it is embraced as a symbol of anti-authoritarianism and defiance. (Figure 23.)

Lucien Greaves says:

> *This inversion is Satan's perception. It asks people to reconsider their cultural grounding, look at the evidence and reconsider their values. ... You have this one-sided vision with institutionalised religion as the arbiters of moral correctness. It prevents them considering whether they could be incorrect today on issues such as gay marriage and reproductive rights.* [82]

These are just a few of the most well-known Satanic symbols. Some Satanists decide to use other symbols from occult traditions or other sources, and some make their own entirely from scratch. It's up to you as to how you approach and use Satanic symbology.

---

82 Morgan, James. "Decoding the symbols on Satan's statue." *BBC News.* August 1, 2015.

Art by Holly May.

SECTION 6
Personalizing Your Practice

With an understanding of the Satanic narrative and ethics, and with ritual and symbols in your tool chest, you're ready to put everything you're learning into making your Satanic practice your own.

Satanism can be especially welcoming to the individual in that it doesn't try to impose a rigid framework that controls all aspects of your life in order to make you more obedient and "righteous" in the eyes of God. Although Satanism is a religion with shared core ethics and a shared narrative, there are no strict rules or scriptures that tell you exactly how to practice your own Satanism. Each Satanist creates their own practice.

The path of Satanism does not offer a set of well-worn footprints to follow, but rather encourages each of us to blaze our own trail, find our own way and realize our authentic self, free of reliance on an external higher power. As Satanists interviewed in *The Devil's Party* express it:

> *Satanism does not say, go and become this and that. ... It says only: Go and stand up!* [83]

> *What I really need is my mind, my free will, self-improvement, the revolt against every force that opposes my nature. I do not need any gods; I am God for myself.* [84]

---

83 Faxneld, Per and Petersen, Jesper Aa, editors. *The Devil's Party: Satanism in Modernity.* New York, NY. Oxford University Press. 2013.

84 Faxneld, Per and Petersen, Jesper Aa, editors. *The Devil's Party: Satanism in Modernity.* New York, NY. Oxford University Press. 2013.

Your Satanic practice may be contemplative in nature; you will be looking inside yourself to uncover your strengths and your own distinctive Satanic approach to life. In doing so, you'll experience an ongoing process of individuation, whereby you discover the particular flame that burns bright in your heart. What follows are my own tips on personalizing your individual Satanic practice.

Self-Compassion

I believe Satanic practice should include self-compassion; after all, the self deserves the same compassion the First Tenet asks us to strive for. Kindness to ourselves is equally important as kindness to others. We need to treat ourselves with patience, love and acceptance and to know we are worthy of understanding, wholeness, and happiness, no matter how broken or undeserving we may feel.

A large part of self-compassion may be doing what it takes to heal the wounds of our past. Many of us have experienced mental and physical trauma from the imposition of religion. There is now a clinical term for this harm inflicted by religion: Religious Trauma Syndrome. According to psychologist and educator Marlene Winell, Religious Trauma Syndrome entails: "... a set of simultaneous symptoms and characteristics that are related to harmful experiences with religion, and are the result of immersion in a controlling religion and the secondary impact of leaving a religious group." Winell writes that "religious indoctrination can be hugely damaging, and making the break from an authoritarian kind of religion can be traumatic." [85]

According to Dr. Winell, "the symptoms compare most easily with Post Traumatic Stress Disorder, although it's important to understand that Religious Trauma Syndrome originates from harmful religious experiences, not just any trauma." Another difference is related to the social context. When someone is

---

85 Lesley, Alison. "What is Religious Trauma Syndrome?"
    World Religion News. August 2, 2015.

recovering from domestic abuse, other people are understanding and supportive. On the other hand, when someone is seeking counseling for Religious Trauma Syndrome, their motives are often questioned and even doubted. Winell writes:

> Those most at risk to developing Religious Trauma Syndrome include people who are raised in their religion, sheltered from the rest of the world, very sincerely and personally involved with their religion, and/or from a very controlling form of religion. The symptoms include cognitive, affective, functional, and social or cultural "dysfunctions": everything from confusion, anxiety, panic attacks, sleep and eating disorders, and substance abuse to difficulty with decision-making and critical thinking, lack of meaning, suicidal ideation and rupture of family and social network. [86]

To heal from Religious Trauma Syndrome, Winell recommends "rebuilding one's life around new values, getting involved with one's community and reclaiming one's creativity and independent self-expression." [87] Satanism can help with all these, providing a better scaffolding upon which to grow and a healthier approach to what a religion should provide. Satanism actively encourages us to express ourselves and treasure our independence and freedom, while providing values (the Seven Tenets), purpose (the fight for justice), and a supportive community.

In addition to trauma related to religion and religious abuses, people suffer from all sorts of issues when they have experienced social rejection. For instance, almost all members of our local TST Chapter have some form of social anxiety. While some of this might be innate brain chemistry, a large factor must also be that we've almost all had numerous bad experiences of being rejected by society. After a while, you begin to believe people when they tell you there's something wrong with you, and that internalized view of yourself as a failure can eat away at your self-confidence and exacerbate depression and other mental issues.

Being a social outcast can have an outsized effect on our basic quality of life. Most people get leads on jobs (and thus healthcare),

---

86 Lesley, Alison. "What is Religious Trauma Syndrome?" *World Religion News*. August 2, 2015.

87 Lesley, Alison. "What is Religious Trauma Syndrome?" *World Religion News*. August 2, 2015.

romantic partners, and even housing from people in their social circles. If we are the Outcast, living without social connection, we miss out on all those opportunities and have no one to fall back on when things like job or housing loss happen. Without family or social support, many of us fall through the giant cracks in our social safety net, and that can make us feel like we're not worthy of help.

So many of us Satanists have a reduced capacity for self-compassion thanks to the rejection and abuse heaped on us by our family, peers and/or society. Many Satanists, including me, have spent most of their lives believing there is something wrong with them, internalizing the messages from others (and indeed, from society itself) that they are unworthy in multiple ways. We are used to being told we don't deserve happiness, wellness or success. Self-compassion entails identifying all the ways you've internalized these unhealthy messages and actively working to overcome them.

You may have spent the majority of your life believing these external messages that there was something inherently wrong with you. Self-compassion urges you to look at those messages with a discerning eye and understand all the ways in which they are fallacious and unnecessarily hurtful. It might not be you; it might be them. Train yourself to recognize these internal voices when they tell you that you are bad, wrong and not good enough and to gently move toward accepting yourself as you are, warts and all. We're all imperfect creatures struggling to do our best in an imperfect world. You are completely valid as a person no matter what those internal messages say.

You deserve to be happy and healthy, as much as life permits. Find tangible ways in which you can begin to heal those past hurts, whether that's keeping a journal, talking to friends, seeing a therapist, finding a support group, or other approaches.

Self-Responsibility

I also believe that with self-empowerment comes self-responsibility; they are two sides of the same coin. In addition to the Just World Fallacy, Abrahamic religions teach what is called the External Control Fallacy: that is, your life is not your own, but rather controlled by God. If something goes wrong, the devil is blamed; if something goes right, it's God's will. You are but a helpless pawn, and the only right thing to do is to give yourself wholly over to the will of God — or at least the will of his church leaders.

Satanism refutes the External Control Fallacy. There is no god and no devil controlling your actions. You are the only one who can point your life in the direction you want.

Knowing you are ultimately responsible for all your choices and actions, that there is no one else who will save you but yourself, can give you a sense of deep empowerment. When you realize you are the only one who can do it, whatever "it" is, you'll understand that you hold the power.

There are limits, of course, and in attempting to take control and better our lives, many of us run into societal prejudice based on our race, our religion, our sexuality, our gender identity, etc. So bootstrapping yourself may not be enough to achieve all your goals. Many of us run into obstacles and unfairness of varying degrees — that's one of the reasons we fight for justice. We want everyone to be free to pursue their own happiness without oppression or discrimination.

Self-responsibility also means taking care of yourself. Find out what you need to nourish your mind and body, what it would take to be healthy and as happy as you can be. If it's available, find the medical care you need. Learn what helps you feel right — things like healthy food, exercise, time in nature, meditation, or whatever else works for you.

You can choose to get secular support for any addiction issues; I recommend checking out the S.M.A.R.T. Recovery program as a non-religious, science-based alternative to twelve-step programs like Alcoholics Anonymous and Narcotics Anonymous. [88] Though twelve-step programs do help some people, I found their insistence on admitting you were powerless and giving your life up to a higher power to be actively damaging to my own sobriety efforts. It was only after I quit NA and learned to rely on my own power instead of a supernatural, external force that I was able to finally end my 17 years of addiction. You can also find good therapists and outpatient and in-patient treatment programs that do not rely on the twelve steps; definitely shop around before you decide on one.

Build up your social support, ideally in person, or over the phone, with a few close friends or nearby Satanists, but if you don't have those options, you can try social media. If you don't have a wide network, start small. Friendship takes work, but if you put in effort with the right people, your connections will blossom and you'll start feeling less alone. If you can get involved with your region's TST Chapter or pre-Chapter group, so much the better — then you have a whole community of fellow Satanists you can get to know and befriend.

It's up to you to build a life of personal meaning. God or external forces won't step in and guide you in the right direction. Satanism teaches us that this life is all we have, so let's learn how to make it count. What brings you most joy? Where is your passion? How can you personally make a difference in creating a more just, compassionate world? Let your own heart lead you.

Break Your Chains

For many, one of the first steps in your Satanic transformation will be to break ties with any previous beliefs, baptisms, religious organizations or people with whom you no longer wish to be associated. Many people are baptized against their will, with religion forced upon them from a young age on. Many have

88 SMART Recovery website. *Smartrecovery.org.*

painful memories of being repressed or abused by religion or religious people.

Part of your journey may include prying off these old confines. Many people have been brainwashed from a young age into fire and brimstone fundamentalism, with its emphasis on fear and obedience. Blasphemy and transgression can be powerful tools to subvert the influence of these repressive traditions.

By daring to blaspheme, we show our irreverence for supposedly infallible doctrine; we are directly undermining the hold it has over us. For example, The Satanic Temple has performed a number of Black Mass rituals, in which participants desecrate Judeo-Christian symbols. Lucien Greaves explains the purpose of these rituals:

> We asked Greaves how he felt about people being upset over him bringing the black mass to Philadelphia. "It's not about them," he says. "What we're doing is not meant to be a calculated insult. This is for us and for the participants. A lot of people come from Judeo-Christian culture and they're trying to shake free of cultural programming. They embrace blasphemy to shake themselves free." [89]

Transgressive acts may be freeing. Many people find that listening to blasphemous music, watching transgressive performances, or engaging with heretical, transgressive art is helpful in making a clean break and leaving the past behind. A wide range of audio, visual, performance and other artists create subversive, blasphemous works that you may find resonate with you on your own journey.

Taboo activities, like ritual nudity; body modification; queer, kinky or "deviant" sex; blood rituals; and consciousness-changing rites can also help you shed your old skin and leave you free to build your own unique practice.

89 Fiorillo, Victor. "The Satanic Temple to Perform a Black Mass In Philly Tonight." *Philadelphia Magazine*. October 12, 2018.

UNBAPTISM RITUALS

In addition to Black Masses, many Chapters of The Satanic Temple have performed Unbaptism rituals for their members and for the public. In an Unbaptism ritual, participants symbolically break their bonds, reject their baptism or religious past, and commit themselves to personal freedom. It doesn't actually require participants to have been baptized; the ritual works symbolically to make a clean break with past religions no matter whether an actual baptism was performed.

In this excerpt from an Unbaptism ritual performed by TST Seattle in 2018, for example, participants were asked to affirm their decision to leave their religious past behind:

> [Participants are bound with red cord to symbolize the bindings of prior religion.]

> **Satanic Clergy:** "Baptism offers false salvation on behalf of an absent god. But we, as flawed humans looking for answers of our own, have within us all that is necessary to free ourselves from outdated superstitions and find our own empowerment. Let us break the chains that have held us back."

> **Clergy:** "Do you reject 'God,' arbiter of superstitious tyranny?"

> **Participants:** "I do."

> **Clergy:** "Do you reject supernaturalism and archaic superstitions?"

> **Participants:** "I do."

> **Clergy:** "Do you believe in yourself, the only sovereign power over your own life?"

> **Participants:** "I do."

> **Clergy:** "Do you believe in the carnal bliss afforded to you by your natural desires?"

> **Participants:** "I do."

> **Clergy:** "Do you believe salvation is to be found solely through your own rational self?"

Participants: "I do."

Clergy: "Do you wish to renounce the faith of your past and be free of its bonds, rejecting your baptism forever?"

Participants: "I do."

Symbolic bonds are cut away and thrown into the fire, along with any baptism certificates that participants want to destroy, and the clergy declares the participants free of any previous religious entanglements.

The rest of this Unbaptism ritual can be found in Appendix 2. You can use it for inspiration in writing your own ritual — solo or group — that helps you leave your religious past behind.

SATANIC DEDICATION

Once you've shed your old religious skin, if necessary, you may wish to make a conscious, purposeful commitment to the Satanic path in the form of vows or a dedication ceremony. This is a good exercise in drawing together your personal symbols and metaphors. Brainstorm on what is most personally meaningful to you. You can undertake this commitment celebration yourself, or have others be part of it. It could be as simple as reading the Tenets aloud and vowing to follow them.

Our TST Seattle Chapter had a short Initiation Ceremony we performed for new members; you can find it in the Rituals Appendix. Even if you only have one other person helping with your commitment ceremony or are doing it by yourself, you could still modify this ritual for your own use — or write your own entirely from scratch.

At the end of our Initiation Ceremony, we presented the new members with Chapter membership certificates designed by one of our artistically talented members. (Figure 24.)

You can also get membership certificates and wallet cards from TST's international Headquarters in Salem, Massachusetts,

161

which you can incorporate into your commitment ceremony even if you're not part of a Chapter. These certificates can be purchased on the main TST website; proceeds go to support The Satanic Temple's extremely important legal activism. You're not required to buy a certificate to become a TST member, however.

You may also choose to perform a daily or recurring ceremony that celebrates your commitment to the Satanic path. As with the Initiation ritual, it works best if you choose to include elements that resonate with you personally. As an example, the recurring Satanic Dedication ritual I do is in the Rituals Appendix; it also contains a Satanic Affirmation ritual written by Venita Na'amah.

Coming Out as a Satanist

Once you've made your commitment to the Satanic path, you can decide how open you want to be about your Satanic beliefs. You can choose to keep your Satanism secret, tell just a few close friends or family, make a conscious choice to purposefully announce it on social media or elsewhere, or just go about your life normally without announcing it or hiding it, recognizing that some folks will notice and ask you about it.

Coming out as a Satanist should be a decision you consider carefully. There is always a risk when you announce your Satanism to the world; we do not yet live in a society that is friendly across the board to Satanism. Plenty of Christians (and some others) believe that Satanism equates with evil no matter what. I've had conversations with people who tell me that even if we don't think we worship Satan, we actually do; I've had people read through our Tenets of compassion and justice and refuse to believe anything other than that we are evildoers. Two of the mothers in our Chapter have had strangers ask them — with a straight face — if they were raising their young children to be eaten.

Sometimes being open about your Satanism can result in threats of violence. For instance, TST founder Lucien Greaves decided he needed to don a bulletproof vest before speaking at a Religious

Liberty rally in Arkansas. The rally was flanked by hostile KKK members bearing loaded assault rifles. Luckily no shots were fired, but the danger was definitely there.

While few Satanists reach that level of public recognition, we still have to carefully consider to whom we reveal our religious identification. Those who don't understand could potentially make life very hard for you — you could lose your job, housing, or child custody battle, for instance. But despite the risks, many Satanists have taken the plunge and come out to their friends, family, and even the public.

I interviewed several Satanists about their Satanic Coming Out stories; you can find their full answers in Appendix 1: "Satanic Voices." Their responses varied widely; each situation was unique. Some only came out to their closest friends, whereas others have publicly identified as Satanists for decades.

People came out for all sorts of reasons — some were outed involuntarily when their parents went through their phone, some decided to come out to fight the rising tide of theocracy, and many just decided they wanted to live true to themselves without hiding their beliefs. Some said they wanted to preemptively explain their beliefs before their friends and family heard about their Satanism and started forming an inaccurate mental picture.

For a number of people who responded to the interview questions, there was no clear demarcation where they decided "I will announce my Satanism"; rather, people around them slowly came to realize that they had become Satanists. Some were already known to be "alternative" in some way, like punk, pagan or goth, so it wasn't so much of a shock to those around them. But some Satanists were inspired to explicitly announce their affiliation by a specific incident, like the documentary "Hail Satan?" coming out or the arrival of their TST membership card and certificate.

As to be expected, there were some negative reactions. Some Satanists' families, particularly older family members, cut ties; one individual had Child Protective Services called on her by a neighbor. One Satanist's mom took away all her journals, art and

Figure 24: My membership certificate for The Satanic Temple, Seattle Chapter. Designed by Kirstin Hill.

music, and another's parents accused her of joining a terrorist organization when they found out she had joined TST. Some family members who are very religious or otherwise close-minded may refuse to make the effort to understand what Satanism actually is. But negative ramifications were surprisingly rare. Some family members were willing to be educated and actually took the time to learn about their loved one's religion, resulting in new understanding.

Being fired for being a Satanist is certainly a possibility, especially in some areas of the US and world and at certain "family values" companies. While it's always a danger, not one individual in the Coming Out survey reported being harassed at work or fired for their beliefs. For most people, it wasn't something that was discussed in the workplace at all. Others spoke of the anti-discrimination rules in place as potential protection. And for others, their Satanism was actually integral to their livelihood, like the artist who crafts Satanic jewelry.

Despite the risks, there were a great deal of positive consequences. Satanists reported feeling a sense of pride in having the courage to come out, as well as a newfound sense of freedom. They no longer had to hide something that was extremely important to their sense of self.

When asked about recommendations for those who were thinking about coming out, those who replied mentioned going slow and coming out to only a few people or groups at a time; building up a support network before you take the plunge publicly; being informed about Satanism yourself so you can educate others; and being prepared to walk away completely if someone just refuses to understand and accept your Satanic identification. Some reminded people not to take others' negative reactions personally and to recognize that there will always be a few folks who just won't understand. But most of the interviewees who did choose to come out felt more empowered to be themselves, free to live openly and proudly as a Satanist.

Despite all these varied experiences, almost everyone agreed on one thing: it's completely acceptable to choose to *not* come out. It's not the right choice for everyone — there are many in situations or geographical areas where announcing one's Satanism could have disastrous consequences. If you do have to keep your Satanism to yourself to avoid problems, that's totally understandable; there is absolutely no shame in having to hide your Satanism from friends, family, or colleagues. All the interviewees agreed that only you can decide if you're in a safe place to come out, and were highly supportive of those who for one reason or another chose not to bare their religious beliefs to their family or the world.

Again, you can read these Coming Out stories in Appendix 1: "Satanic Voices."

Satanic Self-Expression

One of the great joys of Satanism is its emphasis on personal expression and individuality. Inspired by the Satanic symbols, literature, and imagery that resonate with you the most, you may choose to express your own unique Satanic vision via art, style, tattoos, altar-building and other creative endeavors, deepening your Satanic roots and growing in new directions.

Exploring your own Satanic creativity and unleashing the Satanic artist inside you can free you from conformity, dogma and superstition and help you understand your life's meaning in new ways. Lucien Greaves explains:

> *Those of us who were burdened from childhood by archaic tradition-based dogmas, especially in the era of the Satanic Panic, were instilled with an irrational aversion and fear toward the "other," the Satanic. Breaking that barrier, defying such deeply-entrenched cultural programming, embracing the symbols, narrative, and outside status of the Adversary, can be a supremely liberating personal experience, not merely incidentally divorced from superstition, but emblematic of, and vital to, the break with superstition. ... The power of metaphor, the vital necessity of narrative to cultivate and define one's sense of self and purpose, the atavistic desire for art are all self-evident to me.* [90]

Because these creative portions of your Satanic path are intensely personal, they will vary widely — everyone's self-expression will be different. To sample the diversity of Satanic expression, I've included a number of interviews with practicing Satanists in Appendix 1: "Satanic Voices." You can see what others are doing and potentially use it as inspiration to begin your own creative explorations.

---

90 "Never Let Your Activism Be Artless: An Interview With Lucien Greaves of The Satanic Temple." *Haute Macabre*. June 28, 2017.

SATANIC ART

For many, the Satanic path includes creating artwork of some kind — it can offer one way to fully realize your Satanic self-expression. There are a wide array of artistic modes and

25. Artwork by Tanis Lancaster.

genres you can explore, including visual art (painting, drawing, collage), sculpture, sewing, crafting, music, writing, video, dancing, performance, and more. Satanic artists can draw on the rich symbolism of Satanism, the occult, pop culture and many other sources in order to create something new and thought-provoking.

Art can be a meditative process, a way to work through mental illness or other issues and challenges, an act of rebellion, a way to help others think in new directions, a part of an ongoing life practice of Satanism and more. Don't worry if you feel you don't have artistic talent. You don't have to be a professional painter, musician, sculptor or writer to make art. Many times it is the process of creation itself which is the most meaningful to the creator.

You are primarily making the art for yourself, not the public — you should feel free to explore all your creative options without worrying about how others will judge your finished work. But if you feel comfortable with it, I do encourage everyone to contribute to the larger Satanic discourse by sharing their art with others or with the public. Since art is such an important part of Satanic iconry, the more art we can add to that discourse, the richer the body of Satanic imagery will become.

I asked several artists to talk about their work and how Satanism informs it. You can find their interviews in Appendix 1: "Satanic Voices." Their answers provide a window into the thought processes behind such work, including the advice they have for others thinking of expressing their Satanism through some kind of art.

No matter if you're a professional artist or just playing around on your own, creating art can bring you new insight into your Satanic path.

SATANIC ALTARS

Some Satanists find that having a Satanic altar is a useful form of expression. An altar functions in many of the same ways as an art piece; it's meant to use symbols and intention to invoke certain feelings or inspire certain thought processes. Having a space deliberately set aside to represent your Satanic path can help remind you of that path on a daily basis.

Unlike in most religions, a Satanic altar isn't dedicated to worshipping an actual deity; you won't be making offerings to any gods or expecting supernatural results. Your altar should instead be another form of personal Satanic expression, using items and symbols that resonate most strongly with you to represent your

26: Altar belonging to Simon Widdop.

Satanism. Everyone's altar is going to be different. Build yours to represent your individuality.

You can create your altar inside your home, outdoors, or in the space in which your Satanic group meets. Some people use statues of Baphomet, Lucifer, goats, or other symbolic figures that are meaningful to them. Other common items may include cloths to cover the altar or drape behind it, art, candles, bells, knives, chalices, incense holders, and books. But you can use other objects too — use whatever you feel best represents your path.

If you don't have permanent space to set up your altar, you can use a portable altar that can be set up and put away easily.

I interviewed a number of practicing Satanists about their Satanic altars in Appendix 1.

JEWELRY AND CLOTHING

Some Satanists enjoy wearing Satanic jewelry or clothing, either as a religious statement to the world, and/or because it is personally meaningful to them. For instance, most people in our Chapter wear some kind of Satanic pendant to meetings and actions. Looks range from the very subtle, such as one small understated piece of Satanic jewelry, to over-the-top, with multiple bold pendants, rings, and pins. There is no requirement that every Satanist own or wear Satanic jewelry, however. That is completely up to you.

Clothing is also left entirely up to the individual. Looking at photos of the many different Satanic communities, I see a huge range of styles, from flamboyant to conservative. There is no one style engendered by Satanism; wearing a conservative button-down shirt, bow tie and khakis is just as valid as head-to-toe black. I do see a lot of Satanists wearing black T-shirts, often with band logos or Satanic themes, but no one is required to dress any particular way. We have people in our Chapter who wear elaborate dark Gothic fashion, but also folks who prefer to wear pastels or bright yellow. It makes zero difference in the way we treat each other; respect and compassion are unrelated to people's style choices.

The only cases where our Chapter has a dress code are the occasions when we are out in public doing an action or when we're performing a ritual. TST Seattle's dress code for most actions was

27: My collection of Satanic pendants.

usually black and red (in any style), or black and rainbow for Pride events. Members acting as Clergy in our ritual performances, either private or public, have usually worn black robes. We've been lucky to have a talented seamstress in our Chapter who has sewn us a collection of high-quality robes for these occasions, but you can find robes easily at a costume shop or online. Don't feel that you have to use robes in your own rituals, though; again, the choice is entirely up to you.

Be aware that there is always a risk when you announce your Satanism to the world, even in something as subtle as a pendant or hat. While not everyone will know what a two-point-up pentagram means, there is always the chance that someone will realize you're a Satanist and make life hard for you because of it. Certain symbols like the Lucifer sigil or sulfur symbol will be harder to recognize, but the chance is still there, so put some thought into when and where you're willing to be outed before you wear anything that is recognizably Satanic.

28: "Catphomet" tattoo belonging to Elizabeth Mar.

SATANIC TATTOOS

Another way you can personally express your Satanism is with body modification and tattoos. Satanism is so meaningful to some that they permanently inscribe its symbols on their skin. While it's a big commitment, the Satanists I talked to were all still proud of their body art long after the fact, and had no regrets.

What you choose to put on your skin is entirely up to you. You can get a subtle piece that is usually hidden by clothing, or you can go big and bold and get people's attention on a regular basis. Choose the symbols that most resonate with you; they don't have to fall within the traditional Satanic symbolism, just have meaning to you personally. The style is completely your choice as well, whether you want something dark and serious or cute and funny, done in blackwork, full-color, pastels, or stick and poke. Some Satanists choose to mark a specific occasion with a tattoo, while the inspiration for others wasn't tied to a certain event.

I asked several Satanists to talk about their Satanic tattoos; you can find their interviews in Appendix 1 as well.

YOUR SATANIC NAME

Satanism can be a risky endeavor. If people know your real name, they may drag your friends and family members into the mud over it. In the worst case scenario, you could be doxxed and your private information, address and phone number (and possibly those of other family members) spread around for attackers to use. To protect themselves, their friends and their families, many people choose to use pseudonyms for their Satanic activities.

Lucien Greaves explains:

> *A lot of people are worried that publicly being a Satanist will hurt their careers or standing in their community. We do get a lot of threats. And people ask "are they credible threats?" Well, you don't know until somebody comes at you. So, I don't begrudge anybody having a pseudonym. I am mystified though, at how many times people have called me a fraud because I have a pseudonym. People use them all the time — just because an author writes a book under a pen name, it doesn't mean he's not an author.* [91]

In our Chapter, some members use pseudonyms when we are out doing public actions in case someone overhears their name or sees it in the press and uses it to threaten or attack them for their Satanic activities. Some use a different name and/or create

91 Jaremko-Greenwold, Anya. "Speaking with Satanic Temple Co-Founder Lucien Greaves at Sundance Made Me Want to Join His Reasonable Religion." *Flood Magazine*. January 30, 2019.

separate social media accounts in order to compartmentalize their Satanism away from potentially judgemental family members, friends, or employers. Others use Satanic names simply because they prefer them, or as a statement of their commitment to the Satanic path.

Like other portions of your practice, your Satanic name is your own unique expression. Choose one that you feel drawn to. While many Satanists use names drawn from demonology, the occult, and Satanic literature, you can use whatever appeals to you, whether drawn from real life history, pop culture, or anywhere else you find inspiration. In Appendix 1, a number of Satanists explain how they chose their pseudonyms (sometimes playfully called "Satanyms").

Not everyone's practice includes all these aspects of self-expression. These are just examples; in reality your options are myriad. Everyone's Satanic practice will look different — and that's encouraged. Be creative and do things your way. Use whatever works for you.

Cover art for the 1953 edition of *The Revolt of the Angels*, by Anatole France.

SECTION 7:

As part of our Satanic practice, Tenet Two of The Satanic Temple encourages us to take up the fight for justice, whether that means exercising your personal rights to participate in democracy, supporting The Satanic Temple in their legal fights for civil rights, or participating in an approved Satanic Temple action as part of a local Chapter.

Political action is considered a form of worship for Satanists. Instead of praising a supernatural figure and promising obedience, our Satanic worship involves emulating the actions of our hero Satan in our fight against unjust and arbitrary authority.

Many of the Romantic-era writers whose work we as Satanists draw upon were part of a revolutionary movement that fought for freedom and justice for all — the same movement that informed the representational governments (like the American one in 1776) created after revolt had toppled the repressive monarchies of Europe. Satan's rebellion became a rallying cry for these writers, who saw in the Satan of *Paradise Lost* their own heroic fight against unjust and arbitrary tyranny. Satan became the symbol inspiring them to fight for equality and freedom.

Though much progress has been made since the Revolutionary era, our world is still rife with injustice, discrimination, and repression, and it is our duty to fight to make it better. When we actively fight for justice, we emulate our hero's revolt against unjust authority and replicate the Satanic narrative of rebellion. With these actions, we can venerate — and truly embody — the literary Satan.

FIGHTING THEOCRACY

Our Satanic fight for justice is extremely important in today's world. Across the globe, powerful groups are working to undermine representational, secular democracy and instead impose repressive laws based on religious beliefs. In America especially, legislation based on conservative Christian religious belief is rampant, and a broad coalition of evangelical Christians, Catholics, and politicians have made major theocratic inroads on our government.

Part of the irony is that America was founded specifically to get away from religious persecution, and the driving philosophy behind the American revolution and the creation of our democracy explicitly included the idea that religion should be separated from government. The Bill of Rights in the United States Constitution (written by James Madison in 1791) sets in place firm restrictions on the government with regards to religion: "Congress shall make no law respecting an establishment of religion, or prohibiting the free exercise thereof." [92]

The founding fathers had seen firsthand what centuries of religious strife had done to Europe and wanted to avoid this calamity. James Madison wrote: "The purpose of separation of church and state is to keep forever from these shores the ceaseless strife that has soaked the soil of Europe in blood for centuries." [93]

The founders of our American democracy were quite explicit in insisting on the separation of religion from government. Founding father John Adams wrote, "The government of the United States is not, in any sense, founded on the Christian religion." [94]

---

92 *U.S. Constitution.* Amend. I.

93 Madison, James. *Letter objecting to the use of government land for churches.* 1803.

94 *Treaty of Peace and Friendship between the United States of America and the Bey and Subjects of Tripoli of Barbary.* Signed by John Adams in 1796.

He saw religious freedom as one of the major tenets of Enlightenment-inspired democracy: "We should begin by setting conscience free. When all men of all religions shall enjoy equal liberty, property, and an equal chance for honors and power we may expect that improvements will be made in the human character and the state of society." [95]

The framers of the Constitution envisioned a secular government divided by a high wall from religion; they had no wish to see the government push a specific religion onto the citizenry, who themselves held a diversity of beliefs. But beginning in the 1940s, a coalition of evangelical Christians, Catholics, and conservative politicians gave rise to the Religious Right — a right-wing Christian political faction that sought to install theocratic Christian rule in America.

With the "Red Scare," the rise of communist, atheist nations like the USSR seen as bitter, powerful opponents to American-style democracy, the Religious Right persuaded Americans to breach the wall of church-state separation and insert Christianity into government in an attempt to distinguish our nation from the "godless commies." Thus "In God We Trust" was installed as our official national motto in 1956, supplanting the secular "E Pluribus Unum" (meaning "from the many, one") that our founding fathers chose. Around the same time, the words "under God" were added to the Pledge of Allegiance.

Since then, the power of the Religious Right has grown by leaps and bounds. America has now seen the rise of a new coalition called Project Blitz, a massive coordinated effort by Christian Nationalists to inject religion into public education, attack reproductive healthcare, and undermine LGBTQ rights. Thanks to these efforts, America has seen a bevy of religiously-based pieces of legislation put in place, and there is a constant push to convert the country to authoritarian Christian-based rule. The so-called Christian "Dominionists" of Project Blitz believe it is God's will that they take dominion over the government, just as God gave man dominion over the Earth. They reject the founding fathers'

95 Adams, John. *Letter to Dr. Price.* April 8, 1785.

commitment to pluralism and religious liberty — they don't just want an equal place at the table, they want to abolish secular government altogether and replace it with a repressive Christian-based state.

Randall Terry, founder of the anti-abortion organization Operation Rescue, says:

> *Our goal is a Christian nation. We have a biblical duty, we are called on by God to conquer this country. We don't want equal time. We don't want pluralism.* [96]

George Grant, in his book *The Changing of the Guard: Biblical Principles for Political Action*, says:

> *Christians have an obligation, a mandate, a commission, a holy responsibility to reclaim the land for Jesus Christ — to have dominion in civil structures, just as in every other aspect of life and godliness. But it is dominion we are after. Not just a voice. It is dominion we are after. Not just influence. It is dominion we are after. Not just equal time. It is dominion we are after. World conquest. That's what Christ has commissioned us to accomplish. We must win the world with the power of the Gospel. And we must never settle for anything less. ... Thus, Christian politics has as its primary intent the conquest of the land — of men, families, institutions, bureaucracies, courts, and governments for the Kingdom of Christ.* [97]

Project Blitz has a great deal of power in America's political arena. Many Dominionists and evangelical Christians now hold political office, especially in more rural and conservative areas and states. Our current president Donald Trump owes his presidential victory to the support of the evangelical voting bloc. Courts across the country have been packed with Dominionist Christian appointments, and a large amount of Christian-based legislation has already been put in place.

Laws already require some public schools and textbooks to teach Creationism and the false narrative that our nation's laws were founded on the Bible, and in states like Ohio, current law allows

96 Terry, Randall. *The News-Sentinel*, Fort Wayne, Indiana. August 16, 1993.

97 Grant, George and North, Gary. *The Changing of the Guard: Biblical Principles for Political Action*. Dominion Press. 1987.

COMPASSIONATE SATANISM

children to give wrong answers to science questions without penalty if their answers are based in Creationist beliefs. Tax breaks and federal funding have been made available to private evangelical religious schools, and fundamentalist megapreachers have taken advantage of religious tax exemptions and countless donations from gullible flock members to build huge financial empires and buy mansions and private jets.

Christian belief has been prioritized over basic civil rights using federal and state versions of the Religious Freedom Restoration Act of 1993, a piece of legislation that holds the federal government responsible for accepting additional obligations to protect religious exercise. Thus, according to the current courts, the claim of religious freedom can be used to exempt people and businesses from having to comply with civil rights anti-discrimination laws.

This cry of "religious freedom" has been used to deny individuals with uteruses access to reproductive healthcare when their employer is anti-contraception, using the argument that a company has the same right to religious freedom as an individual. [98] Businesses and individuals (including doctors and emergency personnel) have been given the right to refuse service to gay and trans people based on their religious beliefs — whether it's refusing to bake a cake for a gay wedding or denying emergency medical treatment to a trans person. Bigotry based on religion has been codified in our laws and upheld by our courts.

Though the Supreme Court ruled in the 1973 case *Roe v. Wade* that individuals have the constitutional right to an abortion, the religious opinion that personhood begins at conception has been allowed to drive stricter and stricter legislative limitations on abortion, with the goal of eliminating all opportunity for women and others with uteruses to choose, even in cases of rape and incest. As of this writing, the right to an abortion is in great danger from the conservative-packed Supreme Court. Thanks to these religious efforts, abortion may have already been outlawed by the time you read this.

98 BURWELL, SECRETARY OF HEALTH AND HUMAN SERVICES, ET AL. v. HOBBY LOBBY STORES, INC., ET AL. *Supreme Court Case.* June 30, 2014.

The goal of Project Blitz is to transform America into a nation completely under repressive Christian rule, subject to biblical laws and led by religious leaders instead of elected representatives. All religious toleration and plurality would be wiped out and citizens would be forced to submit to the rule of the Christian religion. Christian symbols and beliefs would be an official part of the government, Christian doctrine would be the basis for children's education, and non-Christians would face even more widespread legalized discrimination.

But as Satanists, we are not content to sit still and allow this to happen. We believe it is our duty to stand up to this burgeoning theocratic oppression and fight to stop religious tyranny. It is especially crucial that we stand up and fight now, when Dominionism has gained a real foothold in our government and forces within the legislative, executive and judicial branches are working overtime to turn America into a theocracy. With so many Dominionists in power and Project Blitz working to inject even more Christianity into our laws and institutions, our secular democracy and religious pluralism is in real danger. As Satanists, we must fight to ensure liberty and equality against the threat of religious oppression.

LUCIEN'S LAW

The Satanic Temple is especially well-known for its fight for plurality, working hard to combat theocratic encroachment. Lucien Greaves writes:

> Above the steps to the Supreme Court, one can see the engraved phrase, "Equal Justice Under Law." It is this value, this Constitutional virtue, that The Satanic Temple seeks to uphold with its political actions. [99]

Where religion has been allowed to drive laws and invade the government in ways that infringe on equality and civil rights, The Satanic Temple pushes back.

---

99 Greaves, Lucien. "Letters to a Satanist: If we're not a Judeo-Christian nation, where do our laws come from?" *Orlando Weekly*. January 24, 2015.

The Satanic Temple's activism has its roots in the Seven Tenets, with their emphasis on ethical values like compassion, empathy and justice. While the Religious Right claims to have the moral high ground, painting anyone non-Christian as unethical, Greaves says,

> *In fact, we feel our campaigns embrace the highest of moral callings — from gay rights, to women's rights, to the protection of children against institutionalized abuse. In each of these cases, we fight against regressive mainstream religious thinking. I think that by embracing Satanism, we represent another phase in our civilization's social growth. This is another step toward ensuring that each individual is judged for his or her actual actions in the real world, free of fear from persecution for symbolic crimes and/or "blasphemy." [100]*

The Satanic Temple's strategy involves simply claiming the same legal rights as other religions. If religion has been allowed to infiltrate the government in some way, we want to claim our place at the same table. If public schools are allowed to distribute biblical literature to students, we claim our right to also distribute Satanic literature. If a Ten Commandments monument is allowed to be placed on state capitol grounds, we claim our right to place our Baphomet statue on the same grounds.

Thanks to the Establishment clause of the constitution, the government cannot legally discriminate among religions or give preference to one over the other. If the government allows religion into its workings, public spaces or laws, it must allow all religions in, not just the dominant Christian religion. This is the notion of religious pluralism that the founding fathers envisioned.

Though Dominionists and the Religious Right envision a completely Christian nation and are constantly working to bring religion into the government, they seldom think through the natural consequences of their actions. They often don't understand that other religions — including those they may find offensive or even demonic   would be legally allowed to have the same

100 Ward, Terence P. "Can The Satanic Temple teach Pagans about PR?" *Wild Hunt.* December 9, 2014.

7 • TAKING ACTION

governmental access and support.

Thus when The Satanic Temple claims the same rights, many suddenly realize the problems inherent with allowing religion into government. Many people, especially Christians, do not want Satanism in their government or schools. In this way, the actions of The Satanic Temple expose the hypocrisy fostered by Dominionists and others who are agitating for Christian rule: they think it is fine for the government to include the Christian religion up until religious freedom is invoked and Satanists legally claim those same rights under the law.

If the choice is between allowing religion in — including the Satanists — or keeping it out entirely, in many cases the government changes the laws to exclude all religions, returning to its original secular nature. Thus the actions of The Satanic Temple often bring about the restoration of the separation of church and state, rebuilding the wall that the founding fathers intended to keep religion and government apart.

Pagan speaker Shauna Aura Knight explains these tactics,

> *You want prayers before city council meetings...religious holiday scenes...statuary at public buildings? You want to give out religious texts at school? You want your religion to provide a legal loophole supporting your beliefs on contraception and abortion?*
>
> *Ok. Then Satanists can do that too. People rarely see a problem with the status quo until provoked.* [101]

Author and activist T. Thorn Coyle says,

> *The Satanic Temple is approaching the public square head on, with no apologies. I appreciate that. Their take on things is, "OK. Religious materials in schools? Here's an educational children's book that we are handing out. You ruled that it was fine," and, "Monumental religious statues at the state capitol? Here is one of our own." They are also mobilizing around issues such as reproductive rights and the rights of children to not suffer*

---

101 Ward, Terence P. "Can The Satanic Temple teach Pagans about PR?" *Wild Hunt.* December 9, 2014.

corporal punishment.

The Satanic Temple are unapologetically themselves and move ahead by assuming they already have the same civil rights as other religions. [102]

This strategy has been shown time and time again to be effective — so much so that the phrase "Lucien's Law" (named after Lucien Greaves) was coined by Central Florida Freethought Community's David Williamson to describe it. Lawyer Andrew Seidel explains:

Lucien's Law states that governments will either (1) close open forums when The Satanic Temple asks to speak, or (2) censor The Satanic Temple, thereby opening itself to legal liability. It is, as Hemant [Mehta] has noted, "like the nuclear option of church/ state separation cases." [103]

This process also serves to highlight the fact that belief in the supernatural is not required to claim the rights to the government that other religions have. While The Satanic Temple doesn't believe in a deity, our religious beliefs are still as valid — we share the narrative of Satan as the eternal rebel, the value system codified in our Tenets, and a form of worship in our activism, plus the Internal Revenue Service has legally ruled that we are a religion. What we believe is immaterial to our legal rights as a religion; the courts must give us the same consideration as theistic sects. Lucien Greaves says,

[The symbol of Satan] resonates very deeply with me, even though I'm not theistic. We just simply don't think that superstition should have more benefits in a pluralistic society than atheism. [104]

102 Ward, Terence P. "Can The Satanic Temple teach Pagans about PR?" *Wild Hunt.* December 9, 2014.

103 Mehta, Hemant. "Friendly Atheist: What I Learned from Fighting Back Against Public School Bible Distributions." *Patheos.* May 5, 2015.

104 Berg, Alison. "Satanic Temple co-founder promotes respect, secularism." *Utah Statesman.* October 15, 2017.

THE CONSCIOUS PARIAH

In undertaking political action, the Satanist speaks from the position of the outcast and plays an important role in driving societal change. We embrace our outsider status in unapologetic terms and, from the position of the scapegoat, we rise to challenge the oppression in the system. In an interview on what Pagans can learn from The Satanic Temple's activism, T. Thorn Coyle says,

> *Philosopher Hannah Arendt spoke of the need to become "conscious pariahs" rather than parvenues (assimilationists) or pariahs outcast by society. The conscious pariah rejects and directly challenges the status quo, not from petulant rebellion, but because the status quo is corrupt. There is great power in choosing to be a conscious pariah. I see some Pagan groups wishing to be "just like everyone else" and that can take away some of the power and bite we have in not being like everyone else. The role of the conscious challenger is important to society. I think that Pagans could take some lessons from the ways The Satanic Temple are issuing their challenges and refusing to assimilate. They are acting from their power, rather than begging for it or giving it away.* [105]

THE ROLE OF ART IN ACTIVISM

The Satanic Temple employs art and aesthetic choices in planning some of its most effective activism. Satanists often have a flair for the dramatic, recognizing that artistic elements can make or break a protest or a campaign. People respond to aesthetics on a deep and sometimes unconscious level. To focus attention on your activism, you don't have to send the press a huge, complicated text statement if you have a powerful visual element to your action. Art is one of the most powerful ways to get your message across.

In planning your actions, consider how artistic choices can support your message and intent. Lucien Greaves suggests, "Never separate art and activism. Never let your activism be artless, and never allow your art to be orthodox." [106]

---

105 Ward, Terence P. "Can The Satanic Temple teach Pagans about PR?" *Wild Hunt.* December 9, 2014.

106 "Never Let Your Activism Be Artless: An Interview With Lucien Greaves of The Satanic Temple." *Haute Macabre.* June 28, 2017.

You may choose to use costumes, performance art, acting, props and other elements of drama to convey your statement, whether you are protesting a harmful association of mind-control-believing therapists or counterprotesting anti-abortion zealots at Planned Parenthood. Invocations, monuments, and literature can all benefit from artistic flair.

SAMPLE ACTIONS OF THE SATANIC TEMPLE

The Satanic Temple is incredibly active in fighting for justice, continuously adding new campaigns in the battle for equal civil rights. They are not content to tackle just one or two issues, but instead are highly proactive in taking action against injustice on many levels, including breaches of church-state separation, attacks on religious freedom and bodily autonomy, harmful Satanic panic pseudoscience and more. Here are a few of the TST campaigns that were in motion at the time I wrote this book; more are added all the time as the religious organization continues to fight ongoing theocratic encroachment.

INVOCATIONS

A number of Satanists have given or applied to give Satanic invocations before governmental bodies like city or county councils. Many of these councils have an open policy that allows people from different faiths to lead a prayer or invocation before their meetings. But in many cases, these councils may refuse Satanists the First Amendment rights that they so freely give to other faiths, and in some instances their denial can be grounds for a lawsuit.

For instance, The Satanic Temple took legal action against the city of Scottsdale, Arizona, after the city took back its invocation invitation. The suit was originally filed in February 2017 after TST Arizona chapter head Michelle Shortt's invitation to speak at a meeting in May 2017 was rescinded by council officials, saying that she had a "lack of community ties" to the city. Legal counsel

Stuart de Haan noted that this stipulation was not in effect when the invitation was initially approved in April, and thus it was clearly an attempt at discriminatory backpedaling by the council because they simply did not wish The Satanic Temple to have their say.

Scottsdale Mayor Jim Lane has since publicly bragged about the situation, even going so far as to list it as an "achievement" on his re-election campaign fliers. Two public records requests with the city of Scottsdale also yielded a trove of emails between councilors and "concerned citizens" which ascertained blatant bias against The Satanic Temple – with Councilwoman Kathy Littlefield notably lamenting in one email that "this was taking equality too far."

The Satanic Temple pressed forward with its substantive claim of Establishment Clause violation. In December 2019, the Scottsdale City Council voted to give themselves $130,000 more in taxpayer money to fight against TST's civil rights; the case is still in the courts as of this writing.

MONUMENTS

The Satanic Temple has applied to install a number of monuments alongside other religiously-themed statues and memorials in public spaces. Their most well-known monument is the 8-foot-tall bronze monument portraying Baphomet. The winged, horned, goat-headed figure sits in peaceful repose with two children on either side gazing up at him. (Figure 29.)

The Satanic Temple has sued to place their Baphomet statue on State Capitol grounds next to existing Ten Commandment statues. The Establishment Clause dictates that no religion be given state preference over any other, and that if one religion is allowed on governmental property, all religions share a similar right to that space. Thus, as a religious symbol of Satanism, Baphomet provides a test case for a government body's requisite commitment to religious pluralism, and can show whether the

Figure 29: The Satanic Temple's Baphomet monument;
photo by Dresden Visage.

government is willing to give all religions the opportunity to be showcased on Capitol grounds, or is instead willing to give only Christianity those rights.

The first Baphomet monument lawsuit was filed in Oklahoma and resulted in a win for the separation of church and state:

> *After a statue of the Ten Commandments was donated to Oklahoma City by State Representative Mike Ritze and placed outside the Oklahoma State Capitol, The Satanic Temple offered to donate for display its own religious monument, a statue of Baphomet. By favoring one religion over another, Oklahoma was engaging in viewpoint discrimination, which is expressly forbidden under the US Constitution. Ultimately, the Oklahoma State Supreme Court ordered the removal of the Ten Commandments statue, and The Satanic Temple withdrew their request to place Baphomet on public property. [107]*

In this case, Lucien's Law took effect and the Oklahoma state government withdrew all religious monuments from public property, returning it to a purely secular nature.

At the time of this writing, The Satanic Temple had filed a second lawsuit against the state of Arkansas based on a similar First Amendment violation:

> *Modeled after Oklahoma's bill that was struck down by their State Supreme Court, the Arkansas Legislature passed a bill introduced by State Senator Jason Rapert to install a Ten Commandments statue on State Capitol grounds. Because this violates the First Amendment by allowing the State to privilege one religion over others when the grounds are not open to other religious organizations, The Satanic Temple offered to donate its statue of Baphomet to be erected directly in front of the Ten Commandments. TST's application was blocked by an emergency-session bill that requires all monuments to have legislative sponsorship. Because the purpose of the bill is to affirm the legislature's intent to act in defiance of the Constitution, a lawsuit is pending. [108]*

---

107 "Campaigns." *The Satanic Temple.* www.thesatanictemple.com.
108 "Campaigns." *The Satanic Temple.* www.thesatanictemple.com.

The Satanic Temple also created a veteran's monument meant for Belle Plaine, Minnesota, where the town's public Veterans Memorial Park featured a monument of a soldier kneeling before a cross. The "Campaigns" section of TST's website explains:

Figure 30: The Satanic Temple Veteran's Monument created for Belle Plaine, Michigan; photo by Jason Lloyd.

> *The Freedom From Religion Foundation put the city on notice that this [Christian] display violates the Constitution, and the statue was removed. The City Council then opted to designate a limited public forum where the park could accommodate up to ten displays honoring Belle Plaine veterans so they could re-erect their religious statue. To assure plurality, The Satanic Temple submitted its own monument proposal dedicated to the veterans of Belle Plaine that is consistent with its aesthetics.* [109] *(Figure 30.)*

The monument was a simple, elegant brushed steel cube with pentagrams on the side and an upturned helmet on the top in which park visitors could leave flowers or other offerings in remembrance of veterans. But rather than allow The Satanic Temple to place their tasteful memorial, the Belle Plaine City Council changed their policy and, in a win for church-state separation, reverted to permitting only secular displays.

---

109 "Campaigns." *The Satanic Temple.* www.thesatanictemple.com.

HOLIDAY DISPLAYS

During the winter holiday season, many cities and states allow Christmas Nativity displays on public grounds. But legally they cannot then forbid other faiths to erect their own displays, as long as those displays fit the city or state's technical specifications. The Satanic Temple has successfully applied for and placed holiday displays on Capitol grounds in several states.

After being denied in 2013, the first Satanic display was placed in the Florida State Capitol rotunda during the winter holidays in 2014 after Americans United for the Separation of Church and State threatened a lawsuit. Starting in 2014 with the "Snaketivity" display, The Satanic Temple won the right to install their Satanic displays alongside other religious displays on the grounds of the Michigan State Capitol during the winter holiday season. In 2019, The Satanic Temple - West Michigan installed their Yule Goat display there. (Figure 31.)

Figure 31: TST West Michigan's 2019 Yule Goat holiday display; photo by Christine "Pyretta Blaze" Weippert and Ben "Bendr Bones" Mertz.

Satanic holiday displays have also been placed in the Illinois State Capitol, and The Satanic Temple of Santa Cruz has participated in San Jose's Christmas in the Park tree display with Satanic ornaments they've crafted.

LITERATURE IN SCHOOLS

Many public school districts have adopted a policy whereby religious groups are allowed to hand out literature to students at school. The most common form of literature handed out is Christian bibles, distributed by evangelical Christian groups in order to proselytize to children. However, if a school allows the handing out of bibles, they are by law required to permit other religions to distribute their literature.

The Satanic Temple has created an adorably-illustrated kid's activity book called *The Satanic Children's Big Book of Activities*, with Satanic themes that emphasize compassion, tolerance and friendship. (Figure 32.)

School districts in Florida, when faced with the decision whether or not to allow both bibles and the Satanic Children's activity book to be distributed to students, chose to abolish

Figure 32: TST's Satanic kids' activity book; photo by Lilith Starr.

the distribution of all religious texts rather than allow the Satanic literature to be distributed. However, in response to the ongoing distribution of Gideons' Bibles in Delta County Public Schools in Colorado, The Satanic Temple was actually allowed to distribute their literature to students.

These actions by The Satanic Temple have put other school districts on notice that if they choose to permit the distribution of religious material to children in their schools, all religious organizations must be allowed to hand out religious texts — and that means some kids will learn how to draw a Satanic pentagram as part of their fun activity time.

AFTER SCHOOL SATAN CLUB

The US Supreme Court ruled in its 2001 case of *Good News Club v. Milford Central School* that public schools operate a "limited public forum" and that as such, they must allow religious organizations to hold after school clubs on school campuses, using school facilities. The fundamentalist Child Evangelism Fellowship organization takes advantage of this ruling to run "Good News Clubs" after school where children as young as 5 are terrorized with heavy proselytization that teaches they are wicked, full of sin, and deserving of death and eternal torture. They are also taught to convert their classmates and parents or else their loved ones will suffer for eternity in Hell.

While parents believe these clubs are light-hearted and harmless, many adults who have had Good News Club experiences as children have come forward to testify that the curriculum (which is kept secret from parents and others) is highly abusive and manipulative and inflicts terror and self-loathing upon young children.

To help combat some of this harmful teaching and offer another option, The Satanic Temple founded its After School Satan Club program, which operates only at public schools who already have a Good News Club operating. The After School Satan Club does not proselytize or even teach children about Satanism, but instead focuses on science, reason, and critical thinking skills to help children make up their own mind about the world. Lucien Greaves says:

> It's important that children be given an opportunity to realize
> that the evangelical materials now creeping into their schools are

representative of but one religious opinion amongst many. While the Good News Clubs focus on indoctrination, instilling them with a fear of Hell and God's wrath, After School Satan Clubs will focus on free inquiry and rationalism, the scientific basis for which we know what we know about the world around us. We prefer to give children an appreciation of the natural wonders surrounding them, not a fear of everlasting other-worldly horrors. [110]

GREY FACTION PROTESTS

The Satanic Temple's Grey Faction initiative has undertaken a number of actions and protests designed to expose health care professionals who are still promulgating harmful Satanic Panic delusions of widespread ritual abuse and debunked "recovered memory" techniques.

Starting in 2016, Grey Faction has protested at the International Society for the Study of Trauma and Dissociation's (ISSTD) annual conferences. The ISSTD is a professional organization for mental health professionals who still subscribe to discredited theories related to Multiple Personality Disorder and recovered memories — a therapeutic technique that was thoroughly discredited by research done in the 1990s.

The ISSTD "continues to attempt to put a scientific veneer on the long debunked theories of 'recovered memories' that gave rise to the anti-Satanic moral panic of the 1980s, and hypnotic therapeutic techniques that are used to derive past-life regression narratives, as well as Alien Abduction 'memories.' This is, in no way, science," says Lucien Greaves. [111]

As an example, Grey Faction's 2016 ISSTD conference protest symbolically demonstrated the dysfunctional, harmful relationship between ISSTD therapists and their patients. The mission of this event was to expose the ISSTD organization as instigators of pseudoscientific practices that have been directly connected to the harm of their patients, including the murder of the child Jude

---

110 "After School Satan." *The Satanic Temple.* www.afterschoolsatan.com.

111 "The Satanic Temple crashes professional conference with protest against harmful pseudoscience." *The Satanic Temple.* www.greyfaction.org.

Mirra. Jude's mother, whose therapist encouraged her belief that her son was the victim of Satanic ritual abuse, had murdered him to "save him" from this non-existent threat.

The focal point of the protest was two chained women, kneeling. Five-gallon buckets full of grey ash were poured over them while a man read from the Diagnostic Statistical Manual-5 about Dissociative Identity Disorder as if praying over the patients with the doctrine of pseudoscience. Two individuals stood beside them holding signs that said "ISSTD Kills" and "Killed by Pseudoscience," with Jude Mirra's portrait. Sarah Ponto Rivera, Grey Faction Director, explains:

> *The chains symbolize the mental health consumers' constraints from manipulation by their ISSTD psychiatrists. The patients are held in a metaphorical bondage in order to "get better." The buckets labeled "ISSTD" signify the weight of pseudoscience within the ISSTD organization. The Grey Ash is representative of obscuring truths with a cloud of delusions and imposing a false reality that causes harm to mental health care consumers. The trail of ash off the women's bodies touching pedestrians on the street symbolizes the communities impacted by therapeutic pseudoscience.* [112]

HOW TO SUPPORT THESE CAMPAIGNS

Even if you aren't directly involved in any of these actions, you can still do a lot to help support The Satanic Temple's ongoing fight against tyranny. Use your social media platforms to spread the word about TST campaigns; you can help raise a great deal of support for Satanic actions and projects by reaching out to your personal network this way. Share news stories about The Satanic Temple when they apply to place a monument, give an invocation, or fight for reproductive rights, and any other relevant and objective coverage.

You can also help The Satanic Temple achieve success in their campaigns by supporting them monetarily, either with direct

---

112 "The Satanic Temple crashes professional conference with protest against harmful pseudoscience." *The Satanic Temple.* www.greyfaction.org.

donations or through buying merchandise in The Satanic Temple online store. Money raised goes to fund The Satanic Temple's legal fights for reproductive rights, church/state separation, ending proselytization to children, and other important causes. Legal fees, especially for ongoing lawsuits that take many years to resolve, can cost hundreds of thousands of dollars, so every little bit you donate helps.

TAKING ACTION YOURSELF

Beyond supporting these extremely important TST campaigns, you can also start taking action against injustice on your own. Get involved with your own government, starting with voting but also including canvassing, protesting (when there is a clear goal sought after), and counter-protesting. Find out who your government representatives are, and contact them via letter or email whenever there is an important issue you feel strongly about. Start attending government meetings, like those of your city and county councils, and add your Satanic perspective to the proceedings.

While you can't claim that you're a representative of TST in these individual actions, you can let people know that you're a Satanist, and you can call on your government representatives to fight for plurality and religious freedom for all. Use your voice and your power as a voter and constituent to fight for justice and equality.

If you can join a local TST Chapter, you can do even more. There is strength in numbers. Your TST Chapter may receive permission from TST's governing body to participate in campaigns like applying to give an invocation at your City Council meetings or to place a holiday display at your state Capitol.

By daring to take action against injustice, a Satanist embodies the same spirit as the Satan of *Paradise Lost*: the willingness to rise up and fight against tyranny for the good of all.

TST Seattle members at Seattle Trans Pride, 2019.

SECTION 8
Finding Satanic Community

Until the rise of The Satanic Temple, "Satanic community" was something of an oxymoron. The Satanist was always the Outcast, shunned by most of society, which in most cases also instilled a deep reciprocal mistrust of that society. The result was often a rugged individualism as the Satanist struck out on their own as best they could once they realized there would be no help from their various communities and families. A few groups did form, like Church of Satan's Grottos, but because their doctrine ignored the fact that humans are social animals and instead tended to foster a cut-throat competitive culture, they often did not last long or expand in a major way.

But thanks to the rise of The Satanic Temple, Satanists now have a globally connected community, actively working toward common ends. There are TST Chapters around the globe, with new groups sprouting up on an ongoing basis. In this Satanic community, individualism is honored and maintained, yet members can work together on greater goals and find kindred spirits and friendship along the way.

BENEFITS OF SATANIC COMMUNITY

The benefits to such a Satanic community are many. Working together, you can accomplish a great deal more in terms of community service, public actions, and direct effect on your local city, state, or region. Benefits include:

Increased impact: We have a special role to play in society — as the outcast, we have awakened and we dare to stand up against tyranny wherever we find it. In our fight for justice, we can accomplish a great deal more working together than we can on our own. Having an entire group working on a project or campaign means people can pool their strengths, talents, and contacts, bounce ideas off each other and put in more hours for the cause. You can make a bigger impact on the world as a team.

Shared values: The most exciting part of building a Satanic community for me was meeting so many passionate, intelligent freethinkers and coming together to work on something meaningful. Our Chapter members are all very different, yet we all share the Seven Tenets, the narrative of Satan as rebel against tyranny, and a common goal. Our shared values include compassion and empathy, the willingness to fight for justice, individual freedom, equal rights for all, the inviolability of one's body, and the value of reason and science. Our last Tenet recognizes that humans are fallible, and if we make a mistake, we should do our best to rectify the matter. This spirit of understanding ideally permeates all our interactions as a group; we're not afraid to admit we are wrong.

Understanding: Being around people who totally understand and accept your Satanism is an amazing feeling. In many senses, when our Seattle Chapter came together, it felt like we had found our real family for the first time. We could all openly discuss topics such as Satanism, atheism, body autonomy, and the problems with religious tyranny, and we found ourselves sharing a common passion for truth, justice, and Satanic ideals.

United purpose: As a social club only, I think our community would not be so tightly connected. But we are first and foremost a serious religion that prizes taking action to help local communities and fight for justice, and that gives us a shared purpose that each of us believes in deeply.

This shared purpose gives us a great many ways in which we can contribute. Our mandate for action means we are always hard at work, and it keeps us busy! Religious oppression touches so many in society, we never lack for work to be done. It helps us set aside differences to focus on planning and executing effective actions, events, and community service.

We honor difference: Our group recognizes there is no cookie cutter mold for a Satanist. It is a path that encourages individuality and freedom — and we honor that in our community. We come from disparate backgrounds; we have a wide range of experiences and personalities. There are young people just entering the adult world; there are older folks who've spent their lives fighting the tyranny of religion. We may be extremely different, both from society and each other, but we are united in our belief in the Seven Tenets and our willingness to take an active stand against tyranny. Difference and diversity are recognized as strengths within the organization, not weaknesses.

Camaraderie: For many of us, this is our sole community where we can be free from judgment and bigotry, the one we feel most at home in. For a group of people who almost all have social anxiety, we get along remarkably well. There is a great deal of levity and laughter. I sense we are finally in an environment where we can let the shields down. It's hard to be vulnerable and social when you've had a rough past or faced a great deal of rejection, but each of us has known struggle in our own way, and that helps connect us.

Social support: Along with friendship and purpose, a Satanic community can help provide that social network that so many of us lacked before. We share each other's burdens and hopefully can help make them lighter along the way. Fellow group members can help each other when emergencies strike or when people are looking for housing, jobs, childcare, or other opportunities. We're there for each other if family members, colleagues or others attack or reject us because of our Satanism or other differences. We respect and validate each other's identities just as we are.

Transformation And Change
My Personal Experience

Thanks to my chronic pain and the demands of leading our local TST Chapter, it took me many years to finish this book — I started in 2017 and finished writing in 2020. In 2021, just as my designer and I were finalizing the design for publication, The Satanic Temple launched a major restructuring project that would change the entire way the organization and its local iterations were built. By the time you read this book, it is likely that this transformation project has been finished. That means some of the information in the following sections may have changed — specifically TST's organizational structure and naming conventions. However, I still believe the information is valuable even if the names and leadership arrangements are different.

The point of this deep restructuring is to bring the organization more in line with a traditional church structure. We are a religion, after all. As we've matured over the years, we've undergone a series of changes to better serve our members and execute effective campaigns. In this latest phase, TST will be split into two main pillars: Congregations, which provide local Satanic community; and Campaigns, which will launch actions that are worked on by TST members drawn from many different Congregations (and possibly even members who do not have a Congregation). In this new structure, Campaigns will work independently from Congregations.

In this transformation, TST Chapters will be renamed as Congregations. Instead of Chapter Heads, these Congregations will be led by a Minister who has been officially ordained through TST's Ordination program. This program includes a curriculum of multiple courses and requires renewal every year in order for a Minister to retain their official status (completing this program also grants you the power to officiate weddings in all 50 US states). Instead of a Strategy Council, each Congregation will have a Governing Board. Instead of an International Council that oversees the Chapters, an overarching Governing Board will manage Congregational governance.

TST had just begun working out the details of this restructuring when I was on the final stages of this book. Though when complete, these changes will make some of the naming and structuring information in these next few Community sections of this book outdated, in the interest of keeping a record of where we came from as an organization, I decided not to cut anything.

This book represents my personal experience as a Satanic practitioner and leader. I started The Satanic Temple's second-oldest continuously-running Chapter way back in 2014, just one year after TST's founding in 2013. When I became a Chapter Head, there were only four other Chapters and no governing body above us to create and manage the Chapter process. Executive Ministry (TST founders Lucien Greaves and Malcolm Jarry) were far too busy with our legal battles to guide Chapter leadership. I created the Seattle Chapter from the ground floor up, and I basically had to make it up as I went along, paving the way for the Chapters to come. I published these following sections as a community-building guide in 2016, and I've heard from many Chapter leaders who have told me it was essential when they were starting and building their own Chapters. (It was writing this community-building guide that inspired me to launch the project to write this book.)

Because of this deep experience with leadership within TST, I was actually tapped to be part of the transformation team creating our new organizational structure, though I reluctantly had to say no because I was making this book my top priority. I feel my hard-won personal community and leadership experience may still prove to be insightful after all these years; some issues are perennial no matter what your governing structure or terminology is.

Finding a Satanic Group

If you're interested in being part of a local Satanic community, the chances you'll find an existing TST-related community within a few hours drive of your home grow ever greater with time, as groups are founded, grow, become Chapters, and branch out into sub-chapters.

The Satanic Temple is organized into three official and one unofficial levels, at least at the time of this writing:

1. **The Executive Ministry**, made up of TST's founders, Lucien Greaves and Malcolm Jarry (as well as their support staff). Greaves is the official TST spokesperson as well. The Executive Ministry guides the overall strategy and direction of the organization and makes financial and legal decisions on its behalf. The Executive Ministry also runs The Satanic Temple headquarters and art gallery in Salem, Massachusetts.

2. **The International Council,** a body of directors that manages the Chapters and works on other TST-wide initiatives. The International Council decides which event and action proposals from the Chapters to approve and provides oversight and guidance to Chapter leadership. Each Chapter and group working toward chapterhood has a Point of Contact on the International Council, who acts as their group's advocate.

3. **The Chapters**. Each TST Chapter serves a region, offering a chance for members to come together in a community and work on local issues. At the time of this writing, there is a Chapter or group working towards Chapterhood in every state in America, as well as a number in other countries. Many Chapters, especially those in larger states or regions, have several sub-Chapters — for instance, TST Washington State encompasses sub-Chapters operating in the Bellingham, Seattle, and South Sound regions. These three

groups all meet separately, yet they are part of the greater TST Washington Chapter and fall under that Chapter's management — we're all one big happy family. New sub-Chapters may be added as groups of Satanists come together and form in other areas around the state.

4. **"Friends Of" Groups.** Pre-Chapter groups are termed "Friends Of" Groups, or "FoG," because they generally use that phrase in their name; for example, "Friends of TST Michigan" or "Friends of The Satanic Temple Alabama." These groups are not yet officially part of the TST organization, but they are working toward eventual Chapter status and still fall under International Council management. Each group has a Point of Contact on the International Council who guides them as they form; the group has to prove over time that they can follow IC guidelines and build an effective, stable community that pulls off successful public actions. It may take up to a year or more for a FoG to achieve full Chapterhood.

If you're interested in joining a local Chapter or Friends Of group, you have several options for finding it. Most official chapters are listed on the main TST website, along with links to their Facebook page or group and/or website.

You can also try searching for "the satanic temple" along with the name of your city, state or region, both on the web and on Facebook or other social media. However, if the chapter that comes up in your search isn't listed on the main TST website, there's a chance it's not an actual, official chapter and is using the TST name or graphics in violation of TST's copyright. Try to find out from TST if it is a properly vetted, official chapter registered with TST's International Council.

If your country or region does not yet have an officially recognized Chapter, it's quite possible that there is a "Friends of TST" group working toward official recognition. These pre-Chapter groups are usually harder to find, as they aren't listed on the official TST website. You can do web and social media searches for "Friends of TST" and "Friends of The Satanic Temple" along with your country or region's name. You can contact official Chapters in surrounding states or countries to see if they can point you to your own local group.

To find Chapters and FoGs, you can also ask around your local community, especially atheist, humanist, or skeptic contacts or people involved in the occult, pagan, goth, metal or other alternative scenes.

Be patient; it can take a little while to find your local Satanic community.

GETTING TO KNOW THE GROUP

Most Satanic groups have a web and/or social media presence, like a Facebook page or website. You can generally message the group through these avenues if you have questions. It's also fairly common for Chapters and FoGs to have a Facebook group that you can join to get to know members better and learn about events. Most of these social media groups will have a couple of brief questions for you to answer before they add you.

Observe the community at least briefly to ensure it's a legitimate TST-related group following the Seven Tenets, with no red flags immediately apparent. If it looks like a community you want to be part of, you can start taking steps toward applying for membership.

APPLYING FOR MEMBERSHIP

The process for membership application will vary from group to group. Different Chapters and FoGs will have different ways of vetting and accepting new members. Many Chapters host Meet and Greets or other gatherings open to the public, where interested parties can get to know Chapter members and vice versa. In some Chapters, membership is offered proactively to folks who have attended a number of these Meet and Greets and have proven they're a good fit and an enthusiastic volunteer. In others, like TST Washington State, prospective members have to fill out an application form and undergo an in-person interview.

TST Washington hosts our membership FAQ and application form on our Chapter website. The application asks for contact information and the answers to more in-depth questions like "What drew you to The Satanic Temple?" Every month, our Chapter's New Member Team then takes those applications that meet certain standards and invite those applicants to an in-person group interview at a local coffee shop. If an applicant is accepted at the interview, they become a probationary member of the chapter for 90 days. At the end of the probationary period, if a new member has made it to 4 out of the 6 meetings held in that time period and otherwise seems like a good fit, they are offered permanent membership in TST Seattle.

Be patient when requesting membership. Group leadership is usually very busy and there may not be enough resources to respond to applications quickly. Be persistent, but not annoying, and recognize that it may take a few months before you're properly vetted as a member. In the meantime, try to attend as many of the group's public events as possible.

Starting a Community

Though every state in the US has a Chapter or a FoG now, not all cities or regions within those states have a sub-Chapter. If the FoG, Chapter and/or sub-Chapters in your state meet far away from where you live, and you know other Satanists in your area who are interested in community, you may eventually be able to form a sub-Chapter there within your state's greater Chapter.

To get started, you'll likely need to already be a member of your state's Chapter. You'll work closely with Chapter leadership to build your local group, and they will provide you guidance along the way.

If your country does not yet have a Chapter or FoG, you may be allowed to create one there if there is enough interest. You'll need to get in touch with TST's International Council and follow their application process to start a new FoG. Once you've officially been vetted as a FoG, you'll spend some time building your community internally before doing your debut public event with the guidance of the IC; how successfully you can pull off such an event will help determine if you are granted full Chapter status. The IC will help guide your group along the way as you grow.

QUESTIONS FOR POTENTIAL GROUP LEADERS

If you're motivated to lead a Satanic community in some capacity, you should carefully think about the ramifications a leadership role will have on your life. Here are a few things I had to consider when I started the Seattle Chapter:

First off, are you ready for the increased workload of building a community from scratch? Creating a community where there was none before takes a huge amount of time, energy, and effort. Make sure you have room in your life for the extra work.

Consider who is willing to work alongside you in building the group. When I applied to start a Satanic group, I had to show that I had four other people who were interested in building the community as well. It's easier to start a group when you have help.

Be prepared for difficulties along the way. Interpersonal issues arise in any group, and you'll have to address any drama that bubbles to the surface. Also be aware that trying to work with local organizations, businesses, and politicians can be extremely frustrating; they can be relatively uncooperative with Satanists. But as more people start to understand what The Satanic Temple is all about, you'll likely find your support increasing.

Also, consider the possible repercussions to you for coming out as the leader of a local Satanic organization. As the group grows it's possible you'll have to speak with the press, be photographed, or otherwise put yourself out there. Group leaders face an added level of scrutiny. Are you ready to possibly be outed as the "head Satanist" in your locale? Using a pseudonym can help mitigate these issues.

You have to be especially careful about representing your group to the public — you can't speak as a representative of TST without express permission from the IC. Prospective Friends Of groups can't put on public events or make press statements until authorized by the IC.

Be aware that TST has limited resources and periodically goes through intervals where the IC puts a temporary hold on new FoGs or Chapters. It's quite a workload to manage all the TST organizations around the world, and there's only so much the IC can take on at once. Just be patient and polite and eventually you will get a chance.

HOW TO FIND MEMBERS

You can reach potential members in many ways. These days, I would recommend starting with a Facebook group for your organization. People find TST Washington through all our social media accounts, including Facebook, Twitter and Instagram, but you don't have to have all these; to begin with, a Facebook group for your community is probably all you need. You may want to set a few basic questions for those who want to join. You want members who are already local and looking for in-person meetings.

Though I wish online text interaction in itself could constitute a rich, supportive Satanic community, my experience has proven otherwise. Text-only interaction by itself so often devolves into pointless arguing and petty flame wars. You may find your members online, but you should plan in-person, real-life activities for your group, or at least webcam calls if in-person meetings aren't possible. This is the case as I write this — our Chapter has temporarily had to move to webcam meetings only due to the COVID-19 pandemic. Though we all miss the in-person interaction, the Chapter has managed to survive and even thrive with these group webcam calls; we're still seeing each other's faces and interacting in real-time.

WHERE TO MEET

I recommend holding community meetings or events at least twice a month; these may be a mix of private and public gatherings. In TST Washington, we meet primarily in person, though we've recently started opening these meetings to members who can't make it via webcam.

The Seattle portion of our TST Chapter meets on Sundays in the basement of a local occult bookstore, whose owner graciously allows us to use the space for free. You might end up meeting at a coffee shop or bar, or pooling your money to rent a meeting space.

When I was still Chapter Head and the bookstore wasn't available, we held meetings at my home. Be wary of giving out your home address to strangers; aka, don't post it online where the public can see it. My address only goes out to our private Facebook group or in an email to Chapter members.

We hold our public info meetings at the local library, which has a free meeting room we can sign up for. Our South Puget Sound group holds their public meetings in local parks when the weather is cooperative.

We usually go out to a nearby pub after our meetings, to hang out and spend some social time with each other.

LOOKING FOR THE RIGHT FIT

You're looking for potential members who understand and support TST's mission and values, who are willing to put in the hard work required for activism and community service, and who treat others with compassion and respect.

You should keep an eye out for potential problems when you're vetting applicants for membership. I ran into a few people who were not a good fit for the group. These included:

1. Satanists from other branches of Satanism (like LaVeyanism) who are very big into "might is right" doctrine or who insist your community be focused on their tradition instead of TST. So far this has been just a small percentage of the applicants we've encountered in our Chapter — I myself and many of our other members come from a different Satanic background, and we have no problem seeing humans as cooperative, social animals and fighting for social justice and equality. As TST has become more well-known, we've ended up with fewer of these applicants.

2. Racists, homophobes, misogynists, transphobes, etc. We require that all members respect each other regardless of race, sexual orientation, gender identity, disability status, etc. We've had to remove a member who insisted on using racist terminology and give a stern written warning to another member who was misgendering people (if she hadn't stopped, we would have removed her as well). Bigotry is not acceptable in TST Chapters.

3. People looking to ride TST's fame to their own renown and glory. TST gets a fair bit of press and is well-known for its Satanic activism. Some just want to steal that limelight for themselves and have no intention of contributing to a community. Recognize them by the huge ego they drag in the door.

4. Superstitious people who believe in a real Satan and the supernatural. They may ask about selling their soul, joining the Illuminati, or learning Satanic magic in exchange for money and power. Most people with such notions who contacted us were from Africa, Indonesia and other areas where Satan is often considered a real spirit who can grant wishes.

5. Folks who are looking primarily for a magic or ritual group.

Though ritual is an important part of Satanic practice and almost all Chapters use it, it's of a secular nature, not akin to ceremonial or Pagan magic.

6. People who don't live in the general area served by your Chapter. You want to keep your group focused on local members. In some cases the nearest Chapter to a potential member is in a neighboring state; most Chapters will accept applicants who live nearby even if they're across state lines.

7. Prospective members who saw the documentary *Hail Satan?* or otherwise learned about TST and thought erroneously that it is just an activism group using the trappings of religion ironically to troll Christians. There has been quite the groundswell in interest since the movie came out, and many newbies saw the activism portrayed in it and assumed that's all TST was. If they are willing to listen and open their mind to the fact that TST is in fact a serious non-troll religious organization first and foremost, they can be a good addition, but if they stubbornly refuse to understand and insist that they know TST better than its own leaders, they will only cause disruption in your community.

SECURITY

There can be risks associated with starting a Satanic community and holding meetings and events in your area. While you may have a very progressive family, town, and workplace, you never know who among them might have a deep-seated prejudice against Satanism. We have never been harassed at any of our meetings or picnics, but Seattle is very liberal; it can happen. For instance, in 2019, Satanists having an ice cream social in a park in Belle Plaine Minnesota were verbally accosted by a man who escalated to death threats, requiring the Satanists to call the police. Use common sense and be aware of your surroundings when you meet.

TIPS

- Don't give up if at first it's very hard to get people to come out to meetings. The group will grow organically.

- Be persistent about reminding people about events and meetings. I send out at least three reminders for every meeting.

- Guide your group's ethics by the Seven Tenets. Pay particular attention to number Six: "People are fallible. If we make a mistake, we should do our best to rectify it and resolve any harm that may have been caused."

- Social anxiety is a big problem for almost all of us Satanists. Realize things might be awkward sometimes and be patient with people.

- Make sure your members can communicate with each other if they want to. Our Chapter uses a Google Groups email list to reach everyone at once. We have a members-only Facebook group and group Facebook chat, and a "SatanFam" spreadsheet where members share their neighborhoods and phone numbers in case other members nearby need help.

- If you are the one starting a new group, you will likely have a few others at your side to help. Your role is to be the organizer, meeting facilitator, and leader of your community. You'll reach out to potential members, schedule meetings and drive the group forward.

- It takes a while to build a strong community of any kind. You should expect at first that you, or you and just a few others, will be doing almost all the work. It took me nine months until our chapter grew large and stable enough to expand our leadership council with dependable members. People will come and go, especially at first. Don't give up. It's slow and difficult at first, but eventually you should reach a critical mass and the community you've created will be worth the wait.

- Finally, have fun! A community should be a place to enjoy yourself with others who understand and accept you.

Leadership Tips

The Satanic Temple fights against religious tyranny and arbitrary authority, and it may seem odd to some to have leadership positions in such an individualistic religion. It's true that we don't have a rigid hierarchy with countless unnecessary levels and meaningless titles. In our Chapter and in the larger TST organization, we try hard not to put in place any unnecessary bureaucracy. But we are very active in fighting for justice and compassion, and for a group to pull off successful actions and community service events, leadership, organization and coordination are required.

As your group grows, the IC will provide leadership guidance to help you along the way. Here are my own experiences forming a leadership body.

Top leadership positions for TST Chapters or FoGs include:

- Chapter Head or two Co-Chapter Heads
- Media Liaison

Most Chapters of The Satanic Temple have two Co-Chapter Heads. This provides a level of redundancy. If one Chapter Head has to take a break or leave for any reason, one who can run the Chapter remains. Most Chapters also have a Media Liaison, someone who is authorized to represent TST to the press when necessary.

These are the only positions within the Chapter that are officially registered with the greater TST organization; they report directly to the group's Point of Contact on the IC and have legally agreed to represent TST in their area. They are the ones legally liable to the TST organization for building and running the Chapter. For these positions, TST requires an in-depth application process and interviews with the IC.

Beyond these positions, you may choose to create a Leadership or Strategy Council to help distribute the leadership workload or put in place a structure recommended by your IC Point of Contact.

For those of you just starting a Satanic group, you will probably be able to operate with just one or two leaders for quite a while. Groups do need at least one leader — someone at whom the buck stops, someone who is ultimately responsible for running the group. But beyond one or two leaders, many groups will not require more leadership positions until they grow and mature a bit. If you aren't doing activism or fundraising yet, you might not need a whole roster of official positions.

Two main factors go into deciding when you should form a broader leadership council. The first milestone you will reach will be when your original leadership roster (Co-Chapter Heads and Media Liaison) can no longer handle all the tasks necessary to keep the group running — often when there are more people in the group or you start doing complex activities like activism that require a high level of coordination. For example, our Chapter now has over 80 active members, and we always have at least one major campaign that we're working on. We need a group of people managing our operation.

The second important milestone occurs after you've had the chance to get to know your members and see how much work, enthusiasm and skill they put in, as well as assess their understanding of your group's mission and values. Once you know for certain you have people who would be good candidates for leadership positions, your group will be ready for a more formalized leadership group.

It may take a few iterations before your leadership group takes on its final form. In our Chapter, it took about six months for a stable group to emerge — so patience is essential. And once your group is formed, members will occasionally come and go.

Several people have stepped down from our Strategy Council for one reason or another, and we've had to remove one person after violations of our Code of Conduct.

CHOOSING YOUR LEADERS

Your Chapter or group may choose its leaders in a variety of ways. In the beginning stages of TST Seattle, as Chapter Head I chose my first Strategy Council members myself, and from then on we chose our Strategy Council members by a combination of recommendations from the membership and a vote of the existing Strategy Council. Ask your International Council Point of Contact what strategy they might recommend.

One of the first things to consider is how much responsibility a candidate is willing to take and how much work they are willing to put into the organization. Leadership positions definitely correspond to an increased workload. I chose my first Strategy Council members based on who had already volunteered a great deal of their time and effort — who had already gone the extra mile to ensure our projects and campaigns were successful. A person's skill set was also a factor, but not nearly as much as their enthusiasm and the amount of work they were putting in.

Another really important factor was what each person brought to the table in terms of teamwork. It's essential that your leadership group work well together. In my old career as a manager, I found that the most important contribution to team success was how well the team performed together, as opposed to people's individual skill sets and competencies. Our Chapter's SC had to work closely and function as a greater unit, even while preserving our individual identities and viewpoints. We didn't agree all the time — far from it, as we are all passionate individuals with different views — but we all were willing to put in the hard work to come to a workable agreement.

Lastly, anyone you put on your leadership council should have an excellent understanding of the organization's mission and values. A leadership council member has added responsibility when it comes to properly representing the organization both outside and within your group. You should choose people who you feel will represent your group's mission and values well.

Keep a wary eye out for people who are hungry for power and want a title, but aren't willing to put in the work necessary for the job. There will always be those who simply want authority over others or the added fame of leadership, as opposed to wanting to put in their time and effort in order to make the group better. Leadership is actually a service position. Those interested only in power are ill-suited to helping organize and manage the group.

FUNCTION OF THE STRATEGY COUNCIL

Our Chapter's Strategy Council spread the work of leadership across a whole team of people. We could trust each other to be competent and reliable, to work together to create successful actions and campaigns, and to engage in spirited discussions and the free exchange of ideas in order to guide the strategy and tactics of the group.

 The SC handled the high-level planning for the Chapter. We were responsible for taking the larger goals of The Satanic Temple organization and bringing them to life in our local community. Using input from the rest of the membership, we determined which campaigns and events would be best for the Chapter to pursue, and then we were responsible for putting together teams and coordinating people and resources in order to achieve the Chapter's goals. As Chapter Head, it was my responsibility to file formal Event Proposals with the International Council in order to request permission to do shows, Pride events, community service campaigns, and church-state activism. No Chapter is allowed to proceed with any public-facing event until the IC gives its express permission; filing such proposals also alerts the IC to the fact we might be in need of mentorship for that campaign.

The Strategy Council also decided how Chapter funds were spent.

In addition, we dealt with inter-member issues, such as complaints between members or violations of our Code of Conduct. If someone is causing recurring problems that threaten the health of your organization, it is leadership's job to give them a warning, or even remove them if it has to come to that.

In our Chapter, there is a codified Complaint process to ensure complaints are handled fairly. Violations of our Code of Conduct usually result in one warning, and then if the member continues the behavior, they lose membership. This should be a last resort, but on rare occasions you'll find one person is hurting others in the community or causing problems for the Chapter in general and must be ejected. We've had to do this several times to protect the community. We've removed members who turned out to be racist or who were sexually harassing others.

Our Strategy Council's job was not only to lead the Chapter to success on our actions, but also to foster healthy community within the Chapter. We are a religion with a congregation, and our community ties are integral to our Satanic practice; leadership has the responsibility to look out for our community's well-being.

POTENTIAL POSITIONS

Our Chapter's Strategy Council had varying numbers of seats over the years. When I started the group, there were only three Council members, and we've had up to nine. We liked to remain flexible so we could adjust to what is needed.

Each person on the SC had multiple areas of responsibility. For instance, our Treasurer was also the Merchandise Manager. Sometimes there was more than one person assigned to the area — for instance, we had two New Member Team Leads.

The list below covers various areas of responsibility handled by our Strategy Council, in addition to the larger joint role of setting Chapter direction and high-level strategy. We had these roles permanently assigned to specific people on the SC, but you may choose instead to have Action Committees handle these responsibilities on a more flexible basis or use another system for making sure all your Chapter's needs are covered.

- **Media Liaison:** Handled press interaction, including interviews.

- **Campaign Manager:** Responsible for planning and executing actions — our tactical director. He led our actions in the field.

- **Treasurer:** Responsible for storing, tracking and managing our Chapter funds, including paying expenses and reimbursing members.

- **Secretary:** Took minutes at meetings; reserved our meeting spaces; sent out meeting announcements and reminders.

- **New Member Team Leads:** Responsible for creating and running the process by which new people joined the Chapter.

- **Social Manager:** Organized social events.

- **Design & Print Lead**: Managed all design work and coordination with print shops and other fabricators (for posters, flyers, signs, etc.).

- **Tech Lead:** Managed our technical needs, including building and maintaining our website.

- **Social Media Manager:** Maintained our social media presence on Facebook, Twitter, and Instagram.

- **Merchandise Manager:** Designed, priced, ordered and otherwise managed Chapter merchandise (sold at fundraising events).

- **Community Service Organizer:** Organized charity and community service events for the Chapter to participate in.

- **Documentarian:** Photographed and video-recorded events and managed our media files.
- **Administrative Assistant:** Managed our official membership roll and contact lists.

In addition to these positions, we would often form a special action team within the Chapter to work on a specific project. For instance, we had a team dedicated to organizing and executing each Reproductive Rights benefit show, with people on the team holding positions such as Vendor Coordinator, Talent Coordinator, Green Room Manager, MC, etc.

STRATEGY COUNCIL MEETINGS

We usually had at least one Strategy Council meeting per month. Most often it was in person at one of our homes, but sometimes we had meetings via webcam. This was especially useful when we needed to have a meeting on short notice.

We used Google's free Google Hangouts video chat service (Hangouts is now defunct, but Skype, Zoom or other video chat programs will also work). In general, we liked to use the Google platform for handling Chapter communication and digital resources. We used Google Groups to set up email lists for the Chapter and the Strategy Council. We stored important documents on a Google Drive shared with all Strategy Council members, and we used a Google Calendar to share Chapter events with members. But it is up to you to decide what technology platforms your Chapter should use.

Our SC meetings usually lasted one-and-a-half to two hours. It's a long time, but there was usually a lot we needed to go over. We kicked off those meetings with a brunch potluck, giving us a little socializing time before we got down to business.

LEADERSHIP TRANSPARENCY

It was important to us to maintain transparency so the rest of the Chapter knew what the Strategy Council was doing and was privy to any decisions that we made. After each Strategy Council meeting, we sent out the meeting minutes to the rest of the Chapter, including any votes taken. Then we went over these minutes at our next Members' meeting. Any member could submit a proposal to the SC; we discussed and considered all such proposals.

We also tried hard to avoid stratification within our group. Our Strategy Council members may have had a more official role in the chapter, but we tried to eliminate any "pulling rank" because of this. The SC existed to serve the organization, not support personal quests for power. We strove for equality and required that every member of the Chapter be treated with respect and compassion.

Activities for Satanic Groups

A Satanic community can get a lot done. Our Chapter was always busy, ensuring members had multiple ways to practice their Satanism together. Here are a few ideas for potential activities for your group.

INTERNAL ACTIVITIES

Many of the activities your religious group participates in will be internal-facing activities, meant for Chapter members only, not the public. One virtue of internal activities is that they don't usually require that you submit an Event Proposal to TST's International Council. Within your group, you can do whatever activities you desire.

BOOK CLUBS AND GROUP PRESENTATIONS

You can spend some of your group energy learning. A book club that covers works like *The Revolt of the Angels, Paradise Lost* and other Satanism-related books can engage your members and help advance their understanding of the Satanic path. You can also give presentations internally, having one member give a talk or presentation to the others (a sort of Satanic salon, if you will). We often had a presentation or a facilitated discussion on a topic before our meetings. Some presentation and discussion topics we tackled included: Satanism in Heavy Metal, Why Goats for Satanism, Coming Out to Loved Ones, Ways of De-Escalating Conversations, and The History of Demonology.

GROUP RITUALS

Internal rituals are a nice way to tie the group together. You can work together to write, plan, rehearse and perform the rituals. Our Chapter has a number of rituals we perform at various times, plus we're always planning new rituals. At the end of each meeting, we do a short Invocation in which we jointly recite a text based on an invocation written by Lucien Greaves [113], and bite into apple slices that symbolize partaking of the forbidden fruit of knowledge. See the Ritual Appendix for the full text.

Every few months, we perform an Initiation Ceremony for those who have achieved full membership in the Chapter. In the Initiation Ceremony, initiates declare their intention to become a member of the Chapter and vow to abide by the Seven Tenets. After their Initiation, new members receive their Chapter Membership certificates.

We've also performed a number of Unbaptism rituals within TST Seattle for the members who wanted a clean break with their religious past. The Unbaptisms we perform privately are usually held outdoors, where participants can toss their broken bonds into a fire.

---

113 Abcarian, Robin. "After Supreme Court prayer decision, Satanist offers his own prayer." *Los Angeles Times.* May 5, 2014.

Other internal Chapter rituals have included a Destruction ritual and a Whore of Babylon ceremony, among others. Our group rituals and ceremonies help connect us, mark our transitions, celebrate holidays, and underscore our commitment to the Satanic path.

SOCIAL ACTIVITIES

Then there are the social activities available to you. Our Chapter does a lot together. We go out for drinks after every meeting. People also get together for dinner, movies, club nights, shows, and so on. We have nature walks in good weather. We have celebrations for each of The Satanic Temple's official holidays. And like any other religious group, we have a lot of potlucks — most of our gatherings are bring-your-own-food-and-drinks affairs.

We also go on an annual camping trip. If you want to take a sizable group camping, I recommend reserving the campsites far in advance, as (at least in Washington) the campground reservations fill up quickly and it's hard for us to find three sites next to each other later in the season. We collect money to cover the cost of the campsite, and also to pay for breakfast and dinner on the trip (we pool the money and buy the food in bulk). We also plan carpooling to ensure everyone has a ride.

When planning your social events, do keep in mind people's limitations when it comes to money and other obstacles. Not everyone can afford to go out to a movie, dinner or drinks — plus some people may be under 21 and unable to go to a bar. We have a lot of potlucks because they are all-ages friendly (some members bring their kids) and don't cost much; movie nights at someone's house also don't cost a lot. If someone can't afford to go on the camping trip or another event but really wants to, you can see if your group could pool some money to cover them.

HELPING EACH OTHER

While our Chapter has done a lot of community service for our surrounding Seattle, Tacoma, and other Washington areas, we recently turned our eye inward and launched a "SatanFam" initiative as well — a sort of internal community service, where we help each other out. We want to serve our own Satanic family with compassion just like we do with our surrounding area. So many of us are alone, without any support network. Our Satan-Fam initiative can help bridge the gap.

Whenever a member has a need they can't fill themselves, they bring it up at a meeting and other members sign up to help. For instance, we recently had a member who had surgery and then had to move to another living situation immediately afterwards, before she had time to recover. Other members helped pack and move her stuff, and volunteered to make and bring nutritious meals to her during her 6 weeks of recovery. Another member moved across the country and needed help packing her moving pod.

I've used the SatanFam system several times myself — I've had to ask for help fixing our neighbor's leaking kitchen faucet that was pouring water through our ceiling, for instance, and when we lost our home in a fire, our Satanic community pulled together to help us find and put down a deposit on a new place and pack and move all our stuff. There have been other needs expressed, and people have responded with kindness. We're a religious community that helps each other.

PUBLIC ACTIVITIES

In addition to the activities you do internally, your community will eventually start doing activities that are open to the public. Keep in mind that any activity that will be public-facing will require prior approval from the International Council via a formal proposal that your group submits to your IC Point of Contact. This includes not only political action, but also activities like fundraising, talks, public meetings and community service campaigns, as well as speaking to the press.

Basically, any time you anticipate that people outside your group will be involved or will witness the event, you should have permission from IC first; this helps ensure that TST is being properly represented to the public. It can be all too easy for well-meaning people to misrepresent themselves as speaking for The Satanic Temple and say something that would harm the organization's ability to effectively fight its legal battles.

GET YOUR VOICE OUT THERE

Whether you're trying to find others who are interested in being in your group or you just want your group's voice to be heard, you can benefit from an online presence. One of the first things I did when I started The Satanic Temple - Seattle Chapter was to set this up. If you have someone skilled with tech in your group, their assistance may be helpful in this arena, though many of today's applications need little or no technical know-how.

It's handy to have an email for your group, so people who are interested in joining, the press, and others can reach you. It's best if you create a separate Gmail or other email account for your group, as opposed to using a personal email; that way multiple members of leadership can log in to handle emails and the account can be passed on to new group leadership down the road.

Social media may be a huge part of your online presence. You have many different platforms on which you can broadcast your group's voice. Facebook is one of the biggest social media platforms, and many people will turn there for info about your Satanic group. It's easy to set up a Facebook page for your community that contains your mission statement and links to your website (if you have one). I post a steady stream of articles about TST, Satanism, and church-state separation cases on our Facebook page, usually at least one a day, but you can post far less often than that and still have a useful page. Just remember to check the messages sent to your page on a regular basis, as well as the comments on your posts. Don't hesitate to ban trouble-makers from your page.

Twitter is also a good platform to announce events and share relevant information, so consider making a Twitter account for your group as well. Our Twitter account is used less often, but it's an important platform for our event announcements. It's not essential to use Twitter, but if you're already on it, you may find it fairly useful.

Other big social media platforms include Instagram and Pin-terest, which are focused primarily on visual images. If your group has a lot of photos or images to post, you may consider Instagram, as it's a highly popular platform. TST Seattle does maintain an Instagram account. Pinterest allows you to make collections of images around whatever themes you pick; though we started a Pinterest account in the beginning, we found we never used it.

YouTube is also considered social media, though it's less use-ful for sharing day-to-day info or announcing events. If you frequently have original videos to post (of talks you've given, events you've done, rituals, Satanic philosophy videos, a Satan-ic video blog, etc.), it's a good idea to have a YouTube channel. If you have a Gmail account for the group, you already have a YouTube channel assigned to that account.

A website is also handy, but for many groups, especially in their early stages, a standalone website is optional. You can do a lot with just email and social media. If you do want to build a website, there are many options that make it easy. Our first Chapter website was built by scratch by our tech lead; when she moved away I used Wix.com to build and maintain our website — I found its built-in editing program made it simple to create good-looking websites with no technical know-how. There are other hosting options that provide easy-to-use creation tools as well. If you have members well-versed in Wordpress, that can work. Or if you have the technical skills in your group, you can, as our Chapter initially did, build a custom website from scratch.

CONTRIBUTE TO THE SATANIC DISCOURSE

Satanism is a growing religion, and many are interested in its philosophy and practice. One of the best things about Satanism is that it's an individual path, so adherents will have differing personal perspectives to offer, all of them valuable to understanding Satanism as a whole. Your group can join the Satanic discussion in a variety of ways.

Your group can present informative public talks in your local area. These talks can cover a wide range of subjects, from Satanism 101 to in-depth explorations of Satanic texts or personal experiences with Satanism. I've been invited to give talks to local atheist and skeptic groups and at a horror convention.

You can also hold a public info meeting for your group, where you give a talk about what your group is and what you do, how to join and so on. You can often reserve a room for public talks or meetings for free at your local library. Universities also often have lecture rooms that can be reserved by students, so if any of your members attend college, you may have that option.

When giving a talk, a good rule of thumb for length is not more than 60 minutes total. Usually, our group's talks run for 30 - 45 minutes, with a 15-minute Question & Answer session afterwards.

Another excellent way to contribute to the Satanic milieu is to host an art show. You'll need a place to have the show — usually a gallery, but many other places host art shows too, like clubs, coffee shops and doctor's offices. Though you can populate the show with pieces done only by your group's members, you may have more options if you open submissions to everyone. You might want to have a theme for your show, though "Satanic art" itself could also be a theme. For instance, the Arizona Chapter of TST put on a "7 Deadly Sins" art show.

COMMUNITY SERVICE

The first Tenet of The Satanic Temple is "One should strive to act with compassion and empathy toward all creatures in accordance with reason." Satanists can act in the spirit of this Tenet by engaging in community service.

This can take many forms. Your group can put on a charity drive to collect items for those without homes, in shelters, and otherwise in need. For instance, TST Seattle runs a yearly menstruation product drive (called "Menstruatin' with Satan"); menstrual supplies are a non-optional necessity for many people, and oftentimes they are not donated to shelters and charity organizations. We aim to help destigmatize menstruation along with collecting the items to donate to local shelters. (Figure 33.)

Michelle Shortt, Co-Chapter Head of TST Arizona, explains:

> *Menstruation is definitely something that gets swept under the rug, as something that is icky. Nobody wants to talk about it. Nobody wants to think about it, especially when there's homeless people. What do they do when they have their menstrual cycle and can't do anything about it? This is a way to help the disadvantaged.* [114]

Other TST chapters have run successful drives for other items, like socks, toys, diapers, pet food and winter coats. You can always call local shelters or organizations that help the needy, and find out what they need the most.

To run a drive, you'll need to find local places that will host your donation boxes or collect items. We talked to businesses all over Seattle to find a number that were willing to host our menstrual product donation boxes. Some places prefer not to accommodate a box but are willing to accept donated items. You can also ask people to bring items to an event, like a show or a club night.

You can put together a Wish List on Amazon.com that contains products you'd like people to donate; this allows those outside your geographic area to contribute. We put a QR code that leads

114 Jacobsen, Scott. "An Interview with Michelle Shortt (Chapter Head) and Stuart 'Stu' de Haan (Spokesperson): The Satanic Temple (Arizona Chapter). *Insight: Independent Interview-Based Journal.* September 1, 2017.

Figure 33: TST Seattle's 2018 Menstruatin' with Satan collection; photo by Tarkus Claypool.

to the Wish List on posters for the donation drive; if a business doesn't have room for a donation box, they still may be willing to put up a poster instead.

Our Menstruatin' with Satan posters and publicity include our Chapter's PO box address as well so people have, in addition to using Amazon, the option to ship donations themselves.

Let people know where their items are going. We got permission from a few local charities to list their names as donation recipients. It can be hard to find a charity partner who is willing to publicly work with Satanists, so I recommend starting your charity search early on in the planning process. Our menstrual products went to several local shelters and a comprehensive homeless services provider.

You can also put together care packages to give to homeless people and the needy on your own.

You can volunteer your time at local charity organizations in need. We send a team of people to work at a distribution warehouse for food banks every few months. Check your local youth centers, shelters, homeless encampments, food banks, LGBT support centers and so on for opportunities to volunteer. All our participating members have reported back to the group that they very much enjoyed their time volunteering.

Chapters have helped out in their local communities in other ways. TST Seattle has done a number of blood drives and park cleanups. TST Santa Cruz has adopted a beach that they clean up on a regular basis. TST Arizona volunteered to clean up their local highways — after they put in a certain amount of cleanup work, their name was put on an Adopt-A-Highway sign recognizing their contribution.

You can lend your support to marginalized communities. For instance, our Chapter sends a presence to all our local Pride festivals, including marching in Pride parades and hosting info booths. We've also positioned ourselves along the Seattle Pride parade route near the fundamentalist hellfire preachers who spew hate speech toward gays; we offer a contrasting, compassionate perspective with our LGBTQ-supportive signs.

FUNDRAISING

Though they may be minimal, any organization has costs associated with running it. For example, TST Seattle pays for website hosting; signs and banners; printed informational literature; travel, flyers, and other activism costs; ritual costs; charity campaign costs; event fees (for putting together a show, for instance); and the costs for talk or meeting spaces. We have a donation bucket that members can contribute to at our meetings, but the bulk of our funds come from fundraising events.

You have a lot of options when it comes to what kinds of events to do for fundraising. We've had a great deal of success with benefit shows. Our first big benefit show featured three bands, two dance performance sets, a midnight Unbaptism ritual, vendors, and tattoo artists. You don't need to be that ambitious, though. If you can find one band or a few burlesque performers that want to donate their performance time, you've got a show, albeit a small one. You can also sponsor club nights, where there is only a DJ spinning.

Our experience with putting together our big benefit show was that the first and foremost task was reserving a date at a local club. Many clubs will let you put on a show there for just the price of the sound tech's fee (in our area that's around $150); the club keeps all the money from drink sales, and your group gets the money from the door.

Figure 34: TST Seattle merchandise

You can also start from scratch with a warehouse or other rough space, but in that case, you have to get event licenses and licensed staff to serve liquor, buy all the liquor, and in many cases provide your own stage, lighting and sound equipment. We found it much easier to put on a show at a regular club.

The next step after securing a date at a venue will be to find performers. The saying "If you build it, they will come" often holds here: if you have a date reserved, chances are good there will be performers who want to come perform. We were able to find a whole slew of people in local bands and the burlesque and fusion dance communities who donated their time to our benefit show for reproductive rights. We didn't pay them for their performances, but we did offer them two drink tickets apiece in gratitude.

You may also decide to put on a ritual somewhere and charge admission. We've done a public Unbaptism ritual at our benefit show; other Chapters have done destruction, bloodletting, invocation, Walpurgisnacht, Saturnalia, Babylonian lottery, and Black Mass rituals, among others. Consider sharing photos, videos, or text of the ritual on your social media and website; people are always curious as to what Satanic rituals are like.

If you have an art show, that could also be a fundraiser. Here is the verbiage from TST Arizona's art show info page: "Each artist will be allowed 2 pieces. The first will go into a silent auction with the profits going directly to TST AZ to aid in our community endeavors. The second will be priced according to the artist's desires, and those profits can go where the artist chooses."

You have a lot of different event options for raising money — one TST Chapter even had a Satanic bake sale.

One of your biggest moneymakers may end up being merchandise sold at your events. Many people are thirsty for Satanic goods. If you have a unique logo or a talented graphic artist willing to create original art, you can use those images on your merchandise. Just remember whatever images you use should be large enough to provide a clear, unpixelated image on the final product.

Which products you want to carry is up to you. We have a number of low-cost items, like stickers, buttons, keychains and magnets. We also have drinkware — shot glasses, pint glasses and mugs. You can make DIY patches via screen printing onto black canvas (or pay more for embroidered patches). You can sell screen-printed T-shirts, though it's a slightly harder item to sell as you'll have to carry inventory in all sizes and you can often end up with unsold T-shirts. I've also seen tote bags, flags, posters, enamel pins, woodburned plaques, pipes, and necklaces sold by various Chapters. (Figure 34.)

You may be able to find a small business or individual in your area who can give you a good deal. You can also order customized merchandise wholesale online, which is what we did.

Do some web searching to find the best prices on bulk merchandise orders. There will usually be a minimum order — for instance, the lowest order we can make for pint glasses is 24 glasses. Often the per-unit cost goes down if you order larger batches.

You'll want to mark up your merchandise enough to make a profit, but not so much that no one will buy it. This usually means you price it at a minimum of two times your cost (often three times or more in the case of cheaper items like stickers).

While you can't sell merchandise online (that privilege is reserved for TST's main online store), you can sell your organization's merchandise at events you put on, like benefit shows. You can also reserve a booth where you can sell merchandise at local street fairs, art fairs, and conventions. Some areas have punk rock flea markets or similar events with low entry fees.

Invest in some table decorations and arrange your merchandise booth to be visually pleasing. We have a banner with our logo on it that we hang off the front of the booth, plus a black drape cloth, battery-powered lights, a skull, and various other decorations.

PARTICIPATE POLITICALLY

Getting active politically is part of becoming a Satanist. Your group too can make a difference in your local, state, and federal governments, whether it's with a holiday display on government grounds or giving an invocation at a local governing body meeting. Talk with your TST International Council Point of Contact if you're interested in pursuing political activism — they'll need to walk you through it step by step to ensure you're correctly representing TST. You should also touch base with your Point of Contact before you speak to the press in any capacity; they will have suggestions on what to say or how to interact with the media.

In an article aimed at the Pagan community, Greaves mentioned these tips for speaking to the press:

> *Stay on point and control the dialogue. Don't be pulled into superfluous and irrelevant arguments. If you're asked an unreasonable question, simply answer with whatever message you wish to put forward, whether it addresses the question in any way or not. Move away from meticulously describing what it is you believe and practice. Your material has long been publicly available to the genuinely curious. You simply do not have to justify your religious perspective to anybody to assert your rights as equally regarded citizen[s].* [115]

You have a lot of options as a Satanic group, for activities both internal and external-facing. Working on these together will bring you closer and help your group explore what it means to be a vibrant Satanic community.

Ultimately, what you decide on as far as structure and activities for your own Satanic group is up to you and your IC Point of Contact. There are many approaches that will yield success for your organization; a lot of it will become apparent as you try different options. I invite you to share your own experiences and tips with community-building; the more knowledge we can share, the better we become.

---

115 Ward, Terence P. "Can The Satanic Temple teach Pagans about PR?" *Wild Hunt.* December 9, 2014.

TST Seattle member at Seattle Pride Festival, 2017.

SECTION 9
In Conclusion

These are the basics of my Satanic practice; it's up to you to decide if, when and how you embark on your own Satanic journey. This book is meant as a jumping off point; you can continue your Satanic studies via the rich selection of books, podcasts, talks and articles that expound on the ideas about Romantic Satanism put forth by TST founders and others.

The process of building your own personalized Satanic practice will be ongoing. Over time, your practice will evolve as you yourself grow and change. You'll be able to explore these aspects on a continuing basis throughout your lifetime.

Satanism is for many a "coming home" religion. Many people have described their first encounter with Satanism as not a conversion experience, but rather the feeling that at last they have found a name for the path they are already taking. TST Arizona Co-Chapter Head Michelle Shortt explains:

> *I think everybody has their own coming of age story of coming to Satanism. We have this thing. It is like they are born Satanists. They always had this mentality where we value science and reasoning, and bodily autonomy. And when people discover Satanism, it is almost like they're coming home, "This is exactly what I've always been, and I didn't know there was a name to it."* [116]

---

116 Jacobsen, Scott. "An Interview with Michelle Shortt (Chapter Head) and Stuart 'Stu' de Haan (Spokesperson): The Satanic Temple (Arizona Chapter)." *In-Sight Publishing.* June 22, 2017.

In some senses, building your Satanic practice may feel like work, because it takes energy to fully realize your potential both at the self and larger community levels. Study and research takes effort; finding and getting to know your local Satanic community can take a while. But in many ways, embarking on your Satanic path will simply feel like a waking up, gaining an understanding of who you are as an individual — "coming home," as it were, to a philosophy and a religion that was part of you all along.

Lucien Greaves describes the success of The Satanic Temple as it passes the 100,000 member mark:

> [We have] about one hundred thousand now. I think that's a number where people are going to have to start accounting for Satanists. At the beginning, we felt like we were speaking for a population that wasn't speaking up. And that population rose to the challenge; more and more people are beginning to see this for what it is, and are willing to stand with us. [117]

We are a growing Satanic family bound by ties of empathy and compassion, all in our own way working toward a better society and the end of tyranny. I wish you well on your own Satanic journey!

---

117 Jaremko-Greenwold, Anya. "Speaking with Satanic Temple Co-Founder Lucien Greaves at Sundance Made Me Want to Join His Reasonable Religion." *Flood Magazine.* January 30, 2019.

9 • IN CONCLUSION

239

Ritual Art in Ink & Blood by Lilith Starr.

APPENDIX 1
Satanic Voices

*Thanks to my Interviews Editor Jason Lloyd
for all his help on this section.*

Though there are similarities at the core (such as belief in the Seven Tenets and finding meaning in the narrative of Satan), every person's Satanic practice is going to be different. My experience is limited to my own approach. I wanted to get multiple perspectives, so I interviewed a number of practitioners who were willing to give insight into different aspects of their personal practices. I posted a call for participants on my social media and took whoever volunteered first in selecting interviewees, so this is not a perfectly representational slice of the Satanic community. Still, my hope is that presenting multiple points of view on different elements may help convey a more rounded picture of personal Satanic practice than I could offer on my own.

Elements of Satanic Practice

In this first set of interviews, I wanted to get a high-level picture of the elements each Satanist incorporates into their practice. Since Satanism is such an individualistic religion, everyone's practice is going to look a little bit different. For example, some Satanists may be part of a TST Chapter and others may practice exclusively by themselves. Not all Satanists participate in rituals, either private or public, though many do. I wanted to give readers the chance to see just how diverse each person's practice was and potentially find inspirations for embarking on their own Satanic path.

Questions I asked the Satanic practitioners in this section are:

• How would you personally define Satanism?

    • Tell us a little about your religious background. What drew you to Satanism?

    • How does Satanism fill the role of a religion for you (if it does)? What parts of religion have you kept in your Satanism, and which have you discarded?

    • What roles (if any) do activism and community service play in your practice?

    • Are you part of a Satanic community? What do you get out of it?

    • What role (if any) does ritual play in your practice?

    • What other elements would you say your Satanic practice includes? Some examples: an altar, meditation, making Satanic art, reading Satan-related literature, etc.

    • What challenges have you faced as a Satanist?

    • What have been some of the most rewarding aspects of being a Satanist?

    • What tips do you have for those beginning their Satanic journey?

Siri Sanguine

• *Briefly, I define Satanism as working towards improving the human condition with reason, logic, and community service. Activism is a key component of my practice, fighting for the rights of the oppressed.*

• *When I was young, I was raised in the Evangelical Lutheran Synod, which is quite cult-like in their membership controls — pretty strict and oppressive. I constantly got in trouble for asking too many questions growing up and never felt that Christianity was a good fit. I have been a practicing witch for over 20 years and had been following TST's exploits from early on. The Tenets paired with our fight for reproductive rights and the separation of church and state brought me into the Satanic fold so to speak.*

• *In many ways, Satanism does fill the role of a religion for me. The Seven Tenets speak to my core values and practices, and I frequently meditate on them or use them in writing rituals for myself and my chapter. The service to community that we do as members of TST is very similar to the things we used to do in the church, but without the drive to convert others to our way of thinking/beliefs.*

• *Activism and community are so entwined with my beliefs and ethics that they are a core part of my practice. I serve myself and my community when I participate in actions and community service projects — giving of myself to help others.*

• *Belonging to a Satanic community is also an important aspect of my practice. I am a member of TST Washington State Chapter and the work we do and our vibrant community feeds me. Our interactions in the chapter bring not only a social outlet for my life, but a huge amount of unadulterated joy*

- *Though not every Satanist practices it, I enjoy ritual immensely myself. It is a chance to be creative and express my world view, to create beauty from our struggles, and to connect with my fellow Satanists.*

- *In addition to those elements of practice, I have a working altar that I interact with during my daily meditations and frequently attempt art projects like painting, drawing, writing, etc. with a devotion/focus on my Satanic path. I also read a ton of Satanic-themed literature and try to incorporate that knowledge into my works.*

- *Along the way, I've occasionally faced difficulties, especially as a community leader. Sometimes interactions with other Satanists can be challenging. We are all pretty independent creatures with sizable egos and we distrust authority in general so ... yeah.*

- *Some of the most rewarding aspects of being a Satanist have been supporting my LGBTQIA community at local Pride events and performing acts of activism that have touched the hearts and minds of the public (sometimes making them reconsider their opinions about Satanists along the way).*

- *For those just beginning their Satanic journey, I'd say: Read, ask questions, take what elements work for you and discard the rest — you are responsible for your actions so act accordingly.*

Eric Maldonado

• *To me, personally, Satanism, or at least my personal brand of Satanism, is the act of understanding your own power in the world, and the power of others to affect you. It's considering the consequences of your actions, and pausing to consider the repercussions of the actions others ask you to take before you take them. It's understanding that there is no universal consciousness that provides benefits to people, but instead societal structures, and when one is not privy to those particular structures, one needs to work to create their own structures to support themselves and those like them. It's the act of taking a symbol of rebellion and embracing it to represent yourself and your fight against those who would strive to control you for their own benefit.*

• *I was raised in a household with an atheist mother and Roman Catholic father (though he was not practicing), and my mother established a rule where no religion (or lack thereof) would be pushed on myself or my brother, allowing us to make our own decision. I went through phases of atheism, agnosticism, Wiccan, and finally was introduced to The Satanic Temple through a TST member I met in an atheist group on Facebook.*

Many of the atheists in the group were attacking TST due to a lack of understanding that TST is nontheistic, and even with the minor understanding of TST I had at the time just through doing simple research, I understood that they were wrong, and was attacked in turn when I defended them. In meeting the other TST group members, I dug further, and eventually came to realize that TST embraced ideals and morals that I've held all along, so I took the plunge and became a member.

• *Temple Satanism fulfills the role of a religion for me by way of having a core group of beliefs that help guide you to living a healthy, positive life, as well as allowing for the formation of a community of people following those same guidelines. Temple Satanism is full proof that superstition and a superiority complex are not necessary to have a religion, and I consistently fight to make sure my fellow Temple Satanists avoid the pitfall of deriding all religion and forgetting that Temple Satanism is itself a religion as much as any theistic religion is.*

It is vitally important that theistic religion, and the followers thereof, are not allowed to have total control of the social lexicon regarding the term "religion," as such control then allows them to claim the sole benefits of policies and laws designed to help all religious communities.

• *Regarding activism, I personally strive to allow my religion to guide me in regards to what actions I take as an individual when it comes to being an activist towards movements and political action that affect myself and those I care for, but as a citizen and individual, not as a Satanist. This is because I always strive to remember that associating my activist activities with Satanism has the potential to drive the superstitious to fight even harder to oppose the organizations and movements I associate myself with, making my participation a negative rather than a positive.*

As for community service, supporting and growing my Satanic community, in both size and strength, is a vital part of my Satanic practice, as our community is what gives us the strength and power to be more than we are as individuals, and allows us to exert ourselves in a way we wouldn't be able to otherwise. In my perspective, a healthy and vibrant Satanic community is vital to my religion's ability to empower its members and exert itself for positive change in the world by way of both said aforementioned empowerment of its members, and by way of keeping tabs on its members and their actions. This helps ensure that individuals or sub-groups within the religion are unable to twist or malign the intentions and beliefs of your religion into something it was never intended to be, and/or represent your religion incorrectly to those outside your community.

In regards to the local non-religious community, my Chapter, unfortunately, achieved full Chapter status right before the COVID-19 pandemic, and so our ability to implement any community service actions involving going out and assisting the community more directly was squashed by social distancing and quarantine guidelines. But we have been working on sewing masks for both the general population and the medical community, and have plans ready to implement once the pandemic has passed regarding collecting needed items for single mothers in financially vulnerable situations, assisting organizations like Habitat for Humanity, and otherwise assisting needy people in our local communities.

- *I am one of the Chapter Heads of The Satanic Temple Nebraska, as well as a member of the team that helps other Temple Satanist communities work through a program to achieve Chapterhood in their own local areas.*

  Through my work in leading and developing my local Satanic community, as well as helping the leaders of other Satanic communities work towards Chapterhood in their own right, I am able to feel empowered in the development and direction of my own religion.

  Additionally, I can feel fulfilled by the sense of community and camaraderie that I see displayed by the members of my own community and the communities formed by other Satanic leadership.

- *I don't partake in ritual as much as other Satanists I'm friends with, but I definitely understand its role in our religion, and strive to help create rituals that will benefit myself and my community. I do this both for the obvious psychological benefits ritual can imbue an individual or a community with, and to further provide proof that supernatural belief is not a requirement for something to be a true ritual.*

- *The main other element, beyond the building and growing of my local Satanic community and of Satanic communities across the world, of my personal Satanic practice includes acting as a positive representation of my religion to the outside world. I see myself, as an open and unapologetic Satanist, as an unfiltered representation of what Temple Satanism is to those who are not familiar with it, and so strive to be a positive example of our Tenets and beliefs to those in other communities when the opportunity arises.*

While TST specifically does not proselytize, I always strive to display my Temple Satanism proudly, so that those who are curious about what we are and what we believe can approach me as a representative, and I can make sure they are getting accurate and positive information about us straight from the Satanist's mouth. In the same way, I strive to make connections in the overall religious community, to discover members of other religions that have the capability to understand what we have in common, rather than focusing on what separates us, allowing us to potentially work together on projects where our beliefs overlap. This assists in gathering allies that can speak positively about us within spaces we are generally denied access to, and in further cementing our place as a true religion in the world.

- *Luckily, due to my upbringing, I have not faced the same challenges as other Satanists who have a much more extreme connection to their blood relatives who are deeply religious and judgmental of those who think differently than they do. This has allowed me to avoid the necessity of a Satanic pseudonym, or having to be careful about separating my Satanism from my family or personal relationships. Even living in a very conservative state, I have been lucky to avoid much in terms of attacks against me, verbal or otherwise, during my time spearheading the group that would eventually become my Chapter.*

- *The most rewarding aspects of being a Satanist have been regarding the discovery of a community to belong to, and how dedicated everyone is to helping each other. There is a good reason the Temple Satanist community is often fondly referred to as "SatanFam," as it truly feels like an extended family ... the good kind of family, where everyone supports one another in times of need and lifts each other up. It's through Satanism that I've met some of my closest friends, and the ability to become a leader in the Satanic community has led me to discover many positive things about myself and my capabilities that I likely never would have realized otherwise.*

- *My advice to those just starting on their own Satanic explorations is: Always try to remember that your Satanic journey is your own; your journey might have some of the same steps as the journeys of others, but you should never judge your own journey based on how things happened for others. Take your time, don't be afraid to do your own research, and remember that Satanism is a religion first and foremost; while we celebrate the ideals of self-dependence and rebellion, an organized religion requires ORGANIZATION, and you should be careful not to dispense with connections with your community in your efforts to be rebellious, independent and blasphemous.*

I coined a phrase among my Chapter that became quite popular that I will share here: "Blasphemy with purpose." It means that one should not be contrary or offensive simply for the sake of being contrary or offensive; you should have a positive goal in mind that your blasphemy or rebellion makes a true impact towards achieving.

Hadrian Flyte

• *To me, Satanism is the freedom of self and the acceptance that our actions have tangible effects on the world around us, as opposed to some divine force interceding on our behalf. Satanism in its best form prioritizes rebellion against outmoded tradition and knowledge through exploration and challenge.*

• *I grew up in a family of disparate religiosity and found myself incapable of settling in any theistic tradition because they were all clamoring for the same overworked landscape.*

Left-hand-path practices appealed to me as they were focused on personal accountability as opposed to the right-hand path's subservience to a higher power. Nontheistic Satanism appealed to me in particular because of its focus on self-improvement through knowledge and compassion.

• *Satanism is a religion like any other, if you realize the true intent of religion is often community building and solidification. Satanic communities are integral to the experience and (sometimes despite their best efforts to the contrary) provide open and inclusive spaces. Being able to talk about religious perspective in a group of like-minded people is what I've wanted since I first got an uneasy feeling about theism.*

For now I've discarded most formalized "observances" like sabbaths. However, I think there's some charm in ritualistic practice like holding some days in regard like holidays or resting days. As organized Satanism grows, I think there will be increased interest in the mechanics of religious communities that aren't necessarily bad if they aren't used to oppress congregations and stifle independence.

• *Community service is a major part of my practice. I firmly believe that to make things better for the individual (self) you must be an active part of your community. In the future, I hope to lead my Satanic group in tending a community garden and doing local clean-ups, as well as participating in TST's fundraising initiatives.*

Being active in your community is one of the easiest ways to help yourself and is exceedingly Satanic in times where theistic authority is doubling down on destructive individualism and means-testing for aid.

- *As of writing this I am a co-organizer for Friends of the Satanic Temple Arkansas. I hope in the coming years we can become a full Chapter of The Satanic Temple.*

TST's community and commitment to reproductive rights and bodily autonomy are major factors of why I'm here. I am transgender and finding an accepting religious community can be difficult.

- *Ritual is a focusing element for me. Some days it is the quiet comfort of sinking back in a chair in a dim room listening to an album, other days it is meticulously writing down the poisonous aspects of my thoughts and burning them.*

Ritual is as useful as it feels to you and doesn't require a lot of pomp and circumstance. But if mood lighting and incense help you to refocus or recharge, include them! I'm somewhat modest with my practice and don't go beyond flowers, incense, and the occasional candle. However, I'm always open to learning about other people's rituals and incorporating those ideas into my methods.

I frequently read Tarot cards. I don't give them any supernatural significance but find the supposed meaning of a card can help me to explore my feelings from a different perspective than I might have previously. Tarot is just another tool available to those who enjoy going through motions to bring focus back onto the self.

- *In addition, literature and the pursuit of knowledge are integral to my form of Satanism. I jokingly refer to myself as a Book Satanist but my personal library is built upon a "forbidden knowledge" aesthetic. I collect books on queer history, decadent literature, Satanic literature, biographies — you name it. Access to knowledge should be available to everyone and if my small library can help even one other person, I've succeeded.*

Of course this comes with a lot of awkward conversations when people stumble across my books on occultism and poisons. Having an understanding of something does not mean you practice or utilize it. We as a society should engage with ideas we don't agree with for the sake of understanding others and challenging our beliefs.

- *As a Satanist, there have been some unexpected challenges along the way. I didn't think a religion focused on knowledge and self-improvement would have so much opposition in terms of being "serious," but that's a major hurdle in the greater atheistic/nontheistic world. Mention you're a Satanist to the wrong person and you're in for an afternoon of smug flexing on how moronic talking about the devil is if you want to be taken seriously.*

Never mind the wealth of historical examples of Satan as a rebellious figure being a vital rebellious effort. For some, it's just "so cringe" to be associated with the concept; it's too hard to handle.

I'd honestly prefer theistic hostility over the exhausting efforts of some of the atheistic community to uphold the notion that doing anything in a religious context is poisonous without examining the machinery of religion as chosen community vs. societal control.

- *One of the most rewarding aspects of Satanism is making new and wonderful friends. Satanists can be a cantankerous bunch, but I'm also somewhat cantankerous myself. The reality is that Satanists are passionate about their interests and beliefs and can be seen as "too much" for the general public.*

I have historically had a difficult time making new and long-lasting friendships. Through Satanism, I've made several new connections that already feel like they will last for years to come.

- *For those just starting their Satanic journey, I'd say "Read everything you possibly can." Consume theistic, nontheistic, academic, and casual works on the topic of Satanism and the world. Never stop reaching out and exploring new topics and striving to understand how others view the world. Your perspective will not only broaden but you'll be prepared to discuss and even defend your religion with more success than someone who only reads what immediately aligns with their worldview.*

It's Satanic as fuck to challenge yourself. Do it.

Luna Ereshkigal

• My personal definition of Satanism is a bit complex. In a negative view, anyone who is outside of the belief system of some fundamentalist monotheists is potentially considered Satanic by them just for not believing. A person can be going about their day — gardening, commuting, grocery shopping — and they are a depraved Satanist just for not believing. That is a negative view, but I rather like it, as it makes me feel much more interesting when I am feeding my cat. I have heard people say that Satanism is only about negation — just taking a cross and turning it upside down. But in some ways, negation can be constructive. I like to embrace the idea of "the adversary" — to be a check on unethical behavior, to say "no" and not just go along with injustice. Negation can be the power of protest and working to kick the legs out from under unjust authority. This pushing back against what is wrong helps to make space for what is just — working toward an ethical way of living in this world with other people.

• I came to Satanism in large part because I was eager to learn. I was raised Jewish. I went to Hebrew school three days a week through high school. I was a good student, and I appreciated much of the ethical focus of Judaism, but I was alienated from monotheism by actually reading all of the Jewish Bible – which is a much different picture than you get from selected Bible stories (although many of those were problematic as well). Even as a small child I was fascinated by witchcraft, and in adulthood I have done some Pagan and Wiccan practice, but I always seemed to run up against an expectation of some sort of literal belief — in astrology or in god-forms — when I just don't believe those things. Also, the Pagan/Wiccan community tends to be more crunchy-granola whereas I am more goth.

- *Satanism fills the role of religion for me in providing both precepts (TST's Seven Tenets) and also iconography that resonate with me. A religion does not need a deity, let alone a vengeful patriarchal god. Satanism allows for an ethical focus without a framework of condemning people as having an essentially sinful or defective nature that needs redeeming. A Satanist can have a sense of awe regarding the world as it is, and also revere themselves and others as they are. The natural can be sacred in itself without any need for supernatural trappings. Satanism is more like a contemplative religion in terms of developing self-awareness and perspective, but one that has an emphasis on turning outward toward activism and concrete action in the world. I still consider myself a witch in the Wiccan/Pagan sense, and I enjoy the stories, myths, and iconography as sources of insight.*

- *Activism and community service were what drew me to Satanism. Satanism seems to recognize a duty to work to change or dismantle systems that are unjust, and to also help others in a concrete way — to walk the talk.*

- *I have been a member of The Satanic Temple since 2017. I really enjoy the camaraderie, and also the wealth of knowledge and perspectives from the other members. It is one of the first places I have been where people "get" me. Also, being part of a group allows for impactful, coordinated action that I could not effect by acting singly.*

- *Ritual is part of my practice. Since I have a Pagan/Wiccan affiliation, I have an altar with Anubis for nightly meditation, and I have my own rituals for full and dark moons, as well as the sabbats for the turning of the year. Satanic ritual has been more communal — participating in protests or political actions, or formal rituals at gatherings.*

- *I am a nerd, so as part of my practice I enjoy reading and studying. I have been doing my own Satanic Bible study for the last couple of years — reading the Bibles (Jewish and Christian) with a Satanic*

bent. It's fascinating to see the bits of pre-monotheistic folklore that peep through, and see as through a looking-glass the world that might have developed if Abrahamic religions had not taken over the Western world. By seeing the dystopia that has occurred for what it is, the imagination can spark with what could be.

• As far as challenges go, I have been lucky in that I did not have a fundamentalist upbringing. In Hebrew school I liked to try to stump the Rabbis with questions about the Bible and they were not angry — even the Hasidic Rabbi seemed to just be glad that a student was actually reading the Bible and engaging with the text! So I grew up in an environment where questioning was OK, although I was also considered a weirdo. I also live in a very liberal city, so there is no problem with my friends knowing. I work in a conservative work-place so I cannot be "out" there — but I take pleasure in doing my Satanic Bible study during my lunch breaks, probably appearing to be quite devout, but my more conservative coworkers would probably not appreciate the notes I take.

• The most rewarding aspect of being a Satanist has been "finding my tribe" — finding a group of good people. It is also a relief to have a religion in which I do not have to try to explain away repugnant parts of scripture (as in Abrahamic religions), or contend with a lack of literal belief in such things as astrology that put me out of step with other Pagans/witches.

• I would encourage anyone starting their Satanic journey to follow their own path and find what is right for them. It's great if they find all they need in Satanism. It's also OK if they explore it, and then decide another path is a better fit — that's great, too! It's also fine if Satanism meets some needs but not all, and if people want to be a Sa-tanist and also be involved in another religious tradition or activist group. It may not be realistic to expect one group or religion to be all things to all people. There are no jealous gods here, so you can keep exploring until you find your way!

Harry Hoofcloppen

• *For me, Satanism has been about fully acknowledging my own autonomy, my own strength, and my own worth ... topics that have been difficult for me. Satanism has helped me grow and stand resolute on those points. TST Satanism in particular reinforces everything I believe about inclusiveness, about kindness, and about our responsibilities to each other as members of a community.*

• *I grew up in the small-town Midwest, surrounded by Judeo-Christian mythology. I was born into an agnostic family that didn't try to teach anything, but let the neighbor family take us kids to Sunday School. I was just about to the point of getting baptized when I was kicked out of Sunday school in part because I wouldn't sing the right words to the songs.*

From a young age, the Bible stories demonstrated to me a gross injustice with too many obvious caveats and loopholes to be evidence of a "loving God," and innocent questions usually got put to bed with answers like "Well, God works in mysterious ways." None of it was intellectually satisfying. I wound up waffling between agnostic and atheist for decades, but I eventually settled into resolute non-supernaturalism. Somewhere along the way, I overheard someone talking about Satanists, saying "They think that Satan was the good guy." This struck me as an odd thing to say, but it simmered in the back of my brain for many years. I had resigned myself to being a lonely atheist and secular humanist, but I always felt something was missing.

I first heard about The Satanic Temple probably in 2018 with the showcasing of the Baphomet statue at the Arkansas Capitol for TST's Religious Freedom rally. I instantly fell in love with it and started learning more about Satanism in general, but TST in particular, especially after understanding the difference between TST and the Church of Satan. I soon contacted TST Colorado, and I quickly realized that

APPENDIX 1 • SATANIC VOICES

257

this was the religious community I've longed for all my life.

- *When I joined TST, I was still dubious at the role of ritual; I had decided I was too rational for it to be a useful placebo. I was wrong! With the realization that I needed all of it, including the ritualistic parts, that's when I fully embraced Satanism as a religion that fills a hole I've felt all my lonely atheist life.*

- *In truth, I found TST by way of its activism, so I cringe when I hear people pick on those who joined for that or by way of the "Hail Satan?" movie. People coming in for those things need to understand that this is a religion first and activism is a secondary byproduct, so if that's not okay maybe TST isn't for them. But I think a lot of people come to us for the activism and suddenly realize there's been a TST-shaped hole in their lives all along.*

- *I am overjoyed to be part of my local TST Chapter and wider global TST community. I have never encountered a more accepting, more constructive community than my TST Satanfam. Every collection of humans has its squabbles, but this community has helped me grow, learn, understand myself, and love myself like no other. I am deeply grateful to know so many amazing people.*

- *As far as ritual goes, when I'm stressed, I use a form of meditation to try to relax and recenter. I occasionally do destruction rituals and veneration rituals at my altar as the mood fits.*

- *In addition to those elements of my practice mentioned above, I have explored the rough edges of my understanding of the Tenets. Of note, I explored Tenet 4 by building a blasphemous robot Jesus sculpture, and I do everything I can to give back to my TST community by helping out in my chapter, helping run an online forum, and producing video of rituals and other content for TST-TV. It makes me happy to help others Satan.*

- *I haven't encountered too many challenges due to my Satanism. My family accepts my Satanism even if they don't understand it, and for that I am grateful. As a small business owner, I used to worry what the local community would think if they found out. But the longer I spend Sataning, the more confident I am about it.*

- *The single most rewarding aspect of Satanism has been finally acknowledging and accepting who I am — finally loving my weird self. I am also tremendously grateful to find such a strong community of people helping each other learn and grow and love themselves. It has been an amazing ride.*

- *To those just starting out, I'd say: Learn, learn, learn. Try to approach everything with curiosity and joy. Try everything and keep the parts you like. Embrace yourself and learn to love yourself.*

Jason Lloyd

• *For me, the biggest hallmark of Satanism is personal accountability, plus holding yourself to a standard and applying reason and logic to a situation instead of faith and mysticism to help guide one's actions and views. It's also about equality and standing up to arbitrary authority.*

• *My religious background is varied really. My dad's side of the family is very Pentecostal, but my immediate family was never very religious. I've always grown up more or less the black sheep of the family, since that's the side that I more closely relate to.*

• *Up till now, I've never been overly religious, at least not in any Judeo-Christian sense. I very much consider myself a religious person now though, due to my Satanism. Like most people of any faith, my firmly-held religious beliefs help guide my response and opinions on the world around me and how I interact with it.*

• *I wouldn't say I'm much of an activist, but I do like to work towards causes that promote equality and freedom of choices. LGBTQ+ rights as well as reproductive rights are things that I'm passionate about.*

• *I'm a co-founder and co-organizer of Satanic Kentucky. For me, it's a great sense of community. For so long, being a Satanist was almost lonely in a lot of ways, so to have this group of equally passionate and like-minded individuals is really refreshing and relieving in a lot of ways. I've always envied that sense of community that church-goers experience and have, and now I don't have to envy as I have it myself.*

• *For me, ritual doesn't play a role personally. I find it fascinating, and would love to better expand my use of it at some point, but I've never found it to be something that personally deeply resonated.*

• *I'm big into Satanic literature. I've got a William Blake painting tattooed on my ribs, so obviously I'm a huge fan of his. I also have a quote from Paradise Lost tattooed on my arm. I guess you could say my Satanic interests and pursuits are more "scholarly" in that regard, maybe? That said, I'm always looking for ways to expand my Satanic practices and I'm very open to new ideas and techniques.*

• *I've been lucky in that the challenges I've faced as a Satanist have been really mild, which I guess is weird considering I live in a red state. As I said above, for the longest time, it was rather lonely being a Satanist. This was before The Satanic Temple, and so there wasn't a sense of community like there is now. It was definitely something I wasn't nearly as open about as I am now. But more and more, those various challenges are fading away and more people are open to hearing about my beliefs, which is awesome.*

• *As far as the rewards of being a Satanic go, it's very liberating to simply be yourself. It's difficult to put into words how refreshing it is to wake up every day, knowing that you and you alone are accountable for how your day's going to go. There's no fear of mythical boogeymen or angry deities watching over your every move. I just wake up, and face the day, and that's that.*

• *One thing I always ask of anyone who's beginning their journey in Satanism is, "How do you think a god should be?" And then I challenge them to embrace and embody those traits. If you feel a god should be just and loving, then instead of projecting those traits upon a fictional character, embody them yourself. Remember, you and you alone are accountable for your actions and deeds. Take credit where it's due, and take ownership of your mistakes just as quickly. We all have the ability to shape our own realities, so make yours the one you want!*

Mazikeen Morningstar

• I define Satanism as embracing the rebellious spirit, always questioning everything, having a never-satisfied thirst for knowledge, treating others better than you want to be treated, and a splash of aesthetic.

• I was raised in the United Pentecostal Church International. As a teenager I had been drawn to all of the things the church said was Satanic. If they said something was Satanic I had to check it out. I guess it's like when you see a wet paint sign, like how do you not touch it just to make sure? Ultimately that curiosity, sparked by the church, led me to become a Satanist.

• Growing up, religion was everything. In the UPCI religion, everything has to be for the glory of god. All I was allowed to think about 24/7 was god and religion. Because of my conditioning as a child I view most things I do as Satanic. I've also kept some of the funny language that comes with Christianity. I say things like "Satan knows" or "what the heaven is this." I discarded judging others. In UPCI you view yours as the only correct religion and everyone else is inferior to you. I constantly walked around thinking I was superior to everyone who wasn't UPCI. I discarded that rather quickly after becoming a Satanist. I realized we are all the same species and we're all just trying to make it on this rock.

• Activism was the first thing that drew me to Satanism. I admit that I initially became a Satanist because of the activism I heard of on the Thinking Atheist podcast. The religion aspect grew on me over time. I have toned down my view on activism only because I'm studying and learning so much about the religion. For community service, I've helped out at the local abortion clinic. The parking garage is around the block from the clinic and the clients would have to walk down crowded sidewalks full of protesters. I and others would park our cars at the garage with shuttle signs on our passenger doors. We'd drive *the clients to the clinic so they'd feel safer. As a Satanist I can't stand to see people being harassed. The shuttle program was put on hold due to the COVID-19 outbreak.*

- *I'm part of the Kentucky Friends of The Satanic Temple group. This has turned out to be really huge for me. When I was a kid, a lot of members of our church would go out to dinner after Sunday morning service. We also had a summer picnic potluck every year at a park. Every month, the Kentucky Satanic community has a social event at a restaurant. We even had a potluck at a park in Lexington for Halloween in 2019. I had no clue how much I missed the religious community until I started going to these social events. I feel like this has filled a void I didn't realize I had.*

- *I'm kind of new to ritual. The first ritual I learned about, as I'm sure is the case with most Satanists, is the Destruction ritual. I found that to be very powerful. I try to perform the Destruction ritual at least once a month. I also really want to partake in an Unbaptism ritual. I was coerced into being baptized when I was 13 and it would be hugely symbolic to undo that.*

- *As far as other elements of practice go, I have an altar in my living room. It's mostly for aesthetics but I also use it during my rituals. Growing up, music played a big part in my Christianity. I find music is powerful in regards to Satanism also. Music helps express my Satanism. I like to read Satanic literature like "The Revolt of the Angels," but it doesn't stop there. I really enjoy science and I view that as Satanic also. The church killed people in the past for heresy so I kinda feel like I'm honoring those people by learning about dinosaurs, space, biology, and climate.*

- *The biggest challenge I've faced as a Satanist is having to keep my religion hidden from my family. I'm transgender and they already don't accept that. Satanism would definitely push what little relationship I have with my parents to end.*

- *The biggest advantage I've found is definitely the community. Satanists always lift each other up. If I'm ever feeling down I know I can reach out to my community and they'll be there to encourage me. Also, Satanists don't treat me different because I'm transgender. I'm treated as a human and I hadn't really had that until I joined a Satanic community. Also, I guess just embracing who I am all together. I've always enjoyed D&D, emo fashion, metal music, video games like Dante's Inferno and Diablo, and of course Pokemon — all of the things associated with Satanism. As a Satanist I don't feel taboo enjoying those things anymore.*

- *My tip for those just starting out is: Find a Satanic community and embrace it. These are the nicest, most helpful, coolest people you will ever meet. Ask questions and have fun. Definitely read "The Revolt of The Angels."*

Amy Stanton

• *I would personally define my Satanism as my own journey in the pursuit of knowledge. It is a philosophical belief system that sees Satan as a symbol of rebellion against tyrannical authority, and not as a literal being.*

• *I was raised in an agnostic household. My parents were polar opposites. My mother was caring and loving; my father was selfish and abusive. As a teen, I wanted a way to escape my father. I stumbled across a website that spoke about Satan as the adversary, and a rejection of tyrannical authority. As a teen, that was my father. As an adult, it is the philosophy and community that drew me to Satanism.*

• *Satanism is my religion. It is about deeply held beliefs in science, compassion, community, and rational thought, and also about discarding the notion that religion has to include superstitious belief or worship of a supernatural deity. My Satanism is nontheistic and I do not believe in the supernatural in any form.*

• *My practice does not focus primarily on activism, but it often comes naturally because of my deeply held beliefs in compassion and the pursuit of justice. It serves as a way for me to give back to the world what Satanism has given me.*

• *I am part of a Satanic community; in it I have found a family. It has given me a new lease on life and has helped me grow as a person. Watching other people grow in the community has also given me a great sense of pride. I gain more knowledge by learning from/with my peers.*

• *For me, ritual is largely something personal. I do not have any set times and instead I use rituals when I feel that I need them (for example in times of great stress). I also engage in group rituals as a way to connect with my community.*

• *The other main elements that are part of my Satanic practice are my altar, books and music. My altar is a personal space that represents different parts of myself and my journey. Books are to further my knowledge. Music is a way of expression through song.*

- *The majority of challenges I have faced have been from preconceived notions about what Satanism is. There is sometimes a misconception that Satanists are evil, a cult, and that the myths from the Satanic Panic are true. It is not often that this happens, as most people I've interacted with have understood that isn't what my Satanism is about.*

- *The most rewarding aspect of being a Satanist is the growth I have had as a person. Not only has it helped me in my personal journey, but it's helped me in my relationships and has given me the courage to progress in life. The community I have helped to create with my fellow Satanists is also one of the most rewarding. Watching it blossom and grow is a beautiful thing. It has also opened a whole other realm of conversation with my mother (who I am very close to), who enjoys conversing with me on topics and even now has a Baphomet statue in her living room.*

- *My tips for beginners: Not all journeys are the same. You might not completely fit in one organisation or another, and that's okay. As Satanists, we must continue to learn and evolve. Do as much research as you can, but at a pace that is comfortable and that suits your needs. Above all, be compassionate, be rational and know that people are fallible. This is your journey, and you've got this.*

Omen Cerberus

• *I believe Satanism for me should be the pursuit of knowledge and freedom of Will. I do not believe in a literal Satan and I believe that Satanism should be divorced from all superstition. It should also be spooky and freak out the squares.*

• *I grew up in an atheist household in TX. I went to various Christian churches as a kid out of curiosity. I picked up a Satanic Bible at age 15 or so. It had hexes and curses in it and contained a lot of woo. I was mystified by it. I identified as a Satanist for a year but never came out to anyone but one close friend. All my other friends in high school became Christians one by one. I got suckered into Christianity at age 18 due to the peer pressure of prospective isolation stemming from non-conformity. I buckled. I was a radical evangelical Christian for a decade. I joined the Church of Satan ("CoS") after that out of spite because I was bitter about my experiences in the church. I was in the CoS for about 4 years but couldn't take all the white pride being espoused.*

I became a militant atheist in college. I joined an atheist church named Sunday Assembly LA in 2015. I went but it wasn't super exciting for me. SALA invited the Chapter Heads of TST LA to speak in 2016. I was enamored. I fell in love with the Tenets that they spoke about. They never contacted me even though I signed up to join the LA Chapter. TST LA became defunct shortly after. I finally saw the Arkansas Rally in the news and decided to join the TST Official Forum on Facebook in 2018. I discovered and studied the TST website and voraciously read everything on it. I loved every bit of it. It felt like coming home. I've been a proud member ever since.

• *Having a church family was important to me as a Christian and that camaraderie still exists for me with my TST friends. When I'm doing rituals with them, it gives me a feeling like I'm with family. I dropped the proselytizing and looking down my nose at people.*

• *I absolutely love serving the communities that my Chapter represents.*

They are vital to my Satanic practice because I feel that living my best life through the Tenets demands helping the less fortunate and the under-represented. My heart explodes with joy knowing that my Chapter has helped and donated to women's shelters, homeless shelters, food pantries, animal shelters, books for prisons, LGBTQ+ programs, programs for abused children, clean-up of beaches and parks, etc. That is as close to sacred acts of worship that I can get as a nontheistic Satanist.

- *I'm a Co-founder and Co-Chapter Head of TST Southern California. I'm the CEO and President of a 501(c)(3) Satanic religious charity. I'm a Chapter Head Liaison for several "Friends of TST" groups (FoGs) in the western United States. I'm an admin of the support group Military Friends of The Satanic Temple. I'm the founder and admin of the Spanish language group Amigos Latines del Templo Satánico. I also serve on various temporary committees for the International Council whenever they ask.*

I get the joy and satisfaction of helping people and animals in my region of SoCal. I get a sense of pride for helping various FoGs become Chapters. I feel honored to serve IC when they ask. I love helping the Latin community because a lot of them were forced into religion against their will. I love serving veterans who are also TST members or allies. I also get appreciation from my Chapter members and my Council who are always there for me. I love them and couldn't do it without them.

- *Being an atheist for many years prior to being a Satanist in The Satanic Temple, I didn't understand rituals. I thought they were silly and had supernatural elements to them. But now that I've been exposed to them from this new perspective as a member of TST, I find them fun and cathartic. They are not based in magic or secret esoteric mysticism. They're meaningful and can be quite touching at times.*

- *Part of my practice is that I'm a vocalist in a black metal band. My Satanic art involves writing blasphemous lyrics and exploring dark subject matter. My band's name is Stygiophilia. It is a term used to* *describe a sexual disorder for the sexual arousal of the idea of burning in Hell. That's fuckin' metal. \m/*

I also enjoy books that deal with Satanic history or classic Satanism. I've been busy as of late and haven't been reading a lot, but I'm enjoying audiobooks and listening to podcasts on Satanism.

I'm in the process of building a personal altar. It's not completed yet.

- *Years ago, when I was a member of the Church of Satan, I came out. I was kicked out of my apartment and people were afraid of me. I learned then that there was a stigma to Satanism and it was difficult to educate people. I was a bit of an asshole then and that probably wasn't helping me either. I figured out early that if you identify as a Satanist, you'll eternally be questioned about it. Usually in a redundant fashion. That was my experience.*

  Today, I'm a closet Satanist. I don't talk about it at work. So no one really knows. Off of work, I dress in a metalhead style and I don't hide my Satanic attire. I think most people don't put 2 and 2 together and figure out that I'm a Satanist. They just see some metalhead dude with pentagrams, inverted crosses, and goats everywhere and shrug it off.

- *Starting a Chapter of The Satanic Temple has been incredibly rewarding. The friends I've made and relationships I've forged will likely last a lifetime. What's even better is that the community keeps growing. I'm getting new friends all the time now. That love and friendship makes it all worth it.*

- *For those just beginning to look into Satanism, I'd say to scour the amazing resources of www.thesatanictemple.com. That site has a wealth of information on it, from recommended reading material to basic fundamentals of Satanism to official events. After that, joining a local group helps to see those Tenets and mission put into practice. Joining a community of like-minded individuals is always refreshing and one can learn a few things from the elder members and have fun helping people in your area. An openness to learning is key.*

Coming Out as a Satanist

Being openly Satanist can be a risky proposition. Though as TST has grown, more and more people have heard of it and support its values and actions, at the same time we're also seeing a new form of Satanic Panic hysteria rear its ugly head. The recent rise of the QAnon conspiracy has convinced millions that those in their government and Hollywood are part of a secret Satan-worshipping, baby-eating cult. Being out about your Satanism can result in discrimination, fear, and even potential danger.

With all that said, however, many Satanists do decide to "come out" about their Satanism, despite the risk. Others are outed against their will, but have accepted it and even found positives. I interviewed a number of Satanists who had come out about their Satanism. Their experiences varied greatly. In many cases, life went by mostly unchanged, whereas in others, coming out made family relationships hard or created other difficulties. No one mentioned prejudice at their job or job loss, however. There were some major negatives here and there — for instance, one practitioner had Child Protective Services called on her — but for the most part, the positives of coming out far outweighed the negatives.

None of the interviewees looked down on those who couldn't make their Satanism public; everyone accepted that some Satanists are in situations where coming out could have heavy negative consequences or even be dangerous. Only you can decide if it's safe. But everyone offered tips for those considering coming out.

I asked the interview respondents these questions about their coming out experiences:

- When did you come out as a Satanist?
- Who have you come out to or been outed to — who in your life knows you're a Satanist?
- How did you come out as a Satanist? Was it intentional, or were you outed involuntarily?
- What prompted you to come out?
- Do you use a pseudonym for your Satanic activities? If so, why?
- Did coming out affect your relationship with your family, your partner and/or your children, and if so how?
- Did coming out affect your relationship with your work colleagues, and if so how?
- What negative repercussions did you face as a result of coming out as a Satanist?
- What positive changes did you experience in your life after coming out?
- What advice might you give someone who wants to come out? Do you have any tips on dealing with misunderstanding and discrimination?

Ava Noir

- I came out as a Satanist at age 15, but it's still ongoing.

- Family, friends, and random people who see my tattoo all know I'm a Satanist ... just not my current coworkers.

- My family found out about my Satanism by accident. My sister saw an exacto knife in the back niche of an art book I was making my freshman year. Wrongly assuming I was cutting myself, she told my mom where to find the knife while we were out of the house. The art book also contained Satanic symbols as well as Anton LaVey's Satanic Sins, Rules of the Earth, and other passages from the Satanic Bible.

  Anyone who becomes Facebook friends with me will eventually stumble upon a Satanic post or could see my religion on my 'about me' section. And as for others, I don't openly tell people, but if they see the sigil of Baphomet tattoo on my back, or if I wear any Satanic jewelry or clothing, then that tends to out me.

- I came out because I never wanted to remain in the broom closet.

- I use a pseudonym for protection while meeting with people I don't know. I have one profile. My old high school friends, distant family, and former coworkers all get to see my Satanic posts. Some have chosen to part ways after those posts. Auf wiedersehen.

- Coming out did have a huge negative impact on my family relationships. My parents were devastated, and my mother still tries preaching to me, 13 years later. We haven't had the same relationship since I converted.

- I know at my last job, my tattoo got exposed plenty while changing into my work shirt. I also happened to mention loving all the little "praise Satan"s and such in the new Sabrina series. Soon after, I *found out there were rumours going around about me regarding Satanism. No one seemed to treat me any differently though.*

- *Back when I was 15 and my sister inadvertently outed me, my mom went through my whole room and took away all of my journals, music, and books. She threw away some of my clothing, posters and art on my wall, and forced me to go to a church camp that summer. She eventually gave my books, journals, and music back (later that summer, except my Marilyn Manson CD that I got back at age 20 when she found it again). I am still missing a journal or two, unfortunately.*

- *Since coming out, I've gained a sense of honesty in my being. I've also gained many friends who have similar beliefs.*

- *My tip for those considering coming out is: If people don't like you for who you are, they don't deserve to be in your life. Period.*

Adam

• I came out fairly recently, just a little over two weeks ago.

• After posting everything publicly on my social media, everyone now knows that I am a Satanist.

• Coming out was very much intentional. I have been a member of TST for years. While I was unable to attend the meetings and events with chapters nearest to me I still felt like I was a part of something special. When the documentary was released it inspired me and gave me the confidence as a Satanist to realize that a difference can be made and those who don't agree with what I believe don't matter, for the bigger picture is far more important than what others would think of me. I decided to order my card and certificate from the TST website. It was the day I received it in the mail that I made a public post on my social media accounts about my excitement on receiving the certificate. It was a very interesting few days that followed, to say the least.

• I was inspired to come out by finally feeling empowered for who I truly am and by wanting to be a part of something I can get behind — something that can make a difference for everyone and not just the select.

• I use all of my personal accounts for my Satanic activities. At this point I have nothing to hide and I am proud of who I am and who I strive to be.

• To be completely honest I was nervous to post because of my parents more than anything. Although they're not church going people, they do believe in God. They have never made it an agenda or forced the idea of God on us growing up. They made it our choice — however, with the stereotype of the term "Satanist," I was afraid they would jump to conclusions. I was surprised that after talking everything *over with them they were very accepting of my decisions. They also expressed a few views they had always thought were unfair about the laws of the church and so on. It was a very positive experience for me with them. My wife knew I was a Satanist long before I went public and always said people should believe in whatever they want. My Facebook, however, was not a great turn out. Many jumped to the stereotype and took me off of their Facebooks and other social media. That is fine. I would prefer to not have close-minded people in my life like that anyways so in the end, it all works out.*

- *I would have to say coming out did not affect my relationship with my work colleagues. Work is work for me and personal life is separate. If I ever were approached by a co-worker about it, I would say just that and allow them the option to talk about it in a non-work environment if they did have questions.*

- *I can say that nothing super negative has happened yet due to my coming out, but I am starting a group in my area so we will see how things transpire as things develop.*

- *Just the fact that I accept who I am and can now empower what I truly believe is the most gratifying part of coming out. People come and go but being who you are is what's most important. Those who love you will accept you.*

- *To those just beginning their Satanic journey, I'd say: No matter the outcome, be true to you and no one else. This world forces people to hide behind society as a pawn to serve and obey. Life was never meant to be this way nor should it. Always respect yourself and what you believe. That should never be taken away from you nor should you feel any less for it. The ones that stay matter and the ones that don't were never meant to. Perspective is everything. Just be you.*

Mel Michael

- I think I've always known I was a Satanist since I was a kid but couldn't actually define it until I came across Lucien Greaves' TST philosophy last year. I was raised very religious by my parents who identified with The Latter Day Saints and Methodist churches. But I never felt comfortable going to these churches and actually loathed it every time we had to. I tried to make it a positive experience by justifying my attendance with the fact that we participated in a few youth group activities (our conservative upbringing also meant that we were not really allowed to go to non-religious friend's homes or playdates etc). That was one of the few times we could just be kids and 'have fun'.

- I have never had to state that I'm a Satanist to my family or very close friends, as they've always known I was a humanist with an atheist bent. They do not recognise any concepts outside of their religious beliefs, so they do not ask me about mine. They love me for who I am and not what I choose to believe in (even though it is very much a part of who I am lol). I am very vocal about my aversion to any organised religion though, especially of the Abrahamic variety. So they would rather avoid that topic of conversation altogether as they find my ideas upsetting. For instance, my stance on being pro-choice with abortion rights is totally against their beliefs. They know how I feel about it. I know how they feel about it. It does not make us love each other any less. Tolerance is key to maintaining a healthy relationship with each other. A few parents at my child's school avoid us like the plague. But that's okay, as it weeds out intolerant people from our life and that's a positive in my books!

- I don't really advertise my Satanism as I am quite a private person anyway. Just like my sexual orientation, if I feel comfortable with *the party/ies in a relevant conversation, then I am happy to state my belief system.*

- *I do not necessarily feel like it was a 'coming out' of sorts as I am generally quite an upfront person. So if it comes up, I will happily converse about it. If it doesn't, then it doesn't. Although I must admit, I do get a kick out of the reactions sometimes. I am one of those conservatively-dressed, librarian-looking single mothers who have everything in its place. I am always gifting baked goodies, and wearing very feminine, pastel/light-coloured dresses. Always up for a coffee, hug or a shoulder to cry on. People have joked that I am like a 'Stepford Mom.' So when someone eventually finds out that I am Satanist, the facial response is gold. I can literally see them utterly confused or in disbelief, trying to reconcile that with their perception of me.*

- *I don't use a pseudonym for my Satanic activities. I am what I am. Take it or leave it, I don't care.*

- *My ex partner was a narcissist. Being Satanic actually snapped me out of that awful rollercoaster ride and I am thankful for that. It also helps me co-parent without hate or bitterness, and he respects that side of me now. My family would love me even if I turned out to be a serial killer. My parents and I make it a policy to love without conditions. It has taken a long time to get to this point and that's partially due to my Satanic beliefs. Our bond is stronger than ever.*

- *My Satanism hasn't really come up in many work conversations but I think that's mostly because I work from home for a company, so I only chat to colleagues via messenger and it's mainly about work, funnily enough! I think I have only told two of my colleagues and they still happily chat with me when we're on the same shift together, so I don't think they hold it against me!*

- *I am very fortunate not to have experienced any negativity, other than from fellow judgemental parents from my child's school who opt not to associate with our family (which is a blessing in itself, trust me).*

- *Since coming out as a Satanist, my life has been blessed with so many wonderful things that it's ALL positive. Being a Satanist hasn't had any significant effect on my life other than being able to finally define my belief system that resonates with my values and lifestyle. My child is also being raised this way but there are no hard and fast rules. If my child decides to follow a different path, it will not affect my love or respect for them.*

- *In giving advice, I can only speak about what has felt right for my situation. I do not try to 'defend' Satanism at all, as I feel that demeans the basic tenets of what it is about for me. Haters are going to hate, no matter what you say or do. It is their purpose. It is not my job to change their minds about Satanism. But if they would like an opportunity to be enlightened on the subject, then sure, I am happy to engage. However I cannot give oxygen to people who just want to grandstand/humiliate me or my family because they cannot allow for other perspectives. Humans nowadays generally only have so many years to live (if we're lucky), and I just don't have a minute to spare for that kind of toxicity. My time is precious.*

Michael Brewer

- *I came out as a Satanist about a year ago.*

- *My family, friends, and co-workers all know I'm a Satanist.*

- *The fact that I'm a Satanist has come up in conversation as well as connections picking up on my social media posts. I made my intentions known about joining TST a while back, so it was definitely intentional, but I don't go wave a Satanic flag in people's faces (except when the Christian flag is waved in mine) — but I also don't hide who I am.*

- *A number of experiences came together to prompt me to "come out" as a Satanist. I've been an out as an atheist since middle school and have been known to be very vocal about it. I refuse to be a doormat for Christian privilege. In fact, being a public atheist attracted its fair share of misery when I was enlisted in the Marine Corps. I remember writing "atheist" in the blank on the paperwork you receive at boot camp that requests your religion and receiving identification tags stating I was non-denominational Christian. When I had the opportunity to stamp my own and placed "ATHEIST" on it, I subsequently had it ripped from my neck during an inspection. I've resisted forced prayer during formations and been forced to speak with Naval chaplains. During this experience I found that my ability to not back down and be quiet led to others not feeling alone and even finding their own voice. Yes, Virginia — there are atheists (and Satanists) in foxholes. So it's one part being a rebel and fighting tyranny and it's one part helping others either battle that loneliness that stems from being in the fringes or to pick up the Satanic standard and carry it into battle beside me.*

- *I do not use a pseudonym or separate social media accounts for my Satanic activities, though I dig a lot of the pseudonyms out there. I completely understand the why behind it, and since I am married and have children, I've thought about it, but I'm spoiled by my white, straight, male privilege and would find it exhausting to try to separate my identity and juggle accounts.*

- *My Satanism has affected my family interactions, though not to a devastating degree. My partner is an atheist, but she sure doesn't like it when I express parts of my identity that could cause friction between her and her friends, family, and co-workers. We have a standing arrangement (predating my conversion to Satanism) to approve any incoming friend requests from her peeps for this reason. For my children, it's just a natural evolution of my atheism.*

- *I actually work at a fairly progressive company, so co-workers haven't expressed anything nor has anything changed in the way they communicate. I should note that I work remotely, so for the most part have very little interaction with my co-workers.*

I've definitely received some "come to Jesus" conversations from religious friends who were tolerant of me being an atheist, but freaked the hell out when I began posting all this Satanic stuff. It's been a hard road of education and I've lost some acquaintances from my friends list, but no one I miss. Surprisingly, I've also received some ignorant responses from atheist cohorts. I attribute it to suffering [brainwashing] from artifacts of the Satanic Panic of the 80s and operating under the impression that Satanists actually worship some deity.

- *As I mentioned before, I have large amounts of privilege, and my negative repercussions are most likely far less than other Satanic sisters, brothers, and nonbinary siblings might suffer. I work remotely for a progressive company. My spouse and children are on board. My family can deal; I don't care if they approve or not — besides, the last 30 years I've been out as an atheist with all of them. I'm not the Incredible Hulk, but my physical presence and flesh color usually means people do not threaten me with violence (and if they did, my background lends itself to dealing with such things). I even live remotely in Montana where neighbors are few and far between*

... but I'd probably get a few chiding words if I wore a Satanic shirt out into town. We'll see what happens if we can ever muster enough Satanists into doing a public social gathering.

- *As far as positives I've noticed from coming out, I'm not sure a lot changed, but what cannot be undersold is not suffering from the anxiety of having to lie or hide my identity, thoughts, and feelings. I do the same stuff I have been doing for the last 30 years, but now officially belonging to an organization of like-minded individuals and applying pressure to seek equality in Christian supremacy is pretty positive.*

- *For Satanists considering coming out, I honestly feel that the more people that are being open about being a Satanist, the faster things will change for the better. That being said, in today's political climate, repercussions can be harsh and personal safety must be evaluated. If you have loved ones you share a space with or who are vulnerable, you need to take that into consideration and they should be the first ones you talk to, if you haven't already. Ask them for their input, letting them know about potential risks to themselves.*

When dealing with misunderstanding, you have to remain calm in the face of the sort of insanity that religion fosters. Be prepared to calmly state in facts what Satanism is and that ritual baby sacrifice is just a myth, but under no circumstance accept discrimination. Record, post, litigate if necessary.

Steven Hoffman

- I came out as a Satanist in June 2019.

- My former workplace knew, and my new workplace hasn't asked yet. I won't be hiding it, but I'm not going to go out of my way to discuss religion in the workplace. My friends on Facebook mostly know; my religious brother and sister don't know though they are on Facebook — the topic hasn't come up or hasn't been noticed by them yet.

- To come out as a Satanist, I casually started mentioning it to friends I trusted. Now I'll point it out when people bring up Christianity and ask my opinion on it.

- I came out nearly immediately when I decided I didn't believe in God anymore. I had always respected TST's work but didn't feel right calling myself a Satanic Christian, so I was merely a supporter of their works before that.

- I don't use a pseudonym for my Satanic activities.

- My wife thinks I joined a cult; she's mostly joking, but only mostly.

- Coming out didn't really affect my relationship with my work colleagues. A few welcomed the change and shared kind words, the rest just asked if that meant I could now work Sunday mornings.

- When you come out, there's always the risk of someone acting from a place of fear, but for now I haven't faced that. My work places have strong anti-discrimination rules in place that I haven't needed to use yet.

- One positive about coming out was that I just felt less hypocritical. It's one thing to support a view from the safety of your home, it's another to face the potential of criticism from holding that view publicly, or even low-key publicly as in my case.

• *To those considering coming out as a Satanist, I'd say: Only you can decide if you're in a safe place to do so. As a 500lb white male, I'm not overly concerned about my physical safety, but that isn't the case for everyone. Come out to those closest to you and have a support network in place before making any grand and sweeping declarations to the world. Always understand that just as it took you time to realize the truth, it takes others time too; be patient with those who think you're evil for turning from their God.*

Cecily Hecate

- *I came out as a Satanist in early 2018. I began attending meetings with the Albany, NY chapter of The Satanic Temple and what is now Western New York Friends of The Satanic Temple. Prior to this I was simply lurking in Facebook groups and talking with a few friends that had some facets of being in Satanism and/ or Left Hand Path.*

- *All of my partners now know I'm a Satanist, as well as most of my friends because of access to my Facebook information. My parents. My ex-spouse.*

- *During early 2018 I was also coming to understand my transgender nature and seeking to pursue medically-assisted physical transition; I was not only coming out as Satanic but also coming out as transgender and pansexual. Satanic fundamentals allowed me a confidence that enabled my gender transition; the timing of coming out as Satanic and gay is more than coincidence. I incorporated Satanic icons into my appearance at the same time that I started to change my gendered appearance. For example, I commissioned my first two tattoos at the same time: the popular sigils for Lilith (sometimes seen amongst transgender women) and Lucifer. An early partner gifted me a Baphomet necklace pendant that I wore almost daily.*

I didn't jump up on a metaphorical soap box and announce to the world that I aligned with Satanism; however I did, and still do, wear a lot of icons that reference Satanism. In the beginning I was fearful of social retribution for being outed as a Satanist, but the icons I wore were typically too abstract for most to identify the Satanic reference. For example, few people outside of Satanism recognize my Baphomet necklace or sigil of Lucifer. I enjoy this balance of wearing a lot of overt Satanic references but not having the general public immediately recognize the significance.

- *Coming out as transgender was the most frightening and destructive experience of my life. I came out as Satanic for protection — if someone was going to throw hate at me, I would much rather someone hate me for being Satanic over hating me for being transgender. If I dressed in Satanic themes, then it was easy to pawn off my non-normative gendered appearance as being "goth," which is significantly more socially palatable than being trans.*

- *I use a pseudonym to protect my family. I accept that I'll deal with hate for being Satanic, but I don't wish for that hate to be targeted at others near me.*

- *My parents intentionally raised me without religion; not atheist, rather just an absence of religious reference. My mother has been sincerely inquisitive about my Satanism; my father is quietly neutral.*

  My ex-spouse was distressed when I first announced that I was Satanic; that was the only time I mentioned it. Out of respect for my ex-spouse who has legal custody of our children, I haven't announced my Satanism to the children and am not expecting to for a long time.

- *Coming out didn't affect my work relationships. I work closely with US military and federal agencies, and so far they have been very protective of civil rights. I've had good conversations with other theistic co-workers about philosophical and social topics.*

- *It's difficult to say if I experienced any serious repercussions from coming out as a Satanist as I came out as transgender during the same time; being labeled as transgender has been very destructive and often a physical security risk.*

- *On the positive side, coming out as Satanic gave me the moral confidence to come out as transgender and pansexual. Since then I've been able to move off of being dependent on a daily regimen of psychiatric medications, and actually begin to find pleasure in life. I cannot do justice to how positively profound exploring a Satanic philosophy has been for me.*

• *My tips for those considering coming out: However one chooses to come out, they should do it with confidence; a confident air can help deter potential hecklers. If one finds themselves the target of unwanted attention, strive to remove emotion from the situation and deescalate; "no" is the most powerful tool anyone will have.*

Satanism is no less "right" or "wrong" than any other religion. Do not fall into the trappings of imagining one's beliefs to be superior than another. Equality — no-one's beliefs are invalid no matter how absurd they may appear relative to another.

Jason Lloyd

- *I'm not sure there's ever really been a pinpoint moment in time when I came out, but I was pretty open about it later in high school and throughout college.*

- *My family all knows, friends, employers ... I had a cousin try to dox me, but nobody really gives a shit what she has to say anyhow.*

- *Coming out was definitely a casual thing. I didn't really advertise it, but if someone asked I didn't lie either.*

- *Why did I come out? Well, I've been more open about it in recent years for various reasons. Part of that is simply a Satanic desire to live my truth, to be open about myself. The other is the political landscape today. Christianity today is so skewed and distorted that these people need to know someone's going to push back against their attempts to legislate their beliefs into law.*

- *I don't use a Satanic pseudonym. I have one, and I'm not sure that I won't ever use it for whatever reason, but for me personally I felt that it was worth signing MY name to. I understand why people use them, I support their decision to, but for me I felt it best to assume the risk and put my name on it. If I use my pseudonym down the road, it'll likely just be for artistic reasons.*

- *Coming out didn't really affect my family relationships. I've always been the black sheep of the family, so to speak, and that's still true. I just tell people that I am what I am, and nothing about me has changed. If folks wanna see me differently once they find out, that's on them.*

- *Thankfully, coming out didn't affect my work relationships. One of my managers has made lighthearted jokes about how I'm not very Christian, but it's all in good fun. We joke with each other like that. Everyone else just accepts that it's "Jason being Jason" and doesn't sweat it.*

- *I've had members of my family try and shut me out because I came out as a Satanist, but who cares? We weren't ever close to begin with. Otherwise, I'm aware that I've been really lucky that I can be open, be me, practice my religion, and have nobody really give me a twist over it.*

- *Positives of coming out include: It's very empowering to simply be.*

- *My biggest piece of advice to those considering coming out is to just be honest with people. Most people, in my experience at least, are curious but they're willing to learn. People fear what they don't understand, so helping them learn really helps to alleviate that fear, that concern that they initially have. I always tell people, no question asked with a desire to learn will ever offend me, no matter how silly it might seem. I've been straight up asked if I sacrifice animals, and I just give a soft chuckle and I answer honestly and openly, and it's nice to see that concern melt from their faces as they learn.*

Hadrian Flyte

- *I came out in 2018 publicly, but it was the conclusion of a lifetime of infernal inclinations.*

- *Most of my friends know I'm a Satanist, and many of my colleagues as well. I'm not at all subtle and now that I'm co-organizing a TST Friends Of group it doesn't pay to keep things under wraps.*

  My parents also know.

- *Coming out was voluntary and not exactly an announcement. People started connecting the dots of my interests and trends and before anyone knew, I was wearing a cheeky Satanic holiday sweater to parties.*

- *I came out to my parents somewhat abruptly as my father was going through classes to convert to Catholicism. We're on good terms but I felt moved to clear the air about my intentions and beliefs and that followed through with everyone else.*

  Theistic religion was not my bag and I was tired of being held to a standard codified within theistic tradition.

- *I've attempted to use a pseudonym for my Satanic activities, but my byline is my brand. I came from journalism where your name is connected to what people know about you.*

  I've tried to use a pseudonym and may broaden its use if things get hectic, but I feel part of Satanism as an actual alternative to theistic practice is embracing it as part of my core identity. I am a Satanist and a friend, child, and co-worker. I am a Satanist and this is my name.

  Of course I have no trouble believing the necessity many have for using an alternative name. If I was less stubborn from the start, I probably would have adopted one, but now I'm on this path.

There's nothing shameful, bad, or cowardly about using a pseud-onym and I want to be clear on that point.

• *Coming out to my family didn't affect our relationships much. I'm known for being contrarian and showy. Coming out as a Satanist didn't really surprise anyone. Now if I'd gone from being blisteringly blasphemous and atheistic to theistic Satanism, that would have been concerning for people I know.*

• *When it comes to my work colleagues, it's the same as above, I'm known to be performative. If anything, it's allowed some to engage with me on a different level, like they finally have a clue to a puzzle.*

• *Nothing truly serious happened to me on the negative side, though friends I know who are extremely religious aren't as fond of me. They weren't fond of my coming out as transgender either so can I really count on them as friends?*

I haven't told my grandparents because the news would actually hurt them, or at least my grandmother. I'd rather not burden her with anything else as her health declines.

• *The greatest positive to coming out has been freedom from expec-tation. Our lives are dictated by religious practice more than we realize, and not participating in that eases a great deal of pressure. On a personal level I feel my life has more direction and I can be more honest about my motivations and problems.*

Personal accountability is paramount when you walk this path.

• *My experience with coming out as transgender and as a Satanist are linked to my sense of self. When coming out, you need to know who you are. When you can express who you are freely and confidently, the world bends around you to some extent.*

Prejudice and injustice will continue to happen and I'm sure I'll meet my fair share of it going forward, but I can meet it with the con-fidence that I own my identity. You can wear anything, be anything, work toward anything if you cultivate the confidence to do so.

So the first step for any life-changing or public image-shifting step you take is first owning the experience.

Missy Morbid

- *I came out last year (2018), around the first of December.*

- *Everyone close to me knows.*

- *I really only came out to my husband and kids. I just brought it up out of the blue, lol. I had researched TST and Atheistic Satanism and knew that I wanted to be a part of it.*

- *I was prompted to come out by my own desires.*

- *I had an individual call the Child Protective Services on me because, and I quote, "She is a Satanist and does rituals around her children." From that point forward I've used a pseudonym.*

- *Coming out didn't really affect my family relationships; my family (mom etc.) are not close. My husband and children are very supportive.*

- *I'm fortunate in that coming out didn't affect my work relationships.*

- *I'm lucky that besides the whole CPS ordeal, I've not had to deal with any major negative repercussions.*

- *On the positive side, I found the most wonderful and supportive community and friends.*

- *My advice to those considering coming out is "Let your actions speak for you."*

Creating Satanic Art

Many Satanists choose to create art as part of their Satanic practice. Our religion is richer for the increasing number of artworks created and shared by practitioners.

However, you don't have to be a professional artist to reap the benefits of creation. Anyone can explore and enjoy artistic avenues without years of training and talent. I encourage everyone to pick up a creative tool that speaks to them and just start playing around. As part of your Satanic practice, anything you create will be meaningful, since it comes directly from your own heart. Don't worry about creating a perfect end-product. Many artists say that the process of creation is more important to them than the finished piece.

In this section, I interviewed a number of Satanic practitioners who create art. As with any aspect of Satanism, everyone's artistic endeavors were highly individualistic. They worked in a great variety of media, ranging from digital drawings to polymer clay, jewelry, wood, and more. Some made a full livelihood from their art, while others created just for themselves. Not everyone was open about their Satanism, but some found their Satanic themes to be a selling point.

I was grateful they shared their work — and I encourage all of you to share yours as well, no matter if you feel it's "professional" or not. The more we share, the richer the Satanic discourse becomes.

Here are the interview questions I asked:

- What role does Satanic philosophy play in your life?
- What does Satanism mean to you?
- What artistic medium(s) do you work in?
- What or who are some of your biggest artistic influences?
- What Satanic themes do you explore with your art?
- Let's talk about your featured piece. What Satanic elements did you incorporate into this piece, and why?
- What challenges did you have to deal with in making this piece?
- What would you like audiences to take away from it?
- Are you open about your Satanism? If so, how do you feel that might affect the reception of your art?
- Any tips for aspiring Satanic artists?

Artetak

- *I'm Satanic. It doesn't define who I am as a person, just the beliefs I align with.*

- *Satanism to me is mostly embracing being the rebel, the other, the outsider. For years and years I watched those who were considered "good" and "right" by society do these awful things and I wanted no part of that. I always thought it was weird that I was the one who was labeled as evil by these people. So I started looking into Satanism and it all just clicked. Finally I feel comfortable in my beliefs.*

- *I work in both digital and traditional media.*

- *Some of my biggest artistic influences are Mark Ryden, Trevor Brown, and kitsch culture.*

- *Satanism has a reputation for being pretty dark and scary, but I've never been any of that. So I love taking these themes and turning them around and making them cute, bring a bit of humor and color to it. I like putting symbols and sigils in my work, sometimes super prevalent to the casual observer and sometimes subtle to where only other people interested in the occult would get it. My art is playful.*

- *The Sigil of Baphomet is probably the most recognized symbol of Satanism out there. So in this piece, I drew my take on it. On her forehead is the Sigil of Lucifer, and in her eyes is the alchemy symbol for sulfur, also known as the Leviathan Cross. I basically jam packed as many sigils as I could into it.*

- *I didn't really have any challenges making this piece.*

- *I would like viewers to take away the fact that Satanism doesn't have to be scary.*

- *I'm very much open about my Satanism, and it has come back to bite me in the ass a few times. I've been uninvited from several events I was supposed to sell my art at because of my Satanic imagery. I've had adults angrily drag children out of my vendor booth before. I've gotten nasty messages from less than stable people threatening to*

hurt me because of it. But for the most part people have been wonderful and I'm constantly used as an example of how Satanism isn't this big evil thing by my non-Satanic friends and acquaintances.

• *My tips for beginners: There are no rules to art. Trust your instincts and just go. Not everyone is going to like what you do and that's totally fine because they're not the ones paying your bills.*

Hada Pixie

- *I do consider myself a Satanist at this point. I fought the term Satanist for a long time because being a Pagan-Goth, everyone jumped to that conclusion, and I didn't like the negative weight that title held — being a Pagan-Goth was weighty enough. Even though I took some of Lavey's tenets to heart and incorporated them into my personal philosophy, I did not consider myself a Satanist until I found TST. I really like the philosophy that The Satanic Temple is founded on and I feel it mirrors much of my belief system. I am all about being true to myself, enjoying my life, and taking the reins of destiny into my own hands to create my place in the world. I am not only responsible for my actions but I am responsible for my reactions to the world around me. I feel like TST is able to help me take a label that was placed on me with fear and remold it into something empowering.*

- *For me, Satanism is about being an empowered individual; making my own choices in regards to my life and my body. It gives us black-sheep strays a community that helps our voices be heard to fight an unjust system that has always seemed stacked against us. It's also a way to filter out those who would judge you without getting to know you. If my look and the labels I have taken as my own are enough to upset or offend someone, then they are not a person I want to waste my time trying to build a relationship with.*

- *My main artistic medium is designing jewelry, but I also am a model and photographer.*

- *Everything I create is an expression of who I am as a person, so really it boils down to my love of literature and poetry when you're talking about my artistic influences. I found goth through my love of writers like Edgar Allen Poe, Percy Shelly, Lord Byron and Bram Stoker. And that lens of finding beauty in darkness colors all that I do.*

- *I started HadaPixie Designs with the motto "Alternative jewelry for creative people." I based my designs on the Catholic Rosary but changed up the number of beads used. 5 or 6 sets of 9 beads*

representing LaVey's 9 Satanic Statements and 9 Satanic Sins. The Y connectors tend to be skulls or inverted crosses. The pendants of course are where the real themes come in; my main designs and best sellers are my Baphomet, Sigil of Lucifer, and Satanic Cross rosaries.

• *In this piece, which I call my Brimstone Rosary, I used quite a few Satanic elements. The Satanic Cross aka the Leviathan Cross is actually the alchemical symbol for sulfur and since sulfur is known in the bible as "brimstone," I thought that would be a fitting name for this piece. The one pictured is "Hellfire Red" since the dyed howlite stone skulls are red, but I also do a version in "Sulfur Yellow" where the skulls are yellow instead. I like using black beads with colored skulls because it really makes the skull imagery pop, forcing the eye to see the skull which reminds us of death, another taboo in mainstream society. I have noticed people only tend to ask about my rosary when they notice the skulls.*

• *This piece had its own challenges as I created it. It's gone through the most incarnations with different pendants and slightly different designs. I want to maintain a high quality to my jewelry and when my supplier quit making Satanic Cross pendants, I had to seek out another source that I felt had a comparable quality. Luckily, Satanic jewelry is much easier to find now than it was even just a few years ago. Really the biggest challenge I have faced with my shop as a whole is balancing the fact that I am a Pagan and a Satanist; many Pagans are afraid of Satanic imagery and many Satanists seem to think that Pagans are silly for believing in the supernatural. I know because of this I have lost sales, but I take comfort in knowing that my customer base is open-minded enough to shop with someone who may not walk the same path as them.*

- *I hope people find comfort and community with my pieces. I have encountered people who come from Catholicism and missed the comfort of using a Rosary for prayer and found using one of my pieces is a way to bridge the gap between the person they used to be/the spirituality they used to have and their present state. I have had people's eyes light up seeing my rosary because they know they aren't alone; one cashier pulled out a Baphomet pendant from their shirt, flashing it at me before quickly stashing it back away. I began my shop with the idea that I was simply sharing my aesthetic with people and have come to find out that they are also our little secret signs to each other, reminding us that we are not alone, that there is so much more to the world than all the bad stuff we see on a daily basis.*

- *I am definitely open about my Satanism. I made the choice a long time ago to refuse to walk in the shadows. I am lucky enough not to be in a position that I have to hide who I am to keep my paycheck. I know the Satanic label may hinder some sales just as my Pagan label can affect my sales, but I know that those who are open-minded and are drawn to my shop will come back. I know that it's worth the reduction in stress to just be open about all of the different parts of me that make me and my shop what they are. I admit I thought seriously about splitting my shop up based on the label each piece fell under, but in the end I decided that would be too much like faking who I was to make some unknown person more comfortable.*

• *My tips for aspiring Satanic artists: Take things at your own pace. Don't be afraid to create a pseudonym, and don't be afraid to split up your shop/social media etc. to have your "normal" stuff separate from your Satanic stuff. Do what you think you need to do to be safe and do what's best for your mental health. Try not to feel pressured by anyone to create a certain way; unless they are paying you no one has any right to tell you what your art should be, and if they are paying you it's because they think your art is worth it.*

Na'Amah Morningstar

- *I am a very proud Atheistic Satanist. Satanism is very much embedded into every aspect of my life. I'm always aware of my actions and my words. I accept responsibility for everything I say and do. Artistically speaking, I am attracted to the darker side of life (or death) but I like to also keep it family friendly. I try to keep a little bit of comedy in my work so as to not scare the little ones too much. I'd like people to understand that Satanism is actually about love and acceptance, and not what they've been conditioned to believe as early as childhood.*

- *Satanism means so many things to me. Acceptance, love, (self) respect, pride, self-worth, self-care, individualism and activism (when necessary). I am very fortunate that I was not raised with religion in my childhood. I've been an atheist my entire adult life and a Satanist for just over 3 years. It has changed my life for the better in so many ways. It's made me a better, more thoughtful and self-loving person. Satanism is so important to me that I've worked hard to attain a position in my state's Satanic Leadership.*

- *I am a Polymer Clay Sculptor as well as an Acrylic & Water Painter. I occasionally write short stories as well.*

- *I'm very much inspired by my fellow Satanic artists! Everyone from Marilyn Manson & Sadie Satanas to Cornelis Galle I and Salvador Dali (who was actually all over the place with his religious beliefs.) I'm also a huge fan of some lesser known Polymer Clay sculptors.*

- *I like to use as many Satanic symbols as possible in my artwork. I feel like the more the people who fear the unknown are exposed to us, the less fearful they will be. It's a cathartic experience for me as well. While I don't believe in the supernatural, I do believe in practising ritual. I tend to put my intentions into my artwork. Some would call that Witchcraft or Spell Work but I call it a special added bonus!*

- *I love ventriloquist dummies. I believe they terrify people and I love that. What could make a dummy even creepier? Add an inverted cross. Again, it's that fear of the unknown that freaks people out.*

Being miseducated about a symbol creates a fear so powerful, it causes people to panic and freeze. This piece also has the intentions of fun and mischief worked into it. My hope for this little guy is that he inspires someone to take things a little less seriously and enjoy the darker things in life. They either love it or they pray for me.

- *I had no challenges with this one! It is one of the less complicated pieces I've created and I enjoyed the time it took to make!*

- *I would like people to embrace their fears and be inspired to educate themselves about things they don't understand. I want people to want something like this in their own lives!*

- *I am 100% open about my Satanism! My left arm is covered in Satanic tattoos and Sigils. It is always a thought in my mind that people may reject my art, and some will. I am dedicated and patient. There is someone out there for each piece of artwork I create. There are many people in the world who embrace the same philosophy and appreciate/value the tenets I follow, and they are the people who will also value my artwork.*

- *My tips for aspiring Satanic artists: Just create it! Don't overthink it. Don't worry about artistic rules or what other artists think. Create from your heart. Be confident!*

Justin Norwood

- *I consider myself a Satanist, and have so for many years. I try to live Satanically by adhering to The Satanic Temple's Seven Tenets. I feel the Seven Tenets challenge me to be a better person and find ways to better myself on a daily basis.*

- *Satanism to me means equality, self expression, and an unending quest for knowledge and self improvement.*

- *I work mostly in graphite and charcoal or ink but recently I have been working with Prismacolor markers and gouache.*

- *My biggest artistic influence would be my high school art teacher Herb Aldrich. A lot of my more recent art is influenced by The Satanic Temple's Baphomet statue. I also struggle with mental illness and I feel creating art helps with treating that. Another influence for my art is the challenge in creating something I can be proud to put my name on.*

- *Many of my pieces revolve around the Baphomet statue, but I also enjoy drawing portraits and have done a few abstract drawings with Satanic themes.*

- *This piece is a layered black and white portrait of The Satanic Temple's Co-founder Lucien Greaves. I feel Lucien is a great role model for all Satanists and any human who aspires to be a more compassionate or intelligent contribution to society.*

- *Mostly the biggest challenge in making this piece was getting back into drawing in general. Prior to this piece, I took a break from creating art and was having a hard time getting back into it.*

- *Mainly what I would like audiences to take away from this piece is to stick with your hobbies, especially if it makes you happy.*

- *I haven't officially "come out" as a Satanist but I also haven't exactly hidden my Satanism from others either. I don't feel like it would negatively affect the reception of my art as most of it is Satanic by nature.*

- *My tips for beginners are: Don't give up. Keep pushing yourself. Don't rely on others to improve your art. Your success is yours to achieve.*

Avante Quard

• To me, Satanism is loving who and how we please. Hating those who spew genocidal pseudologic while they do avoidable harm to undeserving people. It's a religious experience of being apart from the willfully ignorant. It's like pirating psychological airwaves for a limited time to broadcast a message of resistance and existence to my siblings in Satan. It is rational, empathetic, and includes concern for myself and others. It is taking direct action. It is an artistic set of psychic constructions that allow for me to create spaces with my hellbound friends that would not exist under any other circumstance. It is self-motivated achievement in spite of what everyone else would do. It is a middle finger whoopie cushion. It is creating art for art's sake, and not waiting for fetishized/industrial/Holy assholes to notice or give permission/validation. It's acting like I have worth in a world that wants more and more for less and less as time goes on.

• My art suggests another side to all of this. It manifests as a conceptually grey mixture of masochism, victimhood, uniqueness, revolt and fierce compassion. It is the manifestation of a coherent, ethically sound, firmly opposing point of view. I like having community. But I'm not defined by my group. I like having friends. But I'm not a martyr. I think I find a good balance that finds its way into what I do. I don't always operate within neat academic frameworks, like academics. I work out my negative states, and refine who I am, through my art. It's all in there. Sometimes clearly, sometimes cryptically in order to allow the viewer/listener to draw their own contextualization.

• Right now I primarily make music independently and in a couple projects. I also paint and do a little tattooing for friends.

• I come from a conservative, superstitious, working class family in up-state NY. I grew up being shamed for wearing makeup, stretching my ears, only wearing black, painting my nails, dyeing what hair I had for a short time, listening to/playing loud aggressive music, creating/consuming controversial imagery, appreciating the bizarre, macabre, grotesque, white trashy and acting or thinking effeminately. That's all had an effect. I'm also affected by reactionaries from both sides of the political spectrum, and some who identify with a third side, or fourth if you count the center as a position, who willingly shoehorn themselves, and those they can quantify and control, into archaic and psychologically destructive molds as unconsciously conservative means to have a meaning-

less failure of a parodied revolution. My legal experiences with and in relation to the criminal justice system affect me. Reading Marilyn Manson's Long Hard Road Out of Hell introduced me to the Satanic Bible. Manson and LaVey with their music, ritual, aesthetics, performance art, works and parasocial influence provided me with a feeling that it was okay, even desirable, and worth the great cost parental/ societal approval of being myself; whatever that meant. I identified as Satanic around 16, and that's when I remember first being conscious of me as "me." I like to watch Metalocalypse, Superjail, Moral Orel, Tim and Eric, Trailer Park Boys, and Batman movies. Experiencing the American metapersonality through normal people keeps me inspired. There are people that think Trump is a direct tool of their God. The unreality that I'm supposed to believe in, according to social media and television, keeps me more than full of ideas. I like H.R. Giger *and Paul Booth's work as well. Check out "trash polka" tattooing if you haven't heard of it.*

- *I grew up as an only child in a conservative, superstitious family. When I would act as characters from movies as a child, I was always the villain. I've liked horror as far back as I can remember. My Reaganite Republican step-father and my now-more-enlightened mother were practicing Mormons while I was an adolescent. I went to church as I "had to." I didn't really care like I was supposed to. In my late teens I formally quit the cult with my Baphomet on, in corpse paint like I'm wearing as I write this. In 2017 I was arrested for rioting while the Mormon Tabernacle Choir performed not far away for Trump's inauguration. I treasure my federal indictment. Satanism provides a stimulating perceptual framework to express and communicate ideas to others. Under the old racist industrial patriarchy order, I'm Satanic whether I care to identify as such or not. I might as well have a good time since I'm going to Hell for not being repentant anyway. I think I'm another anarchist antichrist chipping away at the irrational fear and tyrannical darkness to exact a manner of Apocalyptic Satanic victory of sorts. "I AM SATAN."*

- *In this piece, I see the suggestion of an aggressive underground Satanic consciousness, even movement, in hostile revolt against the old ways. Its horns came from looking at the Dellamore & Co. Baphomet that I got from shopsatan.com. I keep it on my desk as I work. It holds my eye, and takes me back to seeing the 9ft statue in Salem, which is one of my favorite real-world Satanic experiences. I plan to move to Salem at some point.*

- *I painted this around 5AM. I typically go to bed around 430AM and get up around 12PM. I had the idea, and forced my hand to paint it after a study session, which was inspired but miserable. I hadn't created something new for a period of time and it was making me anxious. If I go too long without creating, I lose something that grounds me. The painting is sort of manic-looking, and was painted with an anxious tension. I had to force my hand to paint every stroke. I like that about it. I had to get it out of my mind and over with despite wanting to just rot in front of Youtube and overeat or sleep. Sometimes artwork is easy. Creation feels almost effortless. Other times I feel almost psychically oppressed by my own artistic endeavor. After everything is over and done with, I'm always happy I took the time to make whatever it is, which inspires the next painting or track. Art is all I care about creating, outside of survival projects for the underserved and abandoned. Anything else feels like I've sold out, or given up.*

- *If this painting resonates with anyone, I hope they feel that, in spite of what upstanding fearmongers would have them believe in order to buy and sell them, they're not alone in their alienation or certain unpopular perceptions and observations. The art I've done lately has led to some great conversations with friends and other artists. I don't plan on stopping what I'm doing any time soon.*

- *I'm loud about my Satanism. My art isn't for everyone. It is just as successful when it resonates with others as it is when it offends those whom I find offensive. It might be silly, but it means a great deal to sell my prints and tracks when I do, although I'm in it for views and listeners.*

- *My tips are: Follow your will and manifest your dreams without permission. Trust yourself. People will make promises they don't intend to keep. People will support you when you have earned their respect. Don't expect a penny. Don't involve anyone in anything that will halt your practice. As a musician, have your own music outside of what you record with bands. Draw outside of what you're going to tattoo. Etc. If you're doing real art, people will eventually notice. Worrying about clout or fame is stupid. The more militant you are in your practice, the more you've made yourself as an artist. Do what makes you feel alive. Civility is slavery. Create outside of the expectations of others. Be patient. Share your work. It may save your, or someone else's, life. Possess yourself, or someone else will.*

Horinawa

- *By the standards of The Satanic Temple I am 100% a Satanist. I used to consider myself more of a left hand tantrist. I came of age very interested in the occult and pre/post colonial tribal shamanism, but mostly with more of a Jungian shadow working angle as opposed to the more traditional New Age light working. For that reason, I never really fit in with the more mainstream Buddhist and Hindu organizations in North America. There were no western Aghori sects to find a guru in, so I just did my own thing with whatever taboo literature I could get my hands on, for better or worse. Literature from the Process Church of Final Judgement really resonated with me in school. They also used the Jungian archetype model. The Abrahamic faiths translated the furious eastern Dharmapalas into demons anyways, so Satanism seemed to be a valid category for me to consider.*

- *I believe that maintaining authenticity, even adversarial nonconformity, in the face of moral tyranny is a pivotal principle of Satanic philosophy. Aleister Crowley's "Liber Oz" had a profound effect on my art and life when I was around 13 years old. "Do what thou wilt shall be the whole of the law" is a very powerful principle for a child to wrap his head around. To me, true Satanism is summarized in the literal definition of liberty: The condition of being free from confinement, servitude, or forced labor, or the condition of being free from oppressive restriction or control by a government or other power.*

- *I work in tattoo, acrylic, watercolor, ink, aerosol, silkscreen, digital, photography, videography, as well as recording and performing arts.*

- *Tattoo and outlaw subculture culture has been a huge part of my life, so tattoo legends like Filip Leu, Paul Booth, Leo Zuluetta, and Horiyoshi III have been very influential for me over the last three decades. The imagery of fringe societal organizations ranging from the yakuza, to the Freemasons, the Russian mafia, occult woodblock printing, fetish photography, or even outlaw biker insignia all drew my attention from a very early age. I find inspiration all over the place! H.R. Giger, being the godfather of occult biomechanical art.*

Ozuma Kaname, Genesis P Orridge, Sugiura Norio, and Indian Larry among others.

- *I enjoy challenging content that moves people from their comfort zone. "Art should comfort the disturbed and disturb the comfortable." - Cesar A. Cruz. In many ways, complacency is stagnation. The act of creation, to me, should have some degree of intent and symbolism. Not just graphic design for the purpose of making rich people's walls pretty.*

- *This piece is my interpretation of balance and transformation through the symbolism of Baphomet. (S)he was intentionally not framed as aggressive or hard as opposed to passively stoic and softer. (S)he transitions between the potentially hostile materialism near the bottom of the canvas towards interconnected consciousness surrounding the flame of illumination. The balance points between the left and right hand paths, male and female divine principles, the light moon of Chesed (mercy) and the dark moon of Gevurah (severity), the eye of Ra and the eye of Horus. I also incorporated the ouroboros to reflect that life feeds off life. Even as the universe is birth and creation, it is also death and atrophy — something that many Abrahamists and other right hand path people forget. I believe more people interested in the symbol of Baphomet would do well to research some of Eliphas Levi's commentary on the principles he incorporated into his design.*

- *The biggest challenge I had with this piece was finishing it! I still feel it is a work in progress.*

- *I want my audiences to take away whatever they will from this piece. It can be pretty, or intimidating, or have depth. Some people see the flower, others will see the fruit.*

- *I am very open about my philosophy, for better or worse. I don't run around trying to hide who I am, though I won't try to pigeon-hole my lifestyle as being specifically "Satanic" either. Many people who define themselves as Satanists disagree with my outlooks as well! I just prefer to stay on the shadier side of twilight without falling too far into darkness.*

- *My tips for beginning Satanic artists: Be authentic. In both life and art. Follow your true bliss and do what you really feel is your calling, regardless of criticism, whether there is any money to be made or accolades. If what you are doing is truly what you are supposed to be doing, you will enjoy it the most, it will work, and other people will see that. If you create your art primarily to impress others, you almost invariably compromise your true self.*

Charles Blackwine

- I do consider myself a Satanist. I was raised extremely religious, in the circles of two protestant ministries that are often labelled as cults these days (Institute for Basic Life Principles and New Horizons Youth Ministries.) As a teenager, I rejected what I saw to be a miserable, unreasonable, and tyrannical belief system and for a short time identified as a Satanist. I considered myself a LaVeyan after the idea that Satan is not a real thing but a symbol, but knew little else of the philosophy and made it up as I went, though as a result of learning science for the first time and starting to view much of what was called Satanism to be an attempt to make shitty personality characteristics seem edgy, focusing on some narrow anti-social elements of human nature while ignoring many others, with the same basic social values as the belief system I had rejected, I considered myself an atheist until Satanism was presented in a form that was coherent with my beliefs.

  The role Satanism plays is more of a descriptive role of my beliefs. I do not do the things I do because I am a Satanist, I am a Satanist because it is coherent with what I believe and do.

  The Seven Tenets largely describe my outlook on life, ways of interacting with others, and understanding the universe, and I believe they hold a decent guide for action in life. As a result of my experiences in life, I have found that opposing arbitrary power is necessary for living in a just society and I try to live up to this, as the consequences of not doing so can be horrific at times.

  Truth and justice have always been very important to me. The idea of this was instilled in me early on, by religious zealots, but when I saw that much of what I was taught was neither true nor just, I abandoned it, but retained the core belief that truth and justice are important guiding principles to action.

- Satanism to me is a philosophy that centers around rebellion and the pursuit of knowledge, and I see those two as necessarily intertwined. I first came to Satanism as a youth as a result of seeking knowledge *and rebelling against what I saw to be morally wrong, and later came back to it for the same reasons.*

Satan as the symbol of the one who brings knowledge and fights against a seemingly all-powerful tyrant who seems to rule and demand love that is closer to Stockholm syndrome is something that the world needs. Tyranny must always be challenged. Knowledge must always be pursued. Enforced ignorance is a form of tyranny itself, and its use leads to horrific abuses of power, as any history book will attest to.

- *I work in wood.*

- *I'm most inspired by Steve Ramsey, who runs the Woodworking for Mere Mortals YouTube channel. His approach is designed around getting newcomers to the craft set up with the skills and confidence they need to make wood things, and this is a welcome change from the elitism that is often seen in such affairs. He exemplifies a great deal of empathy in creating educational material on the craft that is geared towards those who don't know what they are doing and may fall into discouragement when their finished works don't turn out like show-room pieces, and he focuses on continuously learning and improving and taking pride in what one has done. While I feel fairly certain he is not a Satanist or anything similar, I did notice a pentacle and Leviathan cross on an ouija board he made and thought it neat.*

- *As a woodworker who is just getting into the more artistic side of the craft instead of the merely functional, for the time being I am just making Satanic symbols of wood, something which I have not found to be commonly available. Much of woodworking is fundamentally different from other mediums of art, so I am not able to (yet) have the same breadth, but it is something I intend to strive for.*

  Functionality is still much of what my Satanic pieces provide, such as altars, boxes, etc. They are not necessarily designed to be the central piece, but to play a supporting role, though I am starting to venture out of this with the pentagrams and other symbols.

- *Well, this piece is a pentagram. That's pretty much it. I saw an ad on Craigslist for a scroll saw that turned out to be partially broken, so I set out to get it operational, and when I did, the first thing I thought to make was a pentagram, partially because I just wanted a pentagram, and because it incorporates a few different types of cuts (obtuse angles, acute angles, curves, copes, etc.) that would help me use it as a learning experience for further projects.*

- *My main challenges with this piece were unfamiliarity with the tools and techniques I was using. It was my first anything with the scroll saw, so it was all uncharted territory for me.*

- *I would like people to take away from this piece: "The person who lives here is a Satanist."*

I think there should be a greater variety of Satanic art available; not everything has to be ghoulish. I try to make nice looking things with varying degrees of success, and would like to continue improving my skill sets to create well-made items with craftsmanship that stands on its own.

- *I'm open about my Satanism with close friends that would understand, but not all. There are people who would understand, and people who wouldn't. I don't do it for shock value so I don't relish the "making people uncomfortable" aspect of Satanism.*

With the woodwork that I do, it's generally easy to tell whether or not it is Satanic; I make things like tables, jewelry stands, wood boxes, pentagrams and Leviathan crosses, etc., so whether or not the observer knows I am a Satanist is probably less material than their perception of the work itself. However, I wouldn't stress the fact when selling at a local craft fair, as I live in a small rural town where that would not help the reception, so I would opt to not sell overtly Satanic items there.

- *My tips for beginning Satanic artists: Keep going. Find something you like doing and keep doing it. Don't get discouraged when it doesn't work out; look at everything you think you did wrong and learn from it; do it again and make it better. Strive for perfection while accepting that you will never create something perfect. Remember that you are your own harshest critic.*

316

Opal

- *I'm not exactly sure where I fit in yet, I'm still figuring that out; however, within this past year I've been doing a lot of research and reading on Satanism and I do agree with all of the Tenets, and believe that Satanism is a powerful step in the right direction for society. I've never seen an organization like this that stands up so shamelessly for what they believe and are actually active in their communities to do good. If there were a TST Chapter near me, I would love to be a part of it.*

- *Satanism means that you are your own god — you don't have a higher power to lean on so you have to grab your life by the balls and manifest and make it what you want, instead of sitting around in prayer just waiting for the pieces to fall together. That being so, you ARE a god, so you should treat yourself with the same respect and care that others treat their gods with. You should also be able to recognize the potential in others and respect the gods/goddesses that they are inside as well.*

- *I mainly work in digital, traditional drawing, charcoal, and paint.*

- *I find inspiration in the people I love that are artists as well. My brother is a phenomenal artist and constantly blows me away with his work. A few friends of mine are artists too, and I love nothing more than seeing people I love pouring their hearts onto canvases; I find inspiration in that.*

  My dream is to be a tattoo artist, and one of my biggest inspirations (though she doesn't do Satanic work) in that aspect is Ryan Ashley from InkMasters Angels. Her work is phenomenal and I actually got to meet her once — she's such an inspiration to me and I aspire to be as good of a tattoo artist as her one day.

- *I like to create pieces that make the viewer feel liberated and empowered. Satanism, for me, has been just that and I like to try to convey that to the viewer.*

- *In this piece, I incorporated a woman with ram horns levitating above a pentacle on the ground, surrounded by candles, as if she's doing a ritual. I wanted the focus to be on the woman and her expression — she's in complete bliss and recognizing her true power.*

• *Artistically, the only challenge I faced with this piece was the shadowing on her limbs. I got it wrong the first time and had to go redo them.*

• *I want people to look at my piece and feel a sense of power, that this woman isn't a made up god, she's a person, just like you. She's tapping into her inner power and becoming the goddess that she truly is. I want people to look at it and feel like Satanism isn't about sacrificing virgins and killing goats — it's about putting yourself first and recognizing the power that you hold inside, and that you've had it inside of you all along.*

• *I'm not very open about my Satanism — I have an extremely conservative and religious family and would definitely be ostracized if they found out I was exploring this path. However, one day, I hope to find the power within me to be honest about who I am and what I stand for regardless of the outcome, I just haven't made it that far yet.*

• *My tip for those doing Satanic art: Just create whatever feels right. With this piece, I had no idea what I was going to paint before I picked up the canvas. It doesn't have to be perfect, it doesn't even have to be pretty, just create something that comes from within you that YOU can be proud of.*

Jeran Michael

- *The primary role that Satanic philosophy plays in my life is the liberation of self from the bondages of social and religious confinement. It also means freedom from addictions and emotional states of being that bring Hell up from a literary geographic location and into a very real manifested kingdom in which the self, its ego and its body suffers.*

- *Satanism is allure, self-perseverance and truth in a world fashioned by lies and hypocrisy. If Satanism was a painting of the Garden of Eden it would be represented by the beautiful red shine of the forbidden fruit, its sweet and delicious taste, the knowledge that came upon swallowing its flesh and the serpent who was there to offer more of that sweet insight. It embraces the beauty and grace of death, madness and the macabre as not only a human condition but a PRIVILEGE. It offers understanding of the world without fog or filter and delivers us into the best parts of humanity without fear of destruction or ridicule. Satanism represents skinning and discarding the hide of hypocrisy and enjoying the warm and wet feel of human desire WITHOUT evil. Satanism is an appreciation for all things most would consider weird, dark, grotesque or strange. It is a full understanding of those things that most humans would fear. With full understanding comes a complete absence of fear. It means commitment to self-truth, laughing and love, disregard for the judgement others cast upon us and each other. It means consent and care, kindness and giving without expectations, defending those we love and ourselves. Satanism is an illustration of the fallen angel put into the living practice of humankind's BEST qualities. It is helping each other and ourselves and doing what we can to contribute to the truth that the rest of the world needs to see.*

- *I work in painting, music, writing.*

- *My influences include Zdzisław Beksiński, Francisco Goya, Black Metal music, opera, and Charles Adams, among others.*

- *I take inspiration from the hell-scapes of Christianity's view on hell and damnation. I create scenes and characters from a realm that may*

very well be seen as hellish or demonic. But every piece of mine has a "smirk." As if it were saying "You see? THIS is what you believe to be real. It's YOUR Hell. YOU burn in it."

- *For this piece, I was inspired by a combination of UFO conspiracies and the anti-Christian, church-burning exploits of certain individuals in the early Norwegian black metal scene in the late 80's and early 90's, the days of the Satanic Panic. The vision you see of a "Satanic UFO" setting a church on fire with its unholy laser beams represents what is seen through the religious goggles of the deluded, self-righteous right wing. That is to say, there are those who believe UFOs and black metal musicians to be of the same "Satanic" origin. They can only see what they want to see. Instead of pondering the possibility of life on other planets, they see alien life as mere legions of the anti-Christ who come to earth to smite the holy homes of the trinity. Instead of seeing artists of extreme music as individuals expressing their own political/spiritual/social/inner views, they equate them with those very few in the black metal circles who indulged in church arson and mischievous anti-Christian horse-play, sullying the name and image of true Satanism.*

- *The biggest challenge I had making this piece was keeping the cat out of my paints!*

- *I would like this piece to prompt viewers to realize that generalizations and assumptions about things we don't know create unnecessary fear, arrogance and destruction.*

- *I am very open about my Satanism because it is my own. Satanism is unique to the individual and how they practice it to carry out their own will is also unique. I am secure in my Satanism as it is not afraid to ask the questions others won't ask or give the answers others might not give.*

- *For aspiring artists, I'd say: Make SURE you know YOUR Satanism. Make sure you understand it in depth, lest others try to use it as a weapon against you.*

Dee Mendes

- *I am a non-theistic Satanist and TST member.*

- *To me, Satanism is a crucial means to push back against the encroaching theocracy that threatens to take over our government and individual liberties. It also provides a vital community and support system for like-minded thinkers.*

- *I work in fabric, stained glass, pencil, and digital.*

- *My art is influenced by everything from traditional animation to heavy metal graphics, fantasy/RPG art, comics, and occult imagery.*

- *My Satanic themes in art are mostly visual elements such as symbols, and characters like Baphomet & demons.*

- *For this piece, as the unofficial mascot of TST Satanism, Baphomet is pretty much good to go out of the box. It has the pentagram and torch of enlightenment, and I added an inverted cross staff. Plus goats are a symbol of disobedience.*

- *My challenges in making this piece: I have an acquired latex allergy due to chemotherapy cancer treatments, and it was difficult to find a non-latex mask caster. The head gear also restricts my vision, hearing, breathing and temperature control. It can't be worn for extended periods or without a "handler" in public.*

- *I hope the characters I create and perform will give inspiration and solidarity to fellow Satanists, and cause the uninitiated to question some of the ingrained assumptions of society.*

- *I'm not blatantly open about my Satanism, but those who know me well are aware. I always try to gauge the appropriateness of the place and time before bringing it up.*

- *To those just starting to explore their own Satanic creativity, I'd say: Do what inspires you, not what you think will sell. People are drawn to the genuine. Hail yourself!*

photo by Martin Kermit Urzua

323

Violet Azimuth

- *The Seven Tenets of The Satanic Temple really met my heart. I had aligned as a Humanist for a large part of my life without really knowing the name for it. I found the concepts within the Tenets were just a regular function in my mind.*

  I would safely say I'm an ally, but if there is such a thing as a closet Satanist, then, yes, I am. I have a really high bar for claiming to "be" anything particular. I guess I feel I have more work ahead as a Satanist. Satanic elements are becoming true endearments among my floral fare, and I enjoy the subject matter so it multiplies that inspiration.

- *For me, Satanism is a means to a needed place. Belonging without having to be anything in particular, just what you are. No shame, no doubt or fear. That feeling of belonging, but without having to belong.*

- *My end product is digital. I sketch in pencils or pen, and I work for the most part in Illustrator.*

- *Artists that have influenced me along the way are Alphonse Mucha, Koloman Moser, J.W. Waterhouse, Brian Froud, and Maurice Sendak. The biggest influence for my art would be flora and fauna. Nature plays a big part in my creativity. Staring at tall grass is strangely inspiring.*

- *I have incorporated Baphomet into my mental universe along with representations of the pursuit of knowledge, empathy, and compassion, along with indulgence of self, combined with my comforts of plant life and animal life.*

- *I'm creating a coloring book I've named "Satanic Botanicals." This particular piece is "The Moon and The Morning." It's a mixture of nature, knowledge, and Romantic symbolism. I've focused on my interpretation of Baphomet with floral elements influenced by night and day. Using the pistil and stamen of a flower as a nod to the Astral light, I want to imply life and growth. Time also plays in. There are many layers in my thoughts on this one.*

The Moon and The Morning

- *My biggest challenge in making this piece was time, always time. I've got a design brain and an art brain battling through the concept and it can be exhausting trying to finish a piece. I love and desire subtlety in art, so finding that balance was important. I want it to be beautiful and meaningful, offering information or parable.*

- *Some themes I want people to take away from this piece: Personal growth and how the beauty and importance of knowledge blooms over time.*

- *I keep my Satanism to myself with the exception of other members within The Satanic Temple. The area I am in isn't open to concepts of empathy and freewill when connected with the term "Satanism." Ultimately, they will think what they will. Of course, I hope they enjoy it.*

- *To aspiring artists, I would say: find what affects you most about the concepts of the Tenets and let that inspire you. I don't think the portrayal has to be obviously Satanic. I don't think Satanic art requires a goat, a Baphomet image, sigils, or any symbol, as long as the message is there. I started with flowers.*

Satanic Altars

Though it's not a requirement, many Satanic practitioners do find it helpful to set up an altar. These Satanic altars aren't used to worship an external deity; rather, they are made to reflect the practitioner themselves. As with so many other aspects of the Satanic religion, Satanic altars are highly individual; there's no "right way" to set one up. I interviewed practitioners about their Satanic altars and found quite a variety of approaches.

People had a number of different purposes for their altars. Some used their altar as a place of quiet reflection, a space at which to shut out the rest of the world and gather their focus. For some, their altar served as a constant visual reminder of their Satanic path. Others used their altar as a space at which to perform rituals.

What you choose to put on your altar is also totally up to you. The items interviewees chose for their altars varied widely, from the more traditional (like a Baphomet statue and candles) to more unique items like plushies and video game artifacts. Don't worry if you don't start off with a large collection; you'll find your altar will grow organically over time as you encounter more objects that resonate with you.

One thing all respondents agreed upon was that there are no set rules as to how you should create your altar. It's an intensely personal process, where you decide what will be most meaningful to you. Use your own intuition and creativity to make an altar that works for you.

I asked practitioners these questions about their altars:

- What does Satanism mean to you?
- Do you consider this a specifically Satanic altar?
- What purpose does your altar serve for you?
- For each item on your altar: what is it, and what meaning does it hold for you?
- Does your altar change for seasons or holidays? If so, how?
- Any tips for Satanists setting up an altar for the first time?

Clark Boutwell

- *To me, Satanism is a religion without hypocrisy — a fun and inspiring way to express and strengthen my belief in myself and in my comrades, rather than in a supernatural 'higher power.'*

- *I couldn't call my religion anything but Satanism, and I couldn't consider my altar anything other than Satanic.*

- *My altar is a nexus for both my formal and informal magical activity, and it's simply a cool decoration for my sparsely furnished home. Like Thomas Paine, my mind is my church — but my altar is also my church.*

- *The objects on my altar: Baphomet represents gender & sexual liberation, self-determination, respect for non-human creatures, and the Godhead within ourselves. My altar has been in a constant state of flux since it began a few years ago as merely the Baphomet idol sitting on a shelf. I expect the evolution to continue.*

  The black candles symbolize my commitment to freedom of expression, and my solidarity with all the witches and weirdos who were harmed for being too different or for calling upon the 'wrong' gods.

  The bell is a nod to Lilith Starr and her "open-source" magical system.

  The skeleton embodies our mortality. Lovely and soothing Death is coming for us all.

  The altar-box itself was partly inspired by The Satanic Temple Veterans' Monument. The 'blood' enhances the altar's Command To Look, while alluding to the fact that, even though Abrahamic religions are based on shedding innocent blood via animal and human sacrifice, and despite Satanism specifically rejecting such needless cruelty, it is often Satanists who are falsely accused of such deeds.

- *The candle-holder on the left always has Pisces (my sign) facing the front. I periodically rotate the other candle-holder so that the sign corresponding to the current date is facing ahead. (In the pic, it's Aquarius.) However, Pisces are skeptics, so I don't even believe in astrology.*

• *My tips to beginners: Have fun with it, of course, and never consider your altar 'finished.' Altars, like people, must be allowed to change and grow to meet their full potential.*

A final note: I'm proud of my well-behaved cats, because they act respectfully towards the altar and refrain from knocking anything over. Apparently, they are Satanists too.

Harry Hoofcloppen

- Satanism is an expression of individuality, of self-determination, and for me it's a repudiation of the Judeo-Christian surroundings of my upbringing and the pointless restrictions and expectations on myself and on the world. It's helped me be me, and accept and love myself despite my myriad faults and weaknesses.

- I do consider this a Satanic altar.

- I use my altar to re-center myself if I'm having a bad day or a rough depressive cycle, and I use it when I'm working through ideas or decisions. I can't concentrate with silence; there's too many distractions, too many intrusive thoughts. So my altar is at the center of a room filled with speakers, and I pop in earplugs, light my candles and incense, and put on earth-shaking, thunderous Goa Psy-trance music. The eastern themes plus the driving beat somehow always put *my brain into "neutral;" it isolates my thoughts. It's like it sends me a thousand miles away from everything and allows me to focus on myself and my thoughts in a way that silence never could. The candles and smoke give my eyes something to do and the beat is like this electric pounding in my body that keeps my thoughts moving. It generates a euphoria that's hard to explain. When I'm searching for creative ideas, they flow like springwater. When I'm troubled by life or a situation, the Seven Fundamental Tenets are right there to nudge me through the answers.*

- *Let's run through the objects on my altar. On the left is a framed copy of the Seven Tenets. They help keep me on the right track.*

  Baphy sits in the far center, flanked by tall black candles. They and the kids represent balance.

  In the center is a dragon head incense burner. It's just pretty ;).

  On the right point are my earplugs ... they're just necessary.

  I also have a Baphomet hobo coin that I hold and feel and flip if I'm wrestling with a decision that has no clear answer. It helps me be resolute about my decisions.

- *My altar doesn't really change through the seasons, though I do add objects that help me think about problems to solve, depending on my purpose for that session.*

- *Tips for beginners: Build an altar that pleases you and try to put it somewhere that helps you shut out the outside world and focus yourself. It doesn't matter whether it has skulls or daisies, just make it a spot that feels like "you." It can be busy or simple ... whatever you decide you're happy with is the right answer.*

Stephanie Rosenberg

- To me, Satanism means finally being able to free myself from a lifetime of living according to the desires and expectations of others. It means freeing myself from being who I thought I had to be and instead, being who I am — developing an internal locus of support. This also gives me the desire to help others I come into contact with to do the same; to move towards self-realization in order to live their lives more fully.

- My altar is most definitely a Satanic one and has reached this stage from a long evolutionary process that started as a Wiccan altar back in the 90s, and went through a number of transformations which included it being a Buddhist shrine and a Taoist shrine. It morphed into a more left-hand path when I started to discover Satanism a few years ago and finally evolved into the TST version shown in the photo.

- My permanent altar serves as a focal point for my life as a Satanist and freethinker. Every morning I meditate for 30 minutes in front of the altar in which I gather my thoughts and energies for the coming day in order to attempt to experience the best possible day that I can. At the end of the meditation I recite the Seven Tenets. When performing rituals, I erect a separate altar designed specifically for the ritual in which I focus on the meaning behind the ritual and the psychological archetypes that it calls to.

- My altar starts with a crafts table which I bought in the early 90s and which stands as the foundation for everything that has evolved since then.

  The box with the pentagram and moon symbols used to have the pentagram round the other way when it was Wiccan. It seemed pertinent to repurpose it.

  The skull is a reminder that I am mortal and no different than anyone else, and also holds loose incense for my censer.

  The labradorite sphere on the left is something I have treasured for many years and is said to soak up magickal energies for those who

believe. I hold it during meditations as it helps me to get into a good head space.

I use the bell to start and end meditations and rituals.

The rectangular slotted container in front of Baphomet is a stick incense burner that I use during meditations.

The Baphomet is of course the embodiment for me of the Satanic egregore containing the balance of qualities that I aspire to in day to day life, i.e. to develop KNOWLEDGE OF what has to be done, the WILL to go with what is required, to DARE what must be attempted and to KEEP SILENT with discernment.

The painting behind Baphomet was one that I created around 40 years ago and is meant to represent The Big Bang.

- *My main altar doesn't usually change, as I use a separately constructed altar when the need arises.*

- *My tips for a first altar: Start simple and let it evolve. There is no right and wrong when it comes to altars, as everyone's relationship to the Satanic egregore is personal to them. Never let anyone tell you what you can or cannot do or include.*

Josh Rogers

• *Satanism to me is purpose. I grew up in a very devout Christian neighborhood and family. I was incredibly religious myself. Eventually, I began to ask questions and become more of a skeptic. After many years I eventually turned to atheism and was very vocal about it. I wasn't one to shy away from shouting about the injustices of theocracy and the need for separation of church and state. I'm very left-leaning and outspoken, in favor of women's reproductive rights, LGBTQ+ equality, and so much more. When I started to research Satanism, the TST way, I found that I was already following closely what the Seven Tenets stood for. It wasn't long after that I did more research, joined groups, and officially joined TST and declared myself a Satanist.*

• *I would think my altar is Satanic. As I did more and more research I really began to fall in love with the idea of the Romantic character known as Satan, found throughout literature, music, and art. With my altar, I proudly show off my TST certificate along with several Baphomet symbols. My favorite piece is a statue depiction of Lilith. Her story of equality and women's opposition to servitude is inspiring, for any person. I don't think it gets more Satanic than that.*

• *My altar is something that I use for self-reflection and meditation at times. It's a personal altar that can help me focus when I just want to calm myself and become introspective. There are times when I'll relax in front of my altar and read the Seven Tenets that I also have hanging on the wall above. It's a great way to help me prepare for the day mentally and it's cathartic.*

• *I have several Baphomet items on the altar — a statue, candle holder, and an incense burner. Personally, this is one of my favorite symbols used in modern Satanism. To me it's the joining of opposites (as above, so below). I like to think that it stands for equality, even in opposites.*

I also have my TST certificate. I show it proudly as I want people to know that I am serious about my Satanism and a shiny certificate

with Satanic imagery and signatures tends to really solidify that in my eyes, and for anyone else who sees it.

As mentioned I also have a statue depiction of Lilith. Again, her story is one that resonates so well with me. It's an incredible message of standing against unjust authority, demanding equal rights and truly sticking by those beliefs. It's just incredibly inspiring.

Finally, I have a journal with a pentagram/pentacle symbol. This journal is probably the most personal item on my altar. I started by handwriting the Satanic Invocation that TST had written and delivered. It's a good first page to a journal where I write anything and everything that comes to me. It's nice to have an altar and self reflect, but I find that physically writing my thoughts on paper almost makes it feel like I'm manifesting whatever it is I'm feeling at that time. If those thoughts are particularly depressing, writing them out is almost a way of acknowledging them so that I can work to move past them. Again, very cathartic.

- *My altar hasn't changed for the holidays yet. It's still a simple altar but with the announcement of TST's officially recognized holidays, I'm thinking of adding some seasonal spark.*

- *To beginners, I would say to really think about what you want the altar to mean to you. I don't think there's a right or wrong way to create an altar as long as you get something out of it. As for adding items to your altar, the Internet and small independent artists are awesome. And don't feel like you need to get everything at one time. Just as you change, your altar can change with you.*

Tim Furlow

- For me, Satanism is a quest for an understanding of the self, and the confidence to do what's right for the universe within. It means free will of the self and others, and the courage to stand when that's infringed upon.

- I absolutely consider this a specifically Satanic altar.

- My altar is built around a large mirror. It's used for daily reflection and meditation. When I stand before the altar, I stand before myself.

- Let me introduce the elements of my altar. It is built around shelves and a large mirror. The mirror is meant to reflect the self in every action. An Eliphas Levi Baphomet sits at the center. To me it's a symbol of balance on the ultimate scale and reminds me to balance my own emotions and frantic artistic impulses with the ability to live and be a responsible person. To Baphomet's left sits a chalice, also featuring the Levi goat, symbolizing to drink and celebrate life, everything in moderation and nothing to excess. To the right of Baphomet sits a small gong for the sake of tradition. Its primary use is in beginning and ending the ritual. On the far left and right sit skull candle holders, a reminder of the fleeting nature of life.

  In front of Baphomet's feet, a brass offering bowl rests, filled with slips of parchment to be used during ritual. This is cradled by a pair of ram's horns, again representing the balance of Baphomet. The sides of the altar are lined with candles and Satanic rosaries. The rosaries are items I wear daily; each is a small act of personal liberating blasphemy. On the top shelf sits a small bottle full of grave dirt; again to remind of the fleeting nature of life. In the frame of the mirror, I keep prayer cards. Souvenirs from rituals past, they serve as small daily meditations. Crowning all of it are another pair of goat horns.

- My altar is constantly growing. As I meet people within the community, people give small gifts and mementos that end up on the altar. While this doesn't change for seasons, it's always evolving and telling more of the story of my life as a Satanist.

- *For beginners I would say: Plan for it to grow. Don't spend a ton of money on stuff, just be happy with what you have and as you go to events and rituals, you'll keep finding more to add. If you start out with every cool Satanic trinket on the Internet, there will be no room for the things that mean something for you. Keep your altar clean and uncluttered. After all, it's where you go to pay respect to the most important thing you'll ever know.*

Amy Stanton

- *For me, Satanism means freedom of expression, acceptance, community.*

- *I consider this to be my own interpretation of a Satanic altar. It has both traditional items (such as skulls and candles) and things that represent me as a person which not everyone would consider linked to Satanism (music player, games console etc.).*

- *My altar is in my living space, the room I spend most of my time in. I can see it out of the corner of my eye most of the time spent at home. It's a place to focus on the parts I love most about myself. It shows my own journey, how far I've come and how far I plan to go.*

- *The bottom shelf is a space for physical copies of some Satanic books I've acquired, and read, over my time as a Satanist. Looking at them fills me with passion, and reminds me of my lust for knowledge.*

  The middle shelf holds my Nintendo switch, a ouija board given to me and some books on politics/physics. It's my 'fun not too serious' shelf that includes items more specific to me than my Satanism.

  The top shelf is my favourite. It holds my TST certificate, which reminds me of the people I hold dear to me in the community. The knife is the first item I bought for myself many years ago; it was my way of expressing myself in a place I didn't always feel like I could as a teenager. I have always had a love for wolves and the strength they gave me. The sheep skull was a present from a dear friend; my first real animal skull. Two pictures adorn my altar, both painted by a very talented friend. They are beautiful and speak to me in a way I can't describe with words, but with the dropping of my jaw to the floor.

  I also have a Baphomet statue from Nemesis now that I can guarantee is the same on many altars. The image of Baphomet means a lot to me personally; through its image I learnt to accept the good, bad, masculine and feminine sides of me.

  There are two items on here that are unlikely to be on other Satanists' altars. Both are from video games that touched me deeply. Video

COMPASSIONATE SATANISM

games are a way of experiencing another life, and in doing so, thinking deeper about my own. The 'test tube baby' is from a video game called 'Death Stranding' with a very thought-provoking story line that challenges what you know about death, life and the way we are all connected. Its actual name is a 'bridge baby' and they're used to create bridges between worlds (and I don't mean other planets). I also have some other items that are purely aesthetic (because who doesn't love a pretty ornament).

I have a fondness for nice-smelling items so my last item is a black cauldron for burning incense. This is both calming for me, and a way to make my home smell wonderful.

- *My altar does not change seasonally, nor for holidays. It just evolves over time.*

- *I would say to anyone starting to create an altar: Don't overthink it. Put things on it that mean something to you. It doesn't matter what others think, this is something personal. If that means a stack of books and a Satanic plushie go for it. Be you. That's what a Satanic altar is about, in my opinion.*

Missy Morbid

- *To me, Satanism means family.*

- *My altar is Satanic. I add things that I feel can be interpreted as Satanic.*

- *My altar is an artistic display that I use for rituals during holidays.*

- *My altar includes:*

  Black Phillip and my Baphomets: A way to honor Baphomet.

  Framed picture of Lucifer falling from Heaven: Sacrifice.

  Skulls: Death.

  Various occult pins: My love of darkness.

  Pinhead: No altar is complete without the Pope of Hell.

- *Before, my altar sometimes changed for the holidays, but not always. Definitely now it will with the introduction of The Satanic Temple's official Holidays. I try to incorporate items that coincide with the particular Holiday.*

- *My tips for beginners would be: Keep it simple. This is your space; add things that have special meaning to you.*

Dita Von Brohm

- I personally define Satanism as a system of self-awareness, rebellion and opposition to the norm. It's the beautiful realm of satire and reveling in it. It's a place of community and high standards for the self. It's a philosophy dedicated to the fundamental nature of knowledge, reality, and existence through our best scientific understanding. The importance of blasphemy and the heathens that create it. It's passion. It's love. It's finding justice for the 'other.' It's dedication. A thought that holds the same comfort as a safe word. It's a place I call home.

- My altar is specifically used for Satanic purposes.

- My altar is my safe place. It's a place of peace and meditation. It's a spot to clear my mind and to think about what's best for me.

- My altar items and their meaning: The lit candles produce the flame bared to us from Lucifer. My membership certificate from The Satanic Temple depicts the beginning of my journey as a Satanist. The statue of Baphomet represents the ebb and flow of life. The box on which Baphomet sits holds valuables or charms that are most important to me. The books represent the power of knowledge and (some) titles important to the TST community. The bell and singing bowl are traditional items used in other religions for rituals and I feel they are quite relaxing for meditation purposes. The incense burner is an instant classic when it comes to altar design. It produces the aroma that aids me into my state of relaxation. The lanterns are used to showcase the crimson hues and set the mood for my personal ritual(s). The rose was given to me as a pure act of love and compassion which holds true to our First Tenet — a reminder to keep good intent no matter the outcome. The hourglass is a symbol of my growth over time, in addition to the indication that to every beginning is an end and one should live in the now.

- *My altar changes when I feel like there is a dramatic shift in my life. I pay attention to it the most in these times for my own self-reflection.*

- *For those thinking of setting up an altar, I'd say to look for items or materials that scream out to you — what you feel represents you and your being.*

Tabitha Slander

- To me, Satanism is the set of guiding principles I base my understanding of the world around.

- I very much consider this a Satanic altar; this is my first altar.

- I originally built this altar when we had our first Dark Arts (and Crafts) night. My hope was that it would activate the intentions for creativity and bring us closer together as a group. We've recently been using it as a backdrop for our budding YouTube series *Everyday Satanism with Baphomette*. Otherwise it's just a nice thing to gaze at and reflect. It reminds me of who I am and what I'm about.

- For a long time most of the items on the altar were sentimental. I like to think about the people I spend my time with and places I've been while reflecting. Recognising worth in human connection helps me be a compassionate person. I've changed it up a bit recently, as I've learned more about my personal Satanic journey. It is divided by the Baphomet statue in the middle, representing duality, a subject *that I'm trying to work on in my life. Objects like the owl represent wisdom; the dagger, strength. These things aren't in opposition to each other, but represent two halves that are a whole in tandem. Just as all the aspects of my personality and history make me, me! I think altars are deeply personal; since I use it more for reflection/intention most of the symbolism is overt and thought-provoking rather than a place at which I perform ritual. Though I suppose my reflection can be described as its own kind of ritual.*

- *The only time my altar changes is when I borrow items to bring to masses or other ritual events. Since I built it it's gone through three refreshes.*

- *For beginners I'd say: Go for it! The only way to do it wrong is to not do it. Actually, make sure your table is sturdy, otherwise, anything goes! It's quite a rewarding experience.*

Daniel Walker

- *I define Satanism as a religious devotion to employing the myth of Satan for personal gratification, emotional and psychological enrichment, community building, and direct public action (in the spirit of the original revolutionary).*

- *I'll be honest, part of the point of the altar is just to have a place to keep things we use in group rituals. But it's also a persistent reminder: of our Satanic values, of my own experiences and psychological resources, and of my commitment to these ideals. Sometimes in the day-to-day struggle of life you can forget what's most important, so having a prominent visual landmark in your home is a convenient way to reinforce that perspective.*

- *The items on my altar and their meaning: The Baphomet is a showy centerpiece — we have a smaller version, "Travel Baph," for everyday use, so we reserve this larger one for more important ceremonial occasions, and in between it lives here on the altar. I had a black one from the same mold, but decided that the faux "bronze" finish looks more dramatic.*

  The candles are just for illumination and atmosphere, although I've discovered that when they're lit they create a moving silhouette of Baphomet on the ceiling that can actually be quite relaxing to watch. I'm not the type who is patient enough for meditation but sometimes when fatigue is setting in a few minutes of this can be relaxing.

  The stoneware vessel is actually a mortar, but I use it to burn incense. I honestly don't remember where the pestle went.

  The skull is a raccoon—so selected because it fits conveniently on top of the mortar, and because I wanted something on the table to serve as a reminder that, well, life is short.

  Similarly, I'm not that into Tarot, but the deck is there as a reminder that life is random and unpredictable, and sometimes the imagery on the top card gives me something to think about while I'm trying not to think about anything else.

The glass case has dirt collected from various places I've traveled to — nothing particularly special, just a reminder of those trips.

The stone on top was a gift from a friend, supposedly taken from a beach that curses anyone who (you guessed it) steals stones from it. And I did indeed get quite ill almost immediately after he gave it to me — but I got over it in a few days, so now the rock is a helpful reminder that curses are bullshit anyway.

The cup we use in various rituals to hold whatever we need: usually blood or wine, sometimes water — once milk because we were doing a screening of "The Witch" and there's a lot of nursing imagery in that movie, etc. The purple color really stands out from across the room, and it's earthenware and surprisingly sturdy.

The bell is also for ceremonial use — we keep talking about upgrading to a gong, which I don't think will fit on the table.

The knife doesn't often get much use, but it's a common ritual implement for a lot of people, so I keep one around in case it comes up. I'm a big proponent of practicality in these things.

The dried rose is leftover from one of our largest public rituals, conducted in a park in the East Bay last year; the altar setup involved nearly 100 individual flowers, and I kept this one as a reminder.

The pendant was a gift from Tabitha; I wear it whenever we're on Satan business, but keep it here the rest of the time so it doesn't get lost.

The little black book on top is a reproduction of the prop used in the movie The Ninth Gate — it's just for show, as the pages inside say essentially nothing. Beneath it (not visible in the photos) is another little black book in which members sign their names during ritual events, in imitation of the old Signing the Devil's Book superstition.

The painting above the altar is a gift from a Black Mass Appeal listener. He made three of these really gorgeous portraits, one for each of the three hosts — it's one of the most gracious things anyone has ever given me.

As for the turkey's claw? I'll admit I just thought it looked cool. I assume we'll find some use for it eventually. I tell people it's mostly there so that if anyone breaks in and finds the altar they'll be sufficiently spooked to just leave without stealing anything. And actually I might not be kidding.

- *My altar doesn't change for holidays; mostly it just changes with my whims.*

- *My advice to beginners would be that it's perfectly fine to use someone else's as a reference or a template, but at the same time don't feel beholden to anybody's instructions.*

Satanic Tattoos

As part of your Satanic self-expression, you may choose to have your body permanently marked with a tattoo (or other type of body art like branding or scarification) that represents your Satanism. I interviewed a number of practitioners about their Satanic tattoos and found a wide range of artistic choices.

Feel free to choose any design you want for your own tattoo as well; after all, it's your body and you'll be adding art that will last a lifetime. Your design can be obviously Satanic, like an inverted pentagram, or extremely subtle, with a meaning known only to you. You may decide to get a tattoo to mark a memorable occasion, to commemorate your dedication to the Satanic path, or just because you want one. While you can get a tattoo in any shop, I recommend asking around in your community to find a high-quality shop or an experienced tattoo artist that works in the style you prefer.

Before getting a Satanic tattoo, even a subtle one, take some time to consider the potential ramifications. Might it affect your job or put you in danger in your locale? You can prevent many of these reactions by getting your tattoo in a place that is normally covered by clothing, or choosing a design that's not obviously Satanic. Thankfully, almost none of our respondents had experienced negative fallout from their tattoos and none of them regretted getting their tattoos — even the Satanist who chose to get a face tattoo.

Ultimately, the Third Tenet applies here: your body, your choice. You have the right to get permanent Satanic body art of any design and placement if you so desire.

These are the questions I asked interview respondents:

- What does this tattoo piece depict? What Satanic elements does it contain?

- Who was the tattoo artist and/or shop?

- Did you get it to mark a special occasion, and if so, which one?

- What meaning does this tattoo represent for you? How does it relate to your personal Satanic beliefs and practice?

- Have you had to cover it up in certain situations, and if so, why?

- What kind of fallout have you gotten, either bad or good, from getting this tattoo?

- Any advice for someone considering getting a Satanic tattoo?

Attar B'alam

- This is a double tattoo with many Satanic elements, including "Solve et coagula," the Sigil of Lucifer, the Leviathan Cross, crescent moons from Lévi's Baphomet, and a pair of black wings and a pair of white wings.

- It was done by Gary Graves from Graves Ink.

- It was a birthday gift to myself.

- I first found LHP philosophy via occultism. My first encounter of Baphomet was from reading Transcendental Magic by Eliphas Lévi when I was 14 and honestly going through a lot of trauma. Seeing that what was supposed to be a deity of knowledge be considered evil resonated with me as I got sent to Catholic school when I lived in Belize as a young child. I was frequently lashed in school there for asking too many questions during theology; this led me to be an atheist at a very young age, probably around the age of 7 or 8 (I honestly don't remember anymore). However, my encounter made me start looking more into the actual practice of LHP philosophy rather than just gathering information on different beliefs as I had been doing. The biggest influencing factor from all of this was to take ownership for myself and stop blaming my childhood and how I was raised for everything that was wrong in my life at the time. This led to continual self-improvement being the cornerstone of my own personal Satanic practice.

Solve et coagula essentially means to take something apart and put it together again; that is, to transmute; to change. That was the main reason I decided on this tattoo. I also substituted the "O"s in "solve et coagula" after someone in an online TST forum shared their own tattoo with me. I liked that it brought in elements from Lévi's drawing plus to me it also signifies a spectrum from which I can take elements I see fit when striving to be a better self. On my right arm the crescent moon is white, matching the moon Lévi's Baphomet points to and preceding "solve"; closest to my wrists are white wings with the Sigil of Lucifer above them. This is representative of Lucifer *as an angel; the sigil also represents enlightenment and knowledge in this case to me. On my left hand after "coagula," again closest to my wrists, is a pair of black wings with a Leviathan Cross above them. The crescent moon on my left arm is also black. These wings coupled with the Leviathan Cross take the meaning of Satan, i.e. Lucifer, after his fall in mythology, which to me represents rebellion against arbitrary authority and the pursuit of justice. Put together, my right arm, which has "solve," is symbolic of taking myself apart, gathering inspiration from a lesson I may have learned (enlightenment); and then on my left arm is the means of putting myself together anew because to me rebellion and the pursuit of justice are a means to make myself a better person internally before promoting it externally.*

It was not planned but I also find it a bit funny that where I symbolically had the means of reforming myself tattooed is on my left arm, given that Satanism falls under the umbrella of LHP philosophy.

- *I've had to cover it up before, mainly for work functions. I'm*

AD military and when you have a commander and his second in command get up in front of the unit and do a presentation about themselves that claiming faith is one of their cornerstones, it's a better idea to blend in than to be asked what your tattoo means.

• Overall the response has been positive. The only negative response I've gotten was from one of my best friends. He's prior army and also a Silver Star recipient; he's also a devout Christian. I had been trying to tell him I was a Satanist for years and well, because of the tattoo, I finally found an opportunity he couldn't run away from. He got very angry that night, saying this isn't what his brothers died for (half his company got killed in Afghanistan), and that we're a Christian nation. It didn't help that I was the one that was driving that night and the majority of this conversation took place as I was taking him home. He even made me pull over at one point and was gonna have an Uber take him home. Thankfully he apologized the following day and since then I've even been to his church with him, mainly because he's actually one of those kind Christians, so I wanted to see how his pastor preached. Also, to give some context, he's from a small town in East Texas and African American; in his own words "the notion that you don't believe in god is unheard of where I'm from." He always tells me that he has to remind himself that I don't believe in either god or Satan whenever we end up talking about my beliefs, so I think that me finally getting the opportunity to tell him I'm a Satanist and (although at first it didn't go too well) the fact that he accepted it and doesn't treat me any differently now speaks volumes. He supports my role as part of Chapter leadership just as I encourage him to go to mass, because honestly it does help him personally.

• My advice for anyone considering getting a Satanic tattoo would be: Be mindful of your environment; I live in TX so it's not exactly the most accepting type of place. Every religion has extremists, so please take your own personal safety as well as those in your company into account if you get something that would trigger an extremist.

Dex Desjardins

- My tattoo is of the Sigil of Lucifer.
- I got the tattoo at Sacred Art in Tucson, AZ.
- It was a walk-in with my partner, Chalice Blythe, but I'd wanted it for a long time.
- It's a symbol of Lucifer, an archetype with whom I closely identify.
- It's located far enough up my arm that I've never had to cover it.
- Honestly, I haven't noticed any fallout from it, good or bad.
- My advice to someone considering getting a Satanic tattoo would be: Be realistic about your life circumstances and, accordingly, be thoughtful as to symbolism and location.

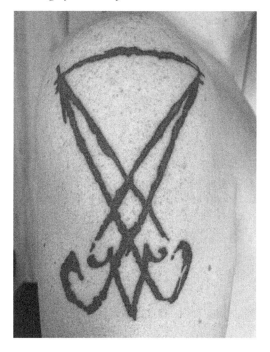

Harry Hoofcloppen

- *My pair of tattoos depict a baby Baphomet goat experiencing the world with enthusiasm and exploration. On the left, he prances in the fall leaves and his flame of knowledge accidentally lights a few on fire ... but he doesn't care, he's having a delightful time. On the right, he's playing with an Acherontia styx death's-head hawkmoth as it alights on his nose.*

- *The original art was done by James Bousema and used with permission, and the ink was done by Chuck Maple at Millennium Gallery of Living Art in Fort Collins, Colorado.*

- *I didn't get it for any particular occasion.*

- *What it means to me: the little goat has broken out of his chains and he's free to enjoy his infernal little life. His unbridled joie de vivre reminds me to have passion and to explore and learn every day. As a mortal being, I intend to take all the knowledge I can to my grave and enjoy the journey along the way.*

- *I haven't had to cover it up — I work in a bar.*

- *I haven't had any negative reactions. They're prominently on my forearms, so people inevitably see them as I'm working. People expect Satanic stuff from me anyway, so they're delighted to see something that is playful as well. Most people usually don't imagine "cute" and "Satanic" in the same image.*

- *My only advice is to remember that if it's someplace visible ... you will eventually get asked about it. But you have no one to answer to; it's your body and your expression and if that's how you choose to celebrate yourself then they can go to hell if they don't like it!*

Kat Zielke

- My tattoo is of Baphomet, done in the style of Lisa Frank. It has the traditional Satanic goat element with a crown of flames, only super cute and cuddly.

- Coyote Tattoo from Washington state did my piece.

- I didn't get it for any special occasion.

- I got this because I entered a time in my life where I could openly be a Satanist and I wanted to have a piece that reminds me of my youth and innocence. I was finally living my childhood dream of working in a scientific field and not doing what others wanted me to do. To me Baphomet is the embodiment of wisdom, and I was finally listening to my younger self and living my best life.

- I've never covered it up because of a situation. I invite people to comment on it and ask its meaning.

- I've received overwhelmingly positive comments on it. I was hospitalized last October with stage IV breast cancer and every nurse that cared for me would say how much they loved my "happy goat." I also met a few Satanic nurses thanks to "Baphy."

- My advice is: don't do what's cool or trendy, do you. Be your awesome, unique self and let your tattoo reflect that.

Jason Lloyd

- *My Satanic tattoo depicts Lucifer's fall and a quote from Paradise Lost.*

- *Kevin "Cabbie" DeVore at Art and Soul in Louisville, KY did it.*

- *I didn't get it to mark any special occasion — I'm just a big fan of Paradise Lost.*

- *I own several different copies of Paradise Lost, which is one of my all time favorite pieces. The depiction of Lucifer's fall is pretty common, but it's such an iconic image that I don't mind having something that others have as well in various forms. As a Satanist, naturally I relate to Lucifer/Satan, and Paradise Lost is pretty much the foundational text in regards to the Romantic image of Satan that eventually led to Satanism as we know it today.*

  The quote, albeit abridged so as to work better for a tattoo, says "Let us live to ourselves, though in this vast recess, free and to none accountable, preferring hard liberty before the easy yoke of servile pomp." The script work actually mimics that of a copy of the poem my wife got me as a gift. As for the quote itself, it's one that deeply resonates with me on a multitude of levels. For one, the Second Tenet of The Satanic Temple states: "The struggle for justice is an ongoing and necessary pursuit that should prevail over laws and institutions." It's easy to shrug and say "the law's the law," but that doesn't always make things right or just, and so we should continue to put in the effort and work for not only our liberties and freedoms, but those of others around us as well. Furthermore, as a Satanist I'm only accountable, ultimately, to myself. It would be easier to live in "servile pomp" and pass the buck for my actions to some fictional character ... but again, it takes effort and work to try and improve myself and to live to my full potential, as opposed to the "easy yoke" of expecting some mythical deity to do the work for me or to simply say "What will be will be."

- *I haven't had to cover it up.*

- *I haven't had any issues with it. Most folks don't immediately*

recognize it as Satanic, actually. In fact, I've gotten quite a few positive comments on it. And honestly, "Paradise Lost" is such a classic piece of literature, whether you're a Satanist or not, that it would be really rather silly to argue against having a tattoo representing it.

• *My advice for someone considering a Satanic tattoo: "One's body is inviolable, subject to one's own will alone."*

If it's what you want, and something you're going to enjoy or has significance to you, I say do it. Find your sense of aesthetics and live deliciously! You should never be ashamed of who you are.

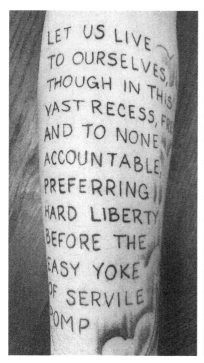

Pope Wonka

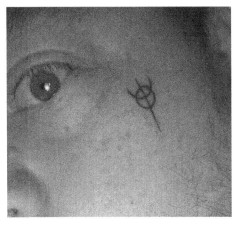

- *This tattoo depicts the Clavicula Nox (The Key of Night). It's a Trident/ Pitchfork inside a circle.*

- *I had it done by Rosaland Daniels of She-Devil Tattoos. It's a professionally done tattoo.*

- *I got it on New Year's Eve of 2018. It was partially to close out a bad year and start fresh.*

- *To me it represents Satan permeating all aspects of my world. It also represents the appropriation of symbolism for personal means*

- *I've never covered it up. I've had my neck and hands tattooed since I was 19; I have intentionally backed myself into a corner to live a life where I don't/can't compromise who I am and what my beliefs are to fill my belly.*

- *I'm sure I've lost some jobs or other opportunities I'm unaware of because of it. I've had Aquaman jokes and some basic ribbing from friends, but nothing unbearable.*

- *My advice to someone considering getting a Satanic tattoo would be to really think about what you're getting and what it means to you. Personalize it. A sulfur cross is cool but what makes it a part of you? Sigils can sneak by because a lot of people aren't familiar with the Seal of Saleos, but a lot of those demons have specific traits that may mirror how you feel or how you want to be. Don't, DO NOT, steal someone else's tattoo. Bring ideas to your artist and allow them to customize it so you're not just a Pinterest board of generic Satanic symbols.*

Darkur NyghtFrost

- My tattoo contains an inverted pentagram.

- I did this tattoo myself using an electric tattoo machine. It was ritually tattooed in the dead of night by candlelight.

- It wasn't for a special occasion per se, but I got it to use as an altar piece. I live in a situation where I cannot have an altar up, but I still feel that having an altar is an important part of my religious devotion and practice. So I realized that the body is an altar, and my body is an altar table waiting to have the tools placed upon it. So I tattooed this on my thigh as a reminder of that and to visualize the altar my flesh is.

- This tattoo represents the primordial darkness that everything requires. It is on my left thigh to show that I walk the Left Hand Path. My view of it is upside down, forming a regular pentacle, which to me is also significant and a reminder of polarities and how everything is part of a continuous spectrum of experience.

- My tattoo is almost always covered due to its location (upper thigh). I have had it exposed at Wiccan events before and some people have asked why it is inverted. The easiest way for me to explain it is 'balance.'

- I love my tattoo because it affirms my religious views and makes me more confident in standing up for my beliefs and my *rights. I have been asked by Wiccans why it is inverted, but because of its location, not many people are aware of it. It was exposed a few times while I was in India and no one thought anything of it.*

- *My advice to anyone considering a Satanic tattoo would be to have it be significant to you personally. I feel that the meaning and story behind my tattoo (being ritually tattooed by my own hand) is way more meaningful than the design or the way it looks. Also having it in a place that is easily coverable can be helpful, and making the location significant to you and easy for you to see also is a good idea.*

Choosing a Satanic Pseudonym

Though the rate of understanding is increasing as more people learn what Satanism actually is, Satanists still face very real risks from those mired in prejudice, hate and fear. To protect themselves and their families, many Satanists choose to use a pseudonym. There are no strict rules about what you call yourself; deciding on your Satanic name is a highly personal endeavor. I asked a number of practitioners how they chose their pseudonym.

Moira Corvid • *I chose Moira as the name of the fates, and the last name was just my obvious love of black flappy screechers.*

Katherine • *There's a (likely untrue) theory that the name Katherine comes from the name Hecate, but I thought it was fun and ran with it.*

Agahnim Moloch • *I was using a different one before, but I was watching some retro gaming videos on YouTube about the Zelda series (which I have been a fan of my whole life). Agahnim is a dark wizard from my favorite Zelda game. Found the name to be very fitting for me.*

Damon • *I'm Damon because it was close to Dante and Daemon but not as explicit.*

Belial Darshan • *I was dating a German guy who introduced me to the Radical Faeries. They, and the Hindu community I was hanging out with, said that I should change my name. I thought "alright, whatever." But then I had this dream. I was being pulled up into the sky by a very big, very black, winged creature and I became frightened. At that moment, the entity, or whatever it was, whispered in my ear, "I am Belial and I will never let you fall." Truth. I woke up the next day and told the German guy that I was dating "I'm going to change my name to Belial." He said "You know that's the son of Satan, right?" I replied "Well, then, I guess it fits me perfectly."*

Evan Blake • *I looked up demon names, and scrolled, and scrolled ... eventually I found one that fit. I took the last name, Blake, from William Blake, and that took about 2 seconds to decide on. After I transitioned I just molded my former first name into a more masc version.*

Marjhani • *I just took my name in reverse. I have also used a method of using all my letters just rearranged. For instance, narjamhi.*

Zita Cross • *Zita from Revolt of the Angels and because I just love the name; Cross came from taking a meandering path from the meaning of my biological mother's maiden name.*

Nikki Crocell • *I looked through the demons in Ars Goetia. I love math and liberal arts so a demon that teaches "geometry and liberal sciences" (Crocell) seemed like a good match.*

Alexander • *Taken from amalgamating different historically relevant sources - Alexander/Zander = Szandor, Aleister, Alexander the Great, which I really enjoyed reading about and reading their literature.*

Harry Hoofcloppen • *I've always been drawn to the Baphomet angle of TST's artistic expression, so I picked "Harry" as a homonym of hairy, and Hoofcloppen because it just sounds like the kind of last name a goat person would have. And it was perfect because it alliterates like my real name does!*

Belial Black • *I became interested in the name Belial years ago after listening to a metal band called Grand Belial's Key. It caused me to look up who Belial was and that research turned me on to Paradise Lost, which ultimately led to me becoming a Satanist. Of course Black, being the negative, the opposite of white, the opposite of clean, the opposite of light, etc. seemed an appropriate, alliterative fit. So considering I am a closeted Satanist, I needed a Satanym in order to post and do all things Satan. Therefore I am Belial Black, Satanist.*

Sly Luna • *My initials + my grandmother's maiden name = Sly Luna.*

Hada Pixie • *My model name came from my HS nickname — I got called pixie-pixie, then as a joke my Mexican friends started calling me Hada since it means fairy in Spanish (and none of them knew the word for pixie; when we looked it up we all thought "hada" sounded prettier).*

Dex Desjardins • *My partner picked my first name at random. My last name is taken from the name of a bank in Montréal.*

Paige Davidoff • *Only used my middle name and grandfather's last name so my pseudonym is inconspicuous and less likely to be reported as a fake name. Plus it helps shield me from potential employers. I purposely set up a brand new account in my legal name with family & childhood friends that I hardly use. It's less suspicious per background snooping to find a boring, bland profile than nothing at all. I set up a new email address in my pseudonym so that nothing is linked in this name to my legal name. The more I use this name, the better I like it than my legal name. I even prefer being called Paige when out and about.*

Lanzifer Eligos Longinus • *I was looking for the most chivalric thing I could find since I'm a jouster. Lanzifer - lance bearer. Eligos - patron demon of chivalry. Longinus - the Roman centurion who put Christ out of his misery, according to legend.*

Attar B'alam • *So the first name I chose is Attar, which is a Canaanite/Mesopotamian deity. Depending on the region there are different associations to them; however, in the Canaanite aspect they are associated with the planet Venus (morning star) and also once usurped Baal as a patron deity. I chose it for blasphemy. B'alam is a lot more personal since it comes from my own personal heritage. Although the broken Mayan I speak is Yucatec since I originally am from Cancun, I grew up in Belize. In the northern districts of Belize (Corozal and Orange Walk), the Yucatec variant of Mayan is vaguely spoken or mixed into the language whether it be Kriol or Spanish, but I grew up in Belize City and it was a mix of Yucatec and K'iche'. B'alam is the K'iche' spelling of the Yucatec Baalam; they both mean jaguar. I chose the K'iche' spelling as a nod to my Belizean heritage since my family is Belmex. There are Mayan kings that also used B'alam in their names as jaguars are revered in Mayan culture. There are also stories of jaguar deities in the Mayan "hell" (Xibalba/Mitnal).*

Venita Na'amah Estella • *I chose something that related to my Jewish ancestry/heritage which would also be blasphemous. I found a few options in The Satanic Bible, which I haven't seen overused in my social circles.*

Crimson • *Crimson — as in the color of blood and all things Satanic that aren't black.*

Ash Phenex • *Ash is the short version of my real first name. Phenex is a goetic demon. A grand marquis of hell, a fallen angel that is a poet, proficient in sciences, and obedient to whomever calls it. It believes it will return to heaven, but it has been deceived and will never return. The symbology of a rising phoenix, rising from the ashes, has always resonated with me. So naturally, so did Phenex.*

Sadaya Jaah • *My Satanic name is Sadaya Jaah. Sadaya is a name given to me by a meditation and yoga teacher in my early 20s. It means "gentle mother." Jaah is Lilith in Hindu.*

Regina Dentata • *My name was mispronounced to other kids' delight so many times when I was a young person, so I started going by my middle name. I guess I missed it, because in adulthood I've chosen not only to embrace the pronunciation but turn it into a rather descriptive term of art/play on words/double entendre.*

Vakker Engel • *When my mother died ... Beautiful angel ... vakker engel is "beautiful angel" in Norwegian. I had to remove myself from everyone at that time in my life. I realised that with my mother gone everyone that has been in my life left. I realised they loved her; I was never part of that I guess. So I moved on and wanted to have a profile free to be myself. I dedicate this account to my mother because she is a beautiful angel. She never judged, she always loved, she was intelligent and a million other positive things. Who else was a beautiful angel? Well we know that answer. Now I use this name for my poetry and books etc.*

Sadie Satanas • *I chose mine when I started doing porn because I wanted to bring Satanism to the trans porn industry and make the world have to see it and us. I based it phonetically on my favorite porn star Sabrina Sabrok, who is also a Satanist.*

Thomasin • *My satanym is Thomasin. This came from the movie "The VVitch." Not only is the movie thematically relevant, but the namesake character is constantly blamed for problems within the family and that really hits home.*

Daniel Walker • *I wanted something low-key. The short story "The Devil & Daniel Webster" was adapted into a one-act play that I did twice in high school — junior year and senior year both, it was well-received — so I picked Daniel based on that association. "Daniel Webster" didn't sound right though and was also, inconveniently, a real, famous personage, so I also tapped the very similarly titled "The Devil & Tom Walker" by Washington Irving, and "Daniel Walker" had a nice ring to it, and that's all there is to it.*

Epona • *Mine is Epona. I chose her as she is a strong warrior-like female, and because she is the mythical goddess of horses, the most beautiful, noble and majestic of animals IMHO.*

Darren Cage • *I got really high and went on a midnight walk and thought about what it is about my worldview that Satanism helps bring into focus for me and helps me express. Darren Cage is a kind of "namification" of the phrase "dark age," which is something I think certain elements of our society are trying to move us back toward.*

Abset (Shi) Midnyte • *At first I didn't have one as Shi means death in Japanese, and I've always loved that. Then, I thought as a just in case, I should figure one out. I chose Abset; it's a name created for a demo of a now defunct US Black Metal band — the demo was called "Blasphomet sin Abset." It tells the story of a demon that falls in love with a goddess. I was even granted permission by the band to use their creation.*

Cinna SinAlma • *Cinna SinAlma: Cinna = old nickname (short for Cinnamon Girl), sounds almost like "sinner"; SinAlma = sin alma = without soul or soulless (play on the fact that I am a redhead). I like alliteration. Together = my playful way of being a soulless sinner.*

Lux Black • *Lux is my favorite character from one of my favorite movies, Virgin Suicides. And means Light. Black because the Harry Potter series is very dear to me and that's a last name used. And because it is "Light Dark" and I like to think of myself that way. Not very satan-y but I like it!*

Maroosha Crowley • *Crowley is from Good Omens (if I was a demon I'd be like him). Maroosha came about during a rough personal period; it was my much stronger alter ego.*

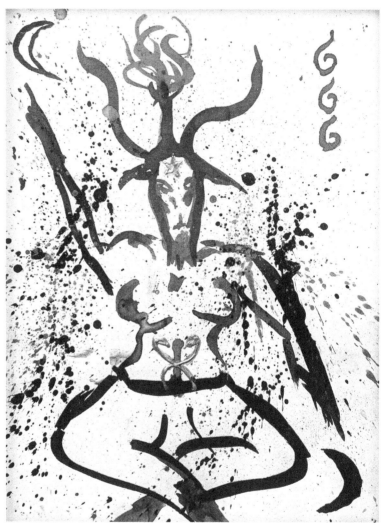

Ritual Art in Ink & Blood by Lilith Starr.

APPENDIX 2:
Sample Rituals

There are no required, rote rituals in Satanism; each ritual is tailored to a specific occasion, intention, and participant or group of participants. But to give you a peek into what Satanic rituals can look like, I've collected a few of the rituals performed by myself and our TST Chapter, along with a few ceremonies created by other individuals who gave their permission for inclusion. I've included a number of rituals celebrating the same theme so you can see differing approaches. I also highly recommend Shiva Honey's excellent book, *The Devil's Tome: A Book of Modern Satanic Ritual*, as a way to delve into Satanic ritual.

Personal Satanic Dedication

by Lilith Starr

This ceremony can be used by you or a group to celebrate your dedication to your Satanic path, either as a one-time performance or an ongoing practice. I use it on a regular basis — not necessarily every day, but several times a week — to reiterate my alignment with my Satanic beliefs. You may choose to perform this dedication at your altar if you have one.

TOOLS

Candle and bell, chime or other sound source. Altar or representation of your Satanism (an image, statue, or other object that symbolizes your Satanic path).

BEGIN RITUAL

Light candle. Ring bell.

> *Ave Satanas!*
>
> *Let the light of Lucifer guide my mind.*
> *Let the power of Satan strengthen my will.*
> *Let justice and compassion work through my hands.*
> *Let the strands of the dark web run through my heart.*
>
> *I vow to walk the Satanic path with full devotion, in every breath, in every moment.*
>
> *And so it is.*

Ring bell.

> *It is done. Hail Satan!*

Satanic Invocation

*by Tarkus Claypool, based on an invocation
    written by Lucien Greaves*

Our TST Chapter ended our meetings with this simple ceremony that our Campaign Manager Tarkus Claypool designed.
It's based on the Satanic Invocation written by Lucien Greaves
in 2014 and performed by Satanists at city councils and other
government meetings across America and beyond. Tarkus rearranged the wording slightly and added the apple, and I modified
it so our whole Chapter could participate in tasting the "fruit of
the tree of Knowledge."

ROLES

Clergy, Assistant, Participants.

PREPARATION

Cut a number of apples crosswise so slices show the five-pointed
star of the seeds. Cut enough slices so each participant can have
one; place on tray. All participants and the Clergy stand in a circle.

BEGIN RITUAL

Assistant comes around circle with a tray of apple slices; participants each take one.

Clergy: *Everyone, please take a big deep breath.*

Clergy rings bell.

Clergy: *Ave Satanas!*

Participants: *Ave Satanas!*

Clergy holds up an apple slice.

Clergy: *Behold, the 5-pointed star, symbol of wisdom and knowledge!*

*Let us stand now, unbowed and unfettered by arcane doctrines
born of fearful minds in darkened times. Let us demand that
individuals be judged for their concrete actions, not by arbitrary*

social norms and illusory categorizations. Let us hold fast only to that which is demonstrably true. Let us stand firm against any and all arbitrary and unjust authority. That which will not bend must break, and that which can be destroyed by truth should never be spared. Let us embrace the Luciferian impulse to eat of the Tree of Knowledge and dissipate our blissful and comforting delusions of old!

Participants all bite into apple slices.

Clergy: *It is done. Hail Satan!*

Participants: *Hail Satan!*

Unbaptism Ritual

By Chalice Blythe and Lilith Starr

This ritual is used to help participants shed their old faith and make a clean break with whatever religious bonds they bear from their past. Some of it came from an Unbaptism script written by Chalice Blythe and performed for TST Utah; I wrote the rest. Please let potential participants know that you do not have to have actually been baptized to participate; the ritual symbolizes general liberation from past and/or imposed faith whether or not there was an actual baptism.

ROLES

- 1 Clergy, 2 Associate Clergy, 1 Assistant
- Unbaptizees
- Observers

PREPARATIONS

If you're using them, fill out Unbaptism Certificates beforehand so they're ready to hand out at the end. At head of ritual space, set up: Gong on stand, table with bell, two goblets of red stage paint and two knives, fire or brazier (you can substitute a bowl of dry ice if indoors).

Unbaptizees are off to one side or in another room. Assistant ties Unbaptizees' hands with red cord or yarn. Observers gather in a circle, holding candles with drip shields.

BEGIN RITUAL

Clergy takes place at head of space, with 2 Associate Clergy to either side.

Associate Clergy lights first candle in circle, and starting there and going counter-clockwise, each person lights the next person's candle until all observers are holding lit candles.

Associate Clergy rings bell

Assistant leads in Unbaptizees to kneel in front of Clergy.

Associate Clergy rings gong.

Clergy: *Hail Satan!*

Crowd: *Hail Satan! [3x]*

Clergy: *Oh Satan,*
Beneficent One,
Seat of knowledge and power,
Indulger of Desires
And Great Rebel of old,
Let us become as you are in myth and legend:
Radiant as the sun
Yet black as a moonless night,
That we may live as we desire,
Free from tyranny and arbitrary law,
Free from superstition and mental chains,
Guided by empathy, compassion and reason
To undertake noble pursuits guided by our own individual will.

Associate Clergy hold red yarn with two hands taut above eye level.

Clergy: *These bindings represent your baptism and bondage to the misguided faith that would shackle your understanding, growth and freedom. Baptism offers false salvation on behalf of an absent god. But we, as flawed humans looking for answers of our own, have within us all that is necessary to free ourselves from outdated superstitions and find our own empowerment. Let us break the chains that have held us back.*

Associate Clergy drop yarn in front of them.

Clergy: *Those gathered here today, do you reject 'God,' arbiter of superstitious tyranny?*

Unbaptizees: *I do.*

Clergy: *Do you believe in yourself, the only sovereign power over your own life?*

Unbaptizees: *I do.*

Clergy: *Do you believe in the carnal bliss afforded to you by your natural desires?*

Unbaptizees: *I do.*

Clergy: *Do you believe salvation is to be found solely through your own rational self?*

Unbaptizees: *I do.*

Clergy: *Do you wish to renounce the faith of your past and be free of its bonds, rejecting your baptism forever?*

Unbaptizees: *I do.*

Associate Clergy use knives to cut the yarn on Unbaptizees' wrists and hand the cut yarn back to each Unbaptizee.

Clergy: *Then behold: your bonds are cut away and your baptism rejected and dissolved. Cast them away forever!*

Assistant leads Unbaptizees one by one to the fire or bowl with dry ice and directs them to toss in their cut yarn. Then Assistant leads Unbaptizees back to kneel in previous location.

Clergy: *With the blood of Lucifer, we bestow upon you the mark of Free Will!*

Associate Clergy raise goblets containing red stage paint above their heads. They then draw an upside-down cross on each Unbaptizee's forehead with stage paint and one by one, motion for them to rise.

Clergy: *You are no longer part of an archaic faith, crushed by conformity and forced to bow before an absent god. Your power is now your own and you are free to walk your own path, to follow your own will, and to soar on your own wings. It is done and witnessed. In the name of Lucifer, you are free!*

Associate Clergy rings gong.

Clergy: *Hail Satan!*

Crowd: *Hail Satan!*

Unbaptizees are led to Observers for congratulatory hugs. Associate Clergy hand out Unbaptism Certificates afterwards, if you're using them.

Satanic Destruction Ritual

Based on a Ritual by TST Los Angeles

This ritual was first performed at a Satanic Mass nightclub event put on by TST LA; I modified it slightly for our own Chapter. It's another ceremony that has been performed by many Chapters and individual Satanists around the world; many participants have reported that it was extremely freeing and empowering for them. To improve safety, I highly recommend putting a heavy tarp or two down under where participants will break their items; we had a bit of trouble when a participant broke a bottle — he put it in a sock first to contain the pieces, but some broken glass still escaped.

ROLES

Clergy, Assistant, Participants, Observers.

PREPARATION

Choose your objects to destroy. Preference is given to something you're holding onto that has a negative association with a person or memory or action. Maybe it's something you hide so it's not in sight everyday to cause you grief, but it's there and you can't let go of it. It could be a possession or gift from someone abusive or cruel, a piece of clothing from the old you, bank statements or receipts from a time you made a poor financial decision, a token of some kind of failure (relationship, friendship, or a personal failure). If something doesn't immediately come to mind, you can improvise. Write angry things you want to get off your chest onto a piece of paper that you can tear up or put in a glass bottle. Ritual organizers should decide in advance whether or not there will be sharp, shatterable items allowed.

Find a good location to do it. This is ideally done somewhere outdoors, where it's safe to get dirty, but it can be done indoors as well. Place plastic or something underneath so cleanup is easy and damage to the surrounding area is minimized. Objects can also be placed on a platter of some kind. A fireplace, bonfire or fire pit is a bonus.

Choose your weapon of destruction. Depending on the object(s) you are destroying, choose your weapon of destruction. Hammers, daggers, baseball bats, crowbars, mallets, and knives work well. It's really up to you and the space available to you. Don't forget safety — if you are destroying something shatterable like glass or ceramics, wear safety glasses and gloves, and wrap your fragile item in a sock or other piece of fabric so you can easily pick up the pieces afterwards.

Before ritual: Gong and a large container for broken pieces are set up at head of ritual space. Plastic dropcloth or tarp is placed in front of where participants will sit. Participants gather their items for destruction, their weapons, and any safety items. Any observers file in and take their places in a semicircle or line well behind the destruction zone.

BEGIN RITUAL

Clergy rings bell.

Assistant leads participants in and guides them to sit in a line facing the Clergy. Each participant lays their object(s) and weapon(s) of choice out in front of them.

Assistant hits gong.

> **Clergy:** *Ave Satanas!*
>
> **Participants and Observers:** *Ave Satanas!*
>
> **Clergy:** *We gather here with tokens of the past*
> *We bear their burden with a heavy heart*
> *Let us take the hammer in our hands*
> *Let us start the work to break these chains*
> *Ave Satanas!*
>
> **Participants:** *Ave Satanas!*
>
> **Clergy:** *These were things that I held in my hands*
> *These were things that belonged to me*

These were things that I held in my heart
These were things that have meaning to me
These things are not dead, because they never carried life
But I gave these things life, because they have carried me

I gave these things my memories
My fear
My secrets
My tears
My blood
My devotion
My hate
My forgiveness
My pain
My pleasure
My love
My disdain

I am the creator of life in these things
For without me, they would not be
And people would seek to profit off what I give
With no mutual heart given back to me

We emancipate ourselves from this material slavery
For without my heart, these things would not be
We liberate ourselves from this endless cycle
Of voids filled with unnecessary greed

Ave Satanas!

Participants: *Ave Satanas!*

Clergy: *I fill my voids with love and compassion*
I fill my voids with clarity
I fill my void with the beauty that surrounds me
I fill my voids with only that which propels me

Ave Satanas!

Participants: *Ave Satanas!*

Clergy: *Raise your weapons!*

Together we raise our arms and unshackle ourselves from the control these things have over us

Together we raise our hammers and daggers, and with them pierce the heart of that control

A power driven by addiction, attachment, consumption, and by a relentless hunger for excess

Ave Satanas!

Participants: *Ave Satanas!*

Clergy: *Repeat after me: 'I do not belong to these things. These things belong to me!'*

Participants *(loudly) as they enthusiastically destroy objects:*

I do not belong to these things
These things belong to me!

[Repeat 10x].

Clergy: *Cast away the pieces of your broken bonds!*

Participants rise and one by one throw their broken pieces into the container, then return to their space; they remain standing.

Clergy: *Thus we break the chains, thus we are free!*
Thus we take our power back
We rise, unshackled from our past
In the name of Satan, it is done!

Assistant hits gong.

Clergy: *Hail Satan!*

Participants and Observers: *Hail Satan!*

Discard the pieces afterwards.

Initiation Ceremony

By Lilith Starr

I wrote this Initiation Ceremony for use by our TST Chapter; we performed it every few months for those who had recently earned their full membership. At the end, we handed out membership certificates designed by one of our artistic members.

ROLES

Clergy, Assistant, Council Members, Initiates, Observers (members who are not being initiated; may also include members' partners).

PREPARATION

Fill out membership certificates for Initiates and put in manila envelopes. Hand out candles and drip shields to Observers. Set bell or gong on a table at the head of the ritual space.

BEGIN RITUAL

Observers form semicircle holding unlit candles with drip shields. Clergy enters and stands at head of group; Council Members stand to either side of Clergy. Assistant leads Initiates in to stand in a line or semi-circle in front of Clergy and hands out candles with drip shields (if outdoors). Assistant lights first candle in row and the flame is passed from Initiate to Initiate, then to Observers til all are holding lit candles.

Clergy: *Let us begin!*

Assistant rings gong or bell.

Clergy: *Ave Satanas!*

All others: *Ave Satanas! [3x]*

Clergy: *Let the banner of Satan be lifted before us,*

Council Members: *Let the light of Lucifer guide the mind!*

Clergy: *Let the Legion among us awake and arise,*

Council Members: *Let the skies fill with the beat of a thousand wings!*

Clergy: *Attend and bear witness, those who watch today! Here stand ready those who would join our band of companions and become our fellows in the unceasing fight for justice. The Satanic path asks much of us: an active Mind, a compassionate Heart, and an individual Will guiding us to noble pursuits. The way may be rocky and the battle fierce, but if we stand together, we may stand triumphant against tyranny. Those here before us today have proven their resolve and dedication to The Satanic Temple Seattle Chapter. Let the Vows of Membership be spoken!*

Clergy: *Do you by your own free will wish to become a member of The Satanic Temple Seattle Chapter?*

Initiates: *I do!*

Clergy: *Do you agree to strive to act with compassion and empathy in accordance with reason?*

Initiates: *I do!*

Clergy: *Do you agree to support the struggle for justice as a necessary pursuit?*

Initiates: *I do!*

Clergy: *Do you agree to respect the bodily autonomy of others?*

Initiates: *I do!*

Clergy: *Do you agree to respect the freedoms of others, including the freedom to offend?*

Initiates: *I do!*

Clergy: *Do you agree that our beliefs should conform to our best scientific understanding of the world?*

Initiates: *I do!*

Clergy: *Do you agree to do your best, as a fallible human being, to rectify any mistake you may make?*

Initiates: *I do!*

Clergy: *Do you agree to heed the spirit of compassion, wisdom, and justice in all things?*

Initiates: *I do!*

Clergy: *You have met the requirements and taken the vows necessary to attain membership in our chapter. In the name of reason and free will, with the authority vested in our chapter by the greater Satanic Temple organization, I declare you full members in The Satanic Temple Seattle Chapter. Hail and welcome! It is done!*

Assistant rings gong or bell.

Clergy: *Hail Satan!*

All others: *Hail Satan! [3x]*

Membership certificates are handed out after ceremony.

Winter Solstice Self-Affirmation Ritual

By Venita Na'amah Estella

It can be interesting to see how different ritual practitioners approach the same theme; you can get a sense of how much creativity and personal meaning goes into each unique ritual. This is the first of two Satanic rituals that focus on the Winter Solstice.

This ceremony was written for the Friends of TST Maine group to celebrate the Winter Solstice. From the writer: "The candle/flame theme is all about adding warmth and fire and energizing the ritual, and watching actual material transformation occur while discussing the ideas of transformation. It symbolizes letting in some light and warmth as we enter into winter and approach the new year."

PREPARATION

Black candles are passed out to group members, along with copies of the Self-Dedication Invocation. One large ritual candle is lit at the head of the ritual space.

BEGIN RITUAL

One by one, group members individually light black candles via one large ritual candle.

INVOCATION

Group reads together: *I vow to My Self*
To continue to do My best,
To honor My Self,
And to acknowledge My own power.

I am My own best friend,
I will love and respect My Self.
I will challenge and grow My Self.
I will celebrate and support My Self.

I vow to forgive My Self,
To let My Self heal and to take My time.

I vow to work every day to be my best Self,
To always learn and improve My Self.
I will lead others by my example,
I will rest when I must rest,
And I will create change when I must create change.

I will embrace the power within My Self,
Liberated by the Light Bringer,
Forgiven by the Fallen Angel,
Empowered by the symbol of Satan.

I will stand up to Tyranny,
I will speak up for Justice,
I will pursue Knowledge,
And I will celebrate Pleasure.

With this invocation,
I dedicate myself to My Self.

Hail Satan and Hail My Self!

There is then a space of time for contemplation and writing down further affirmations to anonymously post up on a board or to share as a group in some form; members can take photographs of the board for individual keepsakes.

At the end, members transfer their black candle flames to smaller tea-light candles, symbolizing the finalization of the affirmation and bringing the transferred words into action and actualization.

By Shiva Honey

This is another ritual approach to the Winter Solstice. As mentioned above, Shiva Honey is the author of *The Devil's Tome: A Book of Modern Satanic Ritual*, an excellent source for a deeper understanding of Satanic rituals.

TOOLS

A fire bowl, strips of paper, pen, matches or a lighter, dead flowers, candle, music player.

SACRED SPACE

A private dark room in your home.

PREPARATION

Perform this ritual on the Winter Solstice (December 21) or before the year's end. Prepare a playlist that puts you in the mood for the cleansing work ahead. Allow yourself at least an hour of time. If you're working through deep and painful issues, identify a friend that you can check in with before and after the ritual to provide support and aftercare.

BEGIN RITUAL

Begin your playlist.

Create a circle of dead flowers and repeat *I cast a circle of protection where I sit in my power* as you lay the circle.

Put the fire bowl, candle, paper, pen, and lighter in the center of the circle.

Step into the circle and sit.

Take 3 deep breaths and allow yourself to sink into your body. Relax. Become aware of the space you occupy.

Light your candle as you say, *Through the darkness of winter, I commit to my illumination. I shed light on that which does not serve me and burn the bridges leading to nowhere.*

Begin to think of people, ideas, beliefs, relationships, and thoughts you want to part with. As they arise, write each down on a separate strip of paper. As you write each down, allow yourself to feel any emotions that come up. Give yourself space and time to process those emotions. Understand you're in a safe space. Cry, scream, grieve as necessary.

After you write each strip, light it on fire saying, *I free myself through the flame.*

Imagine yourself separating from that person, need, or thought as the fire consumes the strip. Watch it burn to completion in the fire bowl.

After you finish lighting all your strips of paper on fire, say *It is done. Non Serviam.*

Collect the ash, dead flowers, and other remnants and dispose of them as you like.

Satanic Wedding Ritual

By Siri Sanguine

Weddings and relationship commitments can be an integral part of a Satanic community; many practitioners want to share their joy and special occasion with the others in their Satanic family. This wedding or commitment ceremony is based on the Seven Tenets, and can be customized as need be. TST Seattle performed this ceremony for two of our members in a park in 2019.

ROLES

Clergy, Seven Witnesses, Two Participants, Guests.

PREPARATION

Table with bell is set up at head of ritual space. Clergy stands at head of space; guests stand in a circle or semicircle around them. Witnesses may stand next to clergy or at points along the circle.

BEGIN RITUAL

Participants enter (to music, if desired) and walk up to stand in front of clergy. Clergy rings bell.

> **Clergy:** *Ave Satanas! In the name of Lucifer, the Lightbringer and Rebel of Old, we bid you greetings and welcome!*
>
> *We are gathered here today to celebrate the love and commitment of these two people, [Participant 1] and [Participant 2], who have decided of their own free will to join their lives together in a true partnership of love and honor.*
>
> *Some of you may wonder why we would call upon the one known as the Father of Lies and The Deceiver to watch over this sacred union. In our religion, we perceive Satan not as a supernatural entity with power over humanity, but as a literary metaphor for standing up to tyranny and arbitrary authority. We embrace the Luciferian principles of encouraging benevolence and empathy among all people, rejecting tyrannical authority, advocating for practical common sense and justice, and being directed by the human conscience to undertake noble pursuits guided by the*

individual will. By honoring these principles and each other, [Participant 1] and [Participant 2] seek to live their lives together in happiness and love.

[Participant 1] and [Participant 2], please join hands and face the Seven Witnesses to proclaim your commitment to each other. By the Seven Tenets of The Satanic Temple, let us begin.

Couple turns or walks towards the Seven Witnesses one by one.

Witness 1: *One should strive to act with compassion and empathy toward all creatures in accordance with reason. Do you commit to treating each other with empathy and compassion, even when life's challenges weigh heavy upon you both?*

Participants, together: *We do!*

Witness 2: *The struggle for justice is an ongoing and necessary pursuit that should prevail over laws and institutions. Do you now vow to treat each other justly and with honor, however you mutually define it at all times, granting the benefit of trust to one another above all others?*

Participants, together: *We do!*

Witness 3: *One's body is inviolable, subject to one's own will alone. Do you choose, of your own free wills, to share your bodies in lust and love willingly, never coercing or threatening the safety of the other?*

Participants, together: *We do!*

Witness 4: *The freedoms of others should be respected, including the freedom to offend. To willfully and unjustly encroach upon the freedoms of another is to forgo your own. Do you reaffirm your commitment to autonomy of self while working together toward your common goals — never encroaching upon each others' freedom while respecting each other with open communication?*

Participants, together: *We do!*

Witness 5: *Beliefs should conform to our best scientific understanding of the world. We should take care never to distort scientific facts to fit our beliefs. Do you vow to strive for honesty in all dealings*

with your partner, even when tempted to take the easier road?

Participants, together: *We do!*

Witness 6: *People are fallible. If we make a mistake, we should do our best to rectify it and resolve any harm that may have been caused. Do you promise to demonstrate the love, honor, and care for your partner by owning your mistakes and making amends whenever appropriate?*

Participants, together: *We do!*

Witness 7: *Every tenet is a guiding principle designed to inspire nobility in action and thought. The spirit of compassion, wisdom, and justice should always prevail over the written or spoken word. Do you commit to treating each other with care and compassion, truth and wisdom, to the best of your abilities?*

Participants, together: *We do!*

Clergy: *In the spirit of Lucifer, you have proclaimed your love for one another and your commitment to creating your lives together guided by these Seven Tenets.*

Clergy holds up rings or other symbols of the union.

Clergy: *Before you I hold these rings, symbols of a life-long commitment with no beginning, and never ending. Before you place the ring upon your partner's hand I must ask one more thing of you:*

[Participant 1], do you take [Participant 2] to be your wedded partner, from this day forward, until such time as your relationship no longer serves?

Participant 1: *I do.*

Clergy: *And [Participant 2], do you take [Participant 1] to be your wedded partner, from this day forward, until such time as your relationship no longer serves?*

Participant 2: *I do.*

Clergy: *With these vows, it is done. Hail Satan! By the power vested in me by the State of Washington, I now pronounce you partners in Life! Congratulations! You may now kiss your spouse!*

Vow Renewal Ceremony

by Lilith Starr

Here is another example of a ceremony that can be used for weddings, vow renewals or handfastings. I wrote this in 2020 for myself and my partner Uruk Black as a celebration of our nine years together, to be performed in front of our friends and Satanic community.

ROLES

Clergy, Assistant, Candle-bearer, Four Lantern-bearers, two Participants, Guests.

PREPARATION

In advance, the couple writes their own Look Back section that describes their past together. Alternatively, you may choose to write a Look Forward or use some other personally meaningful reading.

Before the ritual starts, Clergy stands at the North point of ritual space next to an Assistant with a bell and gong. The Candle-bearer stands next to Clergy. Guests form circle around space. At the four cardinal directions, Lantern-bearers hold unlit candles or candle lanterns in these colors: blue (West), green (North), yellow (East) and red (South).

BEGIN RITUAL

Participants walk into ritual space [to music if desired] and stand before clergy.

Assistant rings bell.

> **Clergy:** *Ave Satanas!*

> **All assembled:** *Ave Satanas!*

> **Clergy:** *It is begun. In the name of Lucifer, the Lightbringer and Rebel of Old, we bid you greetings and welcome! Let us witness the joining of these two individuals, [Participant 1] and [Participant 2].*

Clergy lights Candle-bearer's black taper candle.

Candle-bearer goes to the West and lights blue candle lantern.

Assistant hits gong.

> **West Lantern-bearer:** *Hail Tiamat, serpent of the deep! Let your depths echo the love these two bear for each other. Hail Tiamat!*
>
> **All assembled:** *Hail Tiamat!*

Candle-bearer goes to the North and lights green candle lantern.

Assistant hits gong.

> **North Lantern-bearer:** *Hail Lilith, mother of demons! Let your love cradle these two with caring and joy. Hail Lilith!*
>
> **All assembled:** *Hail Lilith!*

Candle-bearer goes to the East and lights yellow candle lantern.

Assistant hits gong.

> **East Lantern-bearer:** *Hail Lucifer, light of wisdom! May your torch brighten the path these two walk together. Hail Lucifer!*
>
> **All assembled:** *Hail Lucifer!*

Candle-bearer goes to the South and lights red candle lantern.

Assistant hits gong.

> **South Lantern-bearer:** *Hail Satan, burning with strength! May your infernal blessings shower these two who are made one. Hail Satan!*
>
> **All assembled:** *Hail Satan!*

Candle-bearer returns to stand beside Clergy.

> **Clergy:** *Thank you all for coming to bear witness to these two as they renew their vows. Let us look back.*

Read Look Back section; this will be different for each couple:

> **Clergy:** *You met in an isolated coastal town in California,*

*magnetic power sparking when you touched, drawn together in
a relentless tide, the search of heart for heart. Dark worlds moved
when at last you came together. You took your commitment vows
in blood on the night you finally fled the backwaters, alone and
on the run.*

*You began your life together in the whirlwind of change, driven
forth into the cold without a home, rootless, finding only barren
soil in place after place. All looked lost as you found yourself
on the streets, no help in sight. But you survived by working
together as one, keeping each other alive against all odds, guided
by your love toward an unknown beacon.*

*Then in the darkest waters a lifeline of love was thrown, and
another. Old friends laid a tumultuous pathway up to this land
of deep wild forests, passing you hand to helping hand. Here the
dark fecund soil has brought you life, a home, a loving Satanic
community you yourselves helped build. Here you have finally
found peace.*

*Nine years you have spent by each other's side, living in love.
Nine years have you found happiness together, a helpmeet each
for each, both of you lifting up the other to a place of stability
and well-being hitherto unknown.*

*Today we celebrate your vows made so many years ago, and re-
new your commitment to each other in the sight of your friends
and community, held and witnessed within a web of compassion
and love.*

VOWS

Clergy, addresses Participant 1: *[Participant 1], What brings
you here today?*

Participant 1: *Love.*

Clergy: *Do you swear to abide by the tenets of compassion, fairness, reason, understanding and forgiveness in all your relations
with [Participant 2]?*

Participant 1: *I do.*

Clergy: *Do you recognize that you and you alone have the power to continually renew and replenish your relationship?*

Participant 1: *I do.*

Clergy: *Do you vow to offer openness and honesty, connection and strength, warmth and affection in your dealings with [Participant 2], to the best of your ability?*

Participant 1: *I do.*

Clergy: *Do you swear to walk at [Participant 2]'s side, giving mutual support and aid, for as long as it may serve you both?*

Participant 1: *I do.*

Clergy: *Do you wish to renew your vows and pledge your troth anew to [Participant 2] with all the love in your heart?*

Participant 1: *I do.*

Clergy: *Behold the ring, like your love open and never-ending, made of the hardest metal in honor of the strength of your bond. Place it on [Participant 2]'s finger as a symbol of your vows.*

Participant 1 places ring on Participant 2's finger.

Clergy: *It is heard, seen and witnessed!*

Assistant hits gong.

Repeat Vows section for Participant 2.

Clergy: *By my power as priestess, in the names of Tiamat, Lilith, Lucifer and Satan, in the eyes of all here gathered, I declare you bound to each other, your vows made anew, your pledge to each other heard, recognized and sanctified before your community and friends. You may now seal your bonds with a kiss.*

Participants kiss.

Assistant hits gong.

Clergy: *It is done! Hail Satan!*

All assembled: *Hail Satan!*

Satanic New Moon Ceremony

by Jane Thomas

Created for Satanic Bay Area, this is a Satanic variation on a pagan New Moon Ritual, meant to create catharsis and solidarity. Traditionally, the ritual is performed on the night of a new moon with an assembly of femme Satanists, but other users may adapt the ceremony for their own purposes and/or choose to substitute the gender-neutral language I've indicated.

ROLES

Head Clergy, and 3 Patrons who will invoke Lilith, Babylon, and Cerridwen

SETUP

Perform ritual on a dark, dark moon.

Pentagram on floor instead of circle, containing:

- Earth (East) – salt/root vegetables/anything that was grown or foraged by the participants.
- Air (North) – fluffy bread/soda/bubblegum/marshmallows.
- Fire (South) – something spicy, chilis or horseradish.
- Water (West) – water/drinks or seafood.
- Intelligence (Above) – mushrooms, herbs, alcohol.

WELCOME AND SEATING

Participants are invited to place their items on the altar according to the directions and symbolic purpose of their items. Participants are not obligated to sit in position in the circle according to their ritual items, but they might want to.

Invokers of each Goddess should be chosen. Lilith is associated with Fire, Babylon is associated with Earth, and Cerridwen is associated with Intelligence.

Light candles at each point of star.

Starting with Earth, pass the elemental items around the circle to share while discussing their meaning:

- Earth: The physical reality of our bodies, our animal nature and our material needs.
- Air: Freedom, openness, independence.
- Fire: The passions, lust, wrath, ambition.
- Water: Emotions, love, sadness, happiness, depth of meaning.
- Intelligence: Directed intentions, acting on the will.

Pass around stationery/invite participants to write down:

- One grievance
- One goal
- One thing you are grateful for
- A general list of things you want

Patron 1 reads the Invocation to Lilith: *Tonight is the darkest of nights, and we are prepared to journey into the darkness. Lilith, ancient one, we invoke you to guide us into the darkness and introduce us to our most powerful selves.*

Patron 2 reads the Invocation to Babylon: *Mystery, Babylon the Great, you are the Mother of Harlots and Abominations of the Earth. We are drunk with your wine; share with us from the cup of your abominations!*

Patron 3 reads the Invocation of Cerridwen: *Dark Goddess of the Cauldron, rebirthing us from conflicts of the past into the good night of the present, we call you to stand by us as we look into our souls and find the true purposes of our hearts. Hail and Welcome!*

Clergy: *I declare this circle open!*

GUIDED MEDITATION

Clergy (or pre-recorded and played aloud): *You are walking alone in the wilderness, having been separated from your sisters [or 'kin'] during the hunt. The rocks on the mountainside are sharp and uneven, and it has been some time since you've seen a tree. Each step you take, you look in every direction for shelter from the heat, shaking your sweaty clothing, trying to cool off.*

You think you see some trees in the distance, but your progress is slow, balancing on the slope and climbing over thorny shrubs and sharp rocks.

You reach the top of a small ridge and look down into the ravine below, smacking your dry lips pensively. You think you see an outcropping with a dark shadow beneath and you turn toward the shadow, hoping for a few minutes of relief in the shade, not daring to dream of water. As you move closer, a breeze escapes from darkness, covering you in cool relief and energizing you to move more quickly, right past the outcropping and into a dark, empty opening. You realize this is actually a deep cave, and you pause for a few minutes to let your eyes adjust to the darkness. You stare into the shadows but you can't see how far the cave reaches, so you take a few steps further. The cool breezes are washing over you and the deeper you step, the more awake you feel, blinking your eyes and taking in the dark, cool environment around you. The cave begins to slope downward, and you climb deeper into the earth. After a while you hear the sound of running water, and you follow the sound to a still pool deep underground.

You think of your sisters [or 'kin'] as you take off your clothes to bathe in the pool. How did you get separated? Will you ever see them again? Who do you miss the most? What have you left unsaid? By now they must be roasting their kill over an open fire, together. Do you feel cheated? Is it your own fault you got lost, or did they ditch you somewhere? Do you feel better off without them, or are you preparing to find them again soon?

You fill your canteen with clear water, and leave your clothes folded neatly beside the stream and take your first step in. The water is cool but not cold, and each step takes you a bit deeper until you find yourself over knee-deep, bobbing a little bit in waves of your own making. You reach back to the shore for your clothes, rinse them off in cave water, wring them out, and lay them flat on the rocks to dry. Then you feel ready, face the deepest part of the pool, and dive the rest of the way in, coming up for air, then diving back under again. You turn over on your back, floating, relaxing completely in the cool, still water. Your mind wanders freely. You lose track of time for a while.

Five minutes of silent meditation; then Clergy or recording speaks again.

Eventually you feel ready to go walking again and you climb back to your feet on the stone floor of the cave. Your clothes are almost dry, so you pace around in the darkness for a while drying off your skin before getting dressed. As you ascend the path back to daylight, you think you hear human voices, and you pick up your pace. When you reach the mouth of the cave you find your sisters [or 'kin'] have set up their camp fire in this exact spot, and there is a kill roasting already. You share your canteen of cave water with your sisters [or 'kin'] as you rejoin the group.

SHARING

Circling the table counter-clockwise, participants should share a few aspects of what they wrote down earlier, sharing any insights they gained from meditation, and snacking on any leftover ritual foods.

FINAL INVOCATION AND CLOSING

Clergy: *My sisters [or 'kindred'], we are together. Let us reach our goals, overcome all obstacles, and defeat our enemies. Let us be uplifted and empowered.*

The invokers should return.

Lilith: *Let Lilith uncover our deepest desires.*

Response: *Hail Lilith!*

Babylon: *Let Babylon enrich us with abundant treasures.*

Response: *Hail Babylon!*

Cerridwen: *Let Cerridwen empower us with strength and knowledge.*

Response: *Hail Cerridwen!*
And Hail us!
And Hail us!

The circle is now closed.

Food and beverages can now be served.

Satanic Remembrance Ritual

by Satanic Bay Area

Just as weddings can draw together a Satanic community, shared rituals can help participants process grief and find comfort after the death of a loved one or other difficult events. We share our joy, and we share our sadness. Many Satanists who have recently lost someone get bombarded by well-intentioned but infuriating Christian-based condolences from family and others — like "They are in a better place now" or "God must have called them home to Heaven." Ceremonies like this one allow us to support each other in our grief without dragging a non-existent God into the conversation.

From Satanic Bay Area:

> "Composed in 2018 and first performed in early 2019, the Satanic Remembrance Ritual is designed to provide comfort and reflection to people who are grieving, emotionally distressed, or struggling with adversity.

> "As atheistic Satanists we have no formal mourning rituals, no belief in an afterlife or higher power, and no recourse to psychological tools like prayer. As such, society sometimes does not provide us with helpful outlets for dealing with complex or fraught emotions.

> "The Remembrance Ritual is an attempt to provide catharsis and emotional support. Much of the language employed here directly relates to grief and mourning, but in theory this can be employed for any kind of personal difficulty. Indeed, one of the most important provisos of the ritual is that everyone's pain be treated with the same solemnity regardless of the circumstances."

REQUIRED ITEMS

- Altar.
- At least one person to conduct the ceremony.
- One FIREPROOF vessel.
- Matches, alcohol.

- Blood and/or red wine or red paint.
- Cup, bowl, or chalice.
- Tarot cards or playing cards.
- At least five candles. Black is traditional, but whatever works for you.

SUGGESTED ITEMS
- Between four and 12 additional candles for atmosphere.
- Bell or gong.
- Knife or sword.
- Incense.
- Black book.
- One or two additional people to help conduct.

ALTAR SETUP
The altar should be a table high enough for you to comfortably reach everything on it but low enough for everything to be visible to the entire room.

Position the altar either in the center of the room or at one end. If you prefer to conduct without an altar, make sure all of your implements are nearby anyway.

We recommend a centerpiece for the altar, something big and eye-catching to set the mood. In the past we've used a goat's skull or a statue of Baphomet, but whatever seems appropriate for you can serve the same ends.

Cover the table with an altar cloth or just a simple tablecloth — black is generally the default color, but red, deep blue, purple, or even white can work, depending on your mood.

The altar should contain all of your implements. It can also hold additional elements for creating atmosphere — candles, incense, decorative additions, etc. If you're employing a book in your altar setup, make sure that it lies open.

Rather than the altar, the fireproof vessel should be placed on the floor. Around it, create the outline of a perimeter through whatever means you prefer: chalk, electrical tape, string, a painted dropcloth, etc. So long as the five points are distinct and the vessel sits in the center.

INTRODUCTION

Spend a minute or two welcoming your participants and walking them through what to expect. Explain why you're all here and lay out any rules. If you need volunteers, select them now.

Participation in something like this should be consent-based, so give everyone as clear an idea as possible of what the ritual will consist of so they can make a conscious decision to include themselves. (Which they should have done before showing up of course, but even so.)

Given the nature of this ritual, things are likely to get very emotional. Take care to let participants know that they're free to leave the room and compose themselves at any time, but by the same token, if they prefer to remain, that tears or similar expressions are not inappropriate, not a burden on the occasion, and indeed are the entire point.

Normally rituals should be conducted uninterrupted, but in the case of a Remembrance Ritual, if you judge that a break of five minutes or less would be helpful to clear the air after a particularly tough session, then go for it.

PART 1: THE DARK LORD'S PRAYER

You or a volunteer should stand in front of the altar or at the center of the circle to lead the prayer. Since this is an easy task it's a good way to include someone else in.

Conduct the recitation call and response style, first delivering a line and then letting everyone repeat it back:

> *Our Father, who art in Hell*
> *Unhallowed be thy name*
> *Thy kingdom is come, thy will is done*
> *On earth as it is below*

We take this night our rightful due
And trespass on faithless taboos

Lead us into temptation
And deliver us from false piety

For yours is the world
The riches
And the glory
Forever and ever

Hail Satan!

PART 2: TESTIMONIALS

Ask for the help of between one and five volunteers.

Each volunteer will place a single black candle at one of the points of the pentagram, light it, and repeat "Hail Satan" (or whatever other phrase they feel is appropriate).

They should also draw a card from the deck on the altar and lay it next to the candle. Tarot cards are great for the appropriate atmosphere, but playing cards are acceptable if none are handy. Feel free to punctuate each drawing with a ring of the bell.

Once the last elements are in place, tell the assembly:

The burning of the candles reminds us of the passage of time.

The randomness of cards reminds us of the unpredictability of life.

The five-pointed shape reminds us that we are like the pentagram, earthly, knowing, full of the memories of times and bodies past and with emotions, stitched together, but at the same time whole.

Segue with a "Hail Satan" and ringing of the bell, then move on to the next sequence. Feel free to modify this language however you see fit, as long as everyone is clear on what they're doing:

Some people want to say a few words about why they're here tonight. Anyone who wants to speak, feel free to stand in the

pentagram and address the assembly, or if you prefer, go ahead and stay where you are.

You can direct your comments to all of us here or to yourself or to whomever you would like to imagine you're speaking to, you can say whatever you would like to say for whatever reason, you can speak for as long as you'd like, and if you'd like any of us to do or say anything helpful — applaud, repeat after you, do a moment of silence, whatever — just ask.

Everyone else please be accommodating and please respect every-body's feelings, because that's why we're here. Speakers, if you think anything you're going to say might be difficult for other people to hear please provide a little warning up front if need be.

When you're finished, please leave your notes and anything else you might like to be rid of in the vessel at your feet.

At this point those leading the ritual should step aside and allow anyone who wants to address the assembly to speak for as long as they like.

This will probably comprise the majority of the ritual time and involve a lot of fraught emotion, so be prepared. Although there is presumably a finite amount of time set aside for this event, it's best to let everyone talk for as long as they like — only interrupt if there's absolutely no choice.

PART 3: INVOCATION

Once everyone has said their piece, take your place either at the altar or within the pentagram.

One or more of you can deliver the sermon (for lack of a bet-ter word), dividing up the text as you see fit. We've hopefully composed it so that it's fairly easy to move, remove, or add additional statements. Feel free to replace it with other words if you wish.

Whenever the invocation uses the phrase "Hail Satan," it's tradi-tional and appropriate for everyone participating to repeat back,

"Hail Satan." With a big enough crowd this can get quite forceful, which is awesome.

If you have a bell or a gong, punctuate the "Hail Satan" with that. It might be useful to have one volunteer who is just on bell duty.

> We begin life happy, knowing that sin is sweet. We meet no gods, and worldly things are our entire minds.
>
> We fear no rod and no law, use our pride, wrath, and lechery to make the world commendable, and gladly leave the company of angels.
>
> Everyone lives after their own pleasure, because nothing in life is sure, and for what pleasure we make, we owe only ourselves.
>
> We make a long journey, and account to ourselves for bad deeds and good, prove our friends if we can, and that we might escape from sorrow we ask gentle death to spare us a little longer.
>
> For no one living or dead will we happily leave the world, but instead keep time passing until the last minutes.
>
> We eat, drink, love life, and haunt lusty company, and when it's over we keep faith in the things that remain behind: friendship, family, our possessions, our good deeds, and our words.
>
> And for those already gone we carry these things on after them:
>
> We are Pride, daring to go anywhere, and at our feet we demand life pour out perfume and lay down silk.
>
> We are Greed, asking to stock everything in the world in our homes and in ourselves.
>
> We are Wrath, leaping out of a lion's mouth, born in Hell and walking up and down in the world ever since.
>
> We are Envy, wanting all, knowing the goodness of life because we watch it in other lives and see their worth.
>
> We are Gluttony, hungry for 30 meals in a day and born from a royal family of banquets stretching back generations and beloved in every town and city.

We are Sloth, born lying in the sun and wishing we had stayed there ever since, knowing the world does us wrong to take us away from our comforts.

And we are Lust, loving a little just as much as a lot, and apologizing for nothing.

For everything else we offer no confession and no penance, no abstinence and no redemption. Endings cancel all adversities and apologies.

This moral keep in mind: Embrace indulgence, for it will comfort you. Remember that beauty, strength, knowledge, and judgment will last as long as they can. And that after life there are no amends to make.

The stars will move, time will go on, the clock will strike, the devil will come.

Let us live in Hell a thousand years or a hundred thousand, where they say there is no end for souls like ours.

Let our bodies turn to air so that Lucifer might bear us up, or change into drops of water and fall into the ocean, never to be found.

The ugliness of Hell gapes not for us. Because this is Hell now, and these are already the eternal joys of heaven.

PART 4: CLEANSING FIRE

At the conclusion of the invocation, anything that participants left in the cauldron to be destroyed should be CAREFULLY set on fire. If there's a lot in there, start with just a few items and then feed more in as they burn, to maintain a steady blaze. Request a moment of silence while the fire burns out.

PART 5: MARK OF THE BEAST

Blood, paint or wine should be on hand, in an easily accessible vessel. Whereas in the previous step participants approached the altar, this time you should approach the circle or seated participants to administer the mark.

Ask each person whether they prefer to be marked with wine or blood. And where. A simple smudge or X on the forehead or the right hand is sufficient, although feel free to get more creative.

After each marking, have the participant repeat after you:

Hail Satan.

Or any other appropriate sentiment. Once you've made the rounds to everyone, return to the altar for the conclusion.

STEP 6: CLOSING

Once all the fires are out, everyone has said their peace, and hopefully all the tears are shed, return to the altar and close with:

Joyfully, mine and I will return to the earth.

Extinguish the candles and thank everyone.

Illustration by Randy Faust.

APPENDIX 3:
Satanic Holidays

These are the holidays recognized on The Satanic Temple's Official Holidays list; they are celebrated by myself and many other Satanists. Some practitioners choose to ask for some or all of these holidays off at their jobs, exercising their workplace right to freedom of religion.

HOLIDAYS

Lupercalia: *February 15*
Celebration of self-love and self-care, bodily autonomy, sexual liberation, and reproduction. Foods for feast: Milk, figs, lamb. Ritual themes: Mock sacrifice, BDSM, asexual awareness, wolves.

Hexennacht: *April 30*
Celebration honoring those who fell victim to superstition and pseudoscience. Items for feast: Mead and sparkling wine. Ritual themes: Bonfires, music, dance, Destruction rituals.

Unveiling Day: *July 25*
Celebration honoring the unveiling of The Satanic Temple's bronze Baphomet monument in 2015; honors religious plurality and shedding archaic superstition. Ritual themes: Unbaptism or molting.

Halloween: *October 31*
Celebration of indulgence, darkness, and all things spooky. Foods for feast: Corn, root vegetables; sheep, geese, chicken, or

vegan option; and ale. Ritual themes: Bonfires, trick-or-treating, masquerade parties, Hell Houses, Black Mass.

Sol Invictus: *December 25, with feasting on December 23 & 24* Celebration of triumph over superstition and the pursuit and sharing of knowledge. May include gift exchanges, particularly books. Foods for feast: Winter foods and drink, wine. Ritual themes: Candles, Black Mass, Unbaptism, Destruction rituals.

OBSERVANCES

(Not as significant as the holidays, but may still be celebrated):

Anniversary of Roe v. Wade: *January 22*

Devil's Night: *June 6*

Blasphemy Day: *September 30*

Your Birthday: *Floating Observance*

414

APPENDIX 4:
Recommended Reading

PRIMARY TEXTS

France, Anatole. *The Revolt of the Angels*. 1914.

Pinker, Stephen. *The Better Angels of our Nature: Why Violence Has Declined*. 2012.

ROMANTIC AND OTHER PRE-1900 WRITERS

A number of these older texts can be found free online via Project Gutenberg and other web services.

Milton, John. *Paradise Lost*. 1667.

Lanzara, Joseph. *John Milton's Paradise Lost In Plain English: A Simple, Line By Line Paraphrase Of The Complicated Masterpiece*. 2009.

Doré, Gustave. *Dore's Illustrations for "Paradise Lost" (Dover Pictorial Archives)*. 1993.

Blake, William. *The Marriage of Heaven and Hell*. 1790.

Blake, William. *America a Prophecy*. 1793.

Godwin, William. *An Enquiry Concerning Political Justice*. 1793.

Hazlitt, William. *On Shakespeare and Milton*. 1818.

Shelley, Percy Bysshe. *Essay on the Devil and Devils*. 1819.

Shelley, Percy Bysshe. *Prometheus Unbound*. 1820.

Lord Byron. *Cain: A Mystery*. 1821.

De Vigny, Alfred. *Eloa*. 1823.

Baudelaire, Charles. *Les Fleurs du Mal*. 1857.

Sand, George. *Consuelo*. 1861.

Huysmans, Joris K. *La-Bas*. 1891.

LITERARY SATANISM

Schock, Peter A. *Romantic Satanism: Myth and the Historical Moment in Blake, Shelley, and Byron*. 2003.

Murphy, Derek. *Evil Be My Good: An unauthorized Paradise Lost study guide*. 2016.

Faxneld, Per. *Satanic Feminism: Lucifer as the Liberator of Woman in Nineteenth-Century Culture*. 2017.

Forsyth, Neil. *The Satanic Epic*. 2002.

HISTORY OF SATANISM

Faxneld, Per, and Petersen, Jesper Aa. *The Devil's Party: Satanism in Modernity*. 2012.

Dyrendal, Asbjorn; Lewis, James R.; and Petersen, Jesper Aa. *The Invention of Satanism*. 2015.

Van Luijk, Ruben. *Children of Lucifer: The Origins of Modern Religious Satanism*. 2016.

SATANIC PANICS

Bromley, David G. et al. *The Satanism Scare*. 1991.

Demos, John. *The Enemy Within: 2,000 Years of Witch-hunting in the Western World*. 2008.

Frankfurter, David. *Evil Incarnate: Rumors of Demonic Conspiracy and Satanic Abuse in History*. 2008.

Nathan, Debbie and Snedeker, Michael. *Satan's Silence: Ritual Abuse and the Making of a Modern American Witch Hunt*. 2001.

Almond, Philip. *The Devil: A New Biography*. 2014.

Case, George. *Here's to My Sweet Satan: How the Occult Haunted Music, Movies and Pop Culture, 1966-1980*. 2016.

RISE OF THEOCRACY

Kruse, Kevin. *One Nation Under God: How Corporate America Invented Christian America*. 2016.

Green, Steven. *Inventing a Christian America: The Myth of the Religious Founding*. 2015.

Jacoby, Susan. *Freethinkers: A History of American Secularism*. 2004.

CONTEMPORARY SATANISM

Honey, Shiva. *The Devil's Tome: A Book of Modern Satanic Ritual*. 2020.

Wexler, Jay. *Our Non-Christian Nation: How Atheists, Satanists, Pagans, and Others Are Demanding Their Rightful Place in Public Life*. 2019.

Laycock, Joseph. *Speak of the Devil: How The Satanic Temple is Changing the Way We Talk about Religion*. 2020.

Sollee, Kristen J. *Witches, Sluts, Feminists: Conjuring the Sex Positive*. 2017.

Starr, Lilith. *The Happy Satanist: Finding Self-Empowerment*. 2015.

FOR FURTHER READING

The Satanic Temple keeps a comprehensive, updated reading list on its website, thesatanictemple.com. Some TST Chapters also have reading lists on their websites.

ACKNOWLEDGEMENTS

Creating this book has been a whirlwind journey and I've had a lot of help along the way.

I'm especially grateful to my husband Uruk Black, whose love and support sustained me during the long and sometimes difficult years of writing this book.

Thanks also to everyone who gave generously of their time, including my Interviews Editor, Jason Lloyd, who helped greatly with the interviews; my book designer Lena Kartzov, whose enthusiasm and creativity inspired me to keep going; my friend Baal/Gerald, whose edits helped make this book the best it could be; my primary copyeditor, Jennifer Hawk and my associate copyeditor, Dresden Visage, who both put in many volunteer hours on my behalf; and my assistant copyeditors, Eric Maldonado and Evan Blake.

Finally, a special thank you to The Satanic Temple's founders, Lucien Greaves and Malcolm Jarry, for launching the religion that has brought so much joy and meaning to my life.

420

About the Author

Lilith Starr writes about the Satanic religion and personal Satanic practice. She served as Editor-in-Chief of the webzine Satanism 101 from 2012 – 2013. Her first book, *The Happy Satanist: Finding Self-Empowerment*, was published in 2015; it is part of The Satanic Temple's Recommended Reading list and has been featured by Satanic book clubs across the globe. In 2020, she received The Satanic Temple's first ever Anatole France Literary Excellence Award for her writing.

Starr is also a pioneer in Satanic leadership and community-building. In 2014, she founded The Satanic Temple of Seattle, one of The Satanic Temple's first five Chapters, and served as its Chapter Head for nearly five years, building it from a handful of people into a thriving 90-person Satanic community. While there, she directed the Satanic Invocation action that stopped Joe Kennedy, the praying coach at Bremerton High School; organized two highly successful Reproductive Rights benefit shows; helped collect over 800 pounds of menstruation products for the needy; and launched the first functioning After School Satan Club at nearby Point Defiance elementary school. Her writings on Satanic community have helped many other Chapters get their start as well.

Starr holds a B.A. cum laude in English Literature and Language from Harvard University and an M.A. in Journalism and Communications from Stanford University. She lives in Seattle with her husband, Uruk Black. You can find her most recent writing, read her blog, or contact her at **lilithstarr.com**.

OTHER WORKS BY LILITH STARR

The Happy Satanist: Finding Self-Empowerment

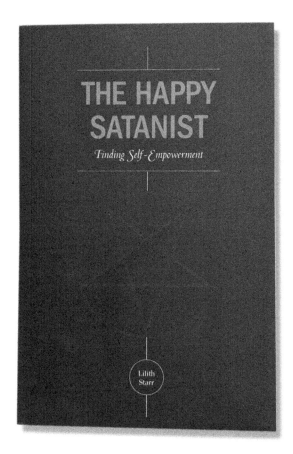